IMAGES
of America

HARMONY

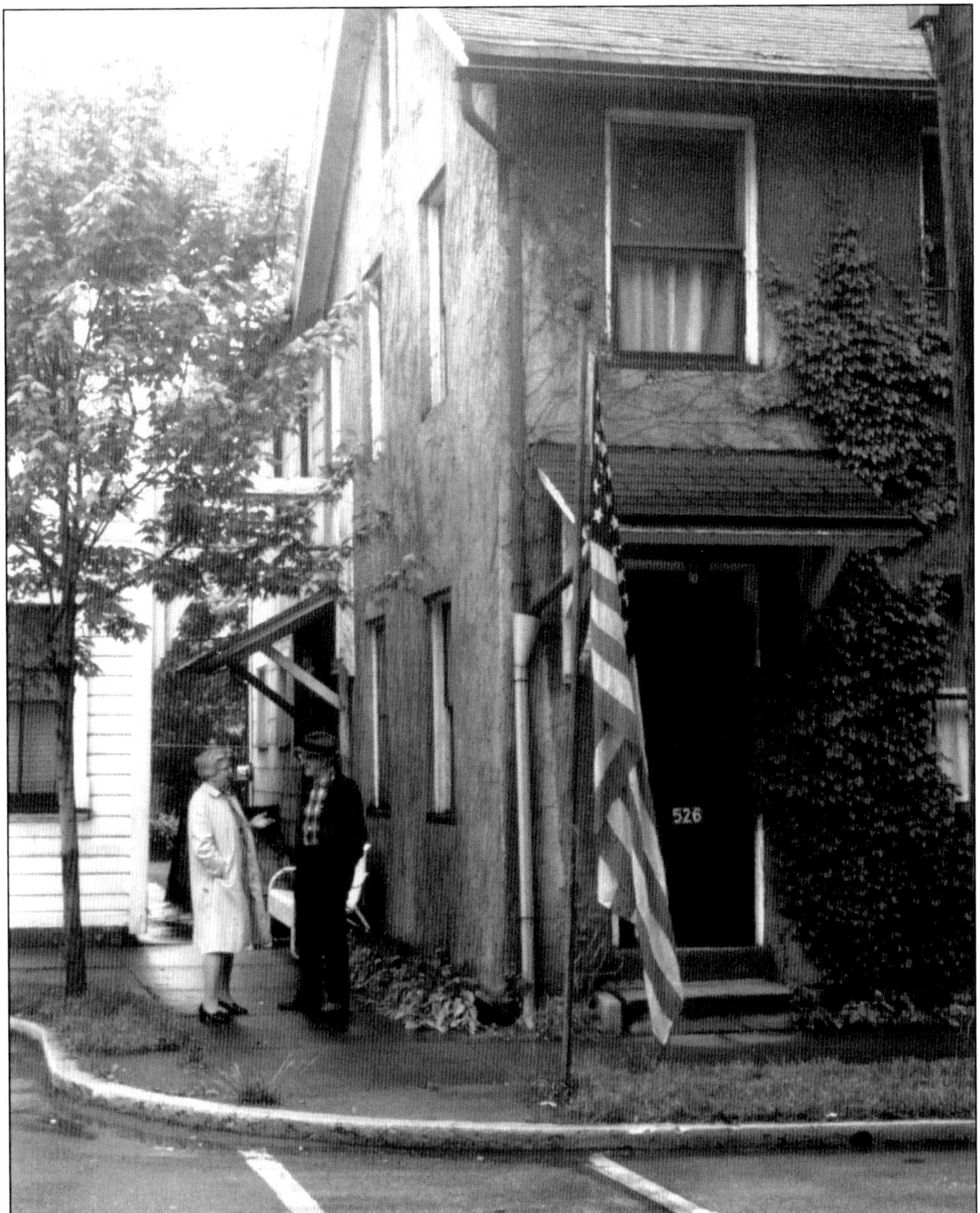

Historic Harmony president Ruth Werner talks with Dr. Arthur Stewart in 1970 during Doc Stewart Day, which recognized his six decades as community physician. His residence and office, in the background, was the home of Harmony Society leader and town founder George Rapp. McPharlin Guitar and Violin shop now occupies the house.

On the cover: Please see page 49. (Courtesy of Historic Harmony.)

IMAGES
of America

HARMONY

Shelby Miller Ruch for Historic Harmony

ARCADIA
PUBLISHING

ISBN 978-0-7385-6527-9

Published by Arcadia Publishing
Charleston, South Carolina

Printed in the United States of America

Library of Congress Catalog Control Number: 2008940082

For all general information contact Arcadia Publishing at:
Telephone 843-853-2070
Fax 843-853-0044
E-mail sales@arcadiapublishing.com
For customer service and orders:
Toll-Free 1-888-313-2665

Visit us on the Internet at www.arcadiapublishing.com

CONTENTS

ACKNOWLEDGMENTS

Harmony's history is best told through the words and pictures of those who lived it. In compiling this volume, I have quoted local residents' memories and impressions, accompanied by pictures they took and treasured. Many of the images and descriptions are from the history notebooks that the late Dr. Arthur Stewart filled with stories and snapshots for decades.

I am indebted to Stewart and to the late Rev. Loran Veith for organizing the historical association now called Historic Harmony, to Harmony Volunteer Fire Company members who founded the museum, and to those early Historic Harmony volunteers who did a great job of planning and arranging the first museum exhibits.

I am grateful to Historic Harmony members who began interviewing older residents in the 1960s and compiled a collection of audiotapes describing life and events in the Harmony area. I have transcribed 40 tapes for the museum library, learning in the process much of the information contained in this book. Special recognition goes to two former Historic Harmony presidents, Ruth Werner and the late Helen Eckstein, for collecting oral history and for their work in acquiring Harmony's national historic landmark district designation.

When asked to compile a book about Harmony that would contain 200 or more pictures, I turned to Ray Thompson, who has been recording life in Butler County for many years. I appreciate his generous contribution of photographs and thank *Butler Eagle* editor John L. Wise III for permitting use of photographs first published in the daily *Butler Eagle* and its weeklies. Thanks to all those who contributed their own photographs, especially Nancy Wiser, Shirley and Henry Burkett, Ruth Werner, Delsa White, Bernice Lewis, Katie Bauder, and Tim Sapienza. Special recognition goes to Jo Annette Cynkar, Historic Harmony webmaster and gift shop manager, who scanned some 170 images for this book and claimed she was having fun doing so, and to Sarah Buffington for scanning images in Old Economy Village archives.

Unless otherwise noted, all images are from Historic Harmony archives.

—Shelby Miller Ruch

INTRODUCTION

As housing developments, shopping centers, and industrial complexes transform surrounding western Pennsylvania farmland, Harmony retains an Old World aura and small-town atmosphere. Its configuration of brick buildings clustered around a market diamond is unusual in western Pennsylvania. Harmony's history is unusual as well, earning national historic landmark district status in 1974. The designation recognizes the community's significance to national heritage and culture as the founding home of the Harmony Society of German Lutheran Separatists. The group went on to settle New Harmony, Indiana, and Economy (now Ambridge).

Preserved in Harmony Museum properties and shared by Historic Harmony volunteers, the area history also includes Native Americans, young Maj. George Washington's near-fatal encounter with a Native American, Mennonite pioneers, farmers, oil speculators, gunsmiths, and road builders. From its earliest days, Harmony has attracted innovators, adventurers, and trailblazers. The wave of new residents continues as rapid development in nearby Cranberry Township spreads to Harmony and neighboring Jackson and Lancaster Townships. The region was not always so friendly to newcomers. A Delaware Indian village was known as Murdering Town when Washington came by in December 1753 on a mission that precipitated the French and Indian War. He narrowly escaped a gunshot fired by a Native American guide.

The millennial separatists, led by charismatic preacher "Father" Johann Georg Rapp, settled the town in 1804. Pennsylvania was not their first choice. Rapp and three others arrived in America in 1803 and eventually chose a site on federal land in Columbiana County, Ohio. Without sufficient cash to make the purchase, Rapp appealed to Pres. Thomas Jefferson for help in speeding the sale. Jefferson received Rapp on July 12, 1804, and explained that only Congress could grant his request. Congress denied the petition, leaving Rapp to quickly find an alternative location for several hundred of his followers. Zelienople founder Baron Dettmar Basse learned of Rapp's search and urged him to locate there. Basse had purchased 10,000 acres that included Revolutionary War depreciation lands in Connoquenessing Township, Butler County (today's Harmony, Zelienople, Jackson, Lancaster, Connoquenessing, and Forward Townships). Basse had founded Zelienople in 1802, envisioning it as the center of a barony in the western wilderness. Rapp and his associates signed articles of agreement to buy 5,000 acres from Basse and began building their town a mile east of Zelienople.

On February 15, 1805, they organized as the Harmony Society, pledging to live as one family until Christ's return, based on the biblical passage, "And the multitude of them that believed were of one heart and of one soul: neither said any of them that aught of the things he possessed was his own, but they had all things common."

They soon built a prosperous town with impressive brick buildings. Their main east–west street was part of the primary route between Pittsburgh and Erie. During the War of 1812, troops marched through town and crossed the society's bridge with supplies for Oliver Hazard Perry's fleet at the battle of Lake Erie. The road came to be called the Perry Highway and was designated U.S. Route 19.

Although the Harmonists focused on spiritual matters while awaiting the second coming of Christ, they were remarkably successful at marketing goods from their factories, mills, and farms. Their business manager Friedrich (Frederick) Reichert Rapp was in charge of agents who sold products in Pittsburgh, Lancaster, and Philadelphia. The Harmonists' approach to business was practical. When society members and businessmen who dealt with them had trouble getting direct postal service, they sent Frederick Reichert Rapp to Washington, where he successfully appealed directly to Pres. James Madison for a Harmony post office.

Visitors were intrigued by the communal group that numbered about 800 in its fifth year. A traveler named Robert Stubbs toured the town in 1809 and found the Harmonists harvesting crops in the fields north of town. He visited the new meetinghouse with an upper story supported by eight pillars that contained space for several thousand bushels of grain. John Melish wrote an extensive description of the society and its properties in 1811 for his book *Travels in the United States of America*. Of his tour with the inn keeper, he wrote, "We passed Conaquenesing creek by a wooden bridge ornamented with flowers, and observed a low meadow on our left, which we were informed had been drained with a good deal of labour and was now converted into excellent pasture grounds, a pleasure garden called the labyrinth and a botanic garden." He met with Johann Georg Rapp (called George Rapp in America) and talked at length with Dr. Christoph Muller, the society's physician who spoke English. Melish noted his trouble in negotiating the maze of labyrinth hedgerows: "The labyrinth represents the difficulty of arriving at harmony. The temple is rough in the exterior, showing that, at a distance, it has no allurements but it is smooth and beautiful within, to show the beauty of harmony when once attained." Muller, the first practicing physician north of Pittsburgh, grew medicinal herbs in the botanic garden.

Reports by Melish and Stubbs were circulated widely, making the society internationally famous. Public curiosity increased after the Harmonists adopted celibacy in 1807, believing it would foster spiritual purity. English poet Lord Byron immortalized the society in a stanza of his poem *Don Juan*: "When Rapp the Harmonist embargoed marriage / In his harmonious settlement (which flourishes / Strangely enough as yet without miscarriage, / Because it breeds no more mouths than it nourishes. / Without those sad expenses which disparage / What nature naturally most encourages), / Why call'd he Harmony a state sans wedlock? / Now here I've got the preacher at a deadlock."

The Harmonists were wealthy by the time they moved to Indiana Territory in 1814. They had constructed 130 buildings and owned 9,000 acres. Most of the Harmonists lived in town, going to work the fields by day and returning home in the evening. To tend flocks and mills, they established three outlying villages: Ramsthal, located just north of Harmony near present-day Mercer and Little Creek Roads in Jackson Township; Olbronn, farther north on Yellow Creek in Lancaster Township; and Edenau, situated about a mile east of town, today called Harmony Junction.

Although the Harmonists left their first Pennsylvania home, they maintained contact with people in Harmony and Zelienople. They helped Dettmar Basse's grandson Rev. William Passavant open the Pittsburgh Infirmary to serve the homeless and destitute sick in 1849. He brought the first Lutheran deaconesses to America to work in his infirmary, the forerunner of Passavant Memorial Hospital.

Mennonite Abraham Ziegler from Lehigh County bought the Harmonists' properties in 1815 and resettled the town with the help of Mennonite descendants of German and Swiss immigrants from eastern Pennsylvania. Unlike the celibate Harmonists who lived close together in town, they preferred individual farms and produced large families. Their meetinghouse, constructed in 1825, is the oldest Mennonite house of worship west of the Allegheny Mountains.

The population became more diverse after Ziegler brought in people to help operate Harmonist factories. Several new churches were organized, and social and fraternal clubs gained popularity. German, along with English, was commonly spoken until the outbreak of World War I. Schools were conducted in Harmony from its earliest days, and elementary classes continued until the

1950s. Harmony High School courses were discontinued in 1932 when local students began attending Zelienople High School. Among Harmony's schoolchildren were songwriter Stephen Foster and baseball pitcher George "Rube" Waddell.

Groups such as the fire company, its auxiliary, and the Harmony Community Club have consistently volunteered their services to area residents. Harmony was incorporated as a borough in 1840, and that year town council purchased the commons, a triangular tract bordering Main Street from German Street to the Zelienople line. Harmony remained an active commercial center boosted by the arrival of rail service in 1879 and the Butler County oil boom. Former U.S. congressman and county president Judge John H. Wilson, who grew up in Harmony during those years, recalled that the town was a thriving business and industrial center surrounded by a rich agricultural district that supplied nearly all of the raw materials for its manufacturing needs. Interurban train service that began in 1908 provided easy commuting between Harmony, Butler, New Castle, and Pittsburgh, and made the Harmony area a popular summer resort destination.

Dr. Arthur Stewart, who came to town in 1906, remembered when Harmony had two hotels; four restaurants; stores selling groceries, clothing, hardware, and furniture; a tailor; two shoemakers; a foundry; two large flour mills; a lumber yard; three blacksmiths; a marble cutter; an oil well supply; as well as an opera house that was the center for entertainment. Stewart practiced medicine in Harmony for more than 60 years and was active in the volunteer fire company.

The relocation of U.S. Route 19 across a new bridge in Zelienople in 1936 left Harmony off the main north–south artery through western Pennsylvania, and business activity shifted to Zelienople. While residential development has blurred the boundaries between the two towns, each retains its individual historical character.

In 1912, Walter W. Stamm, a writer for the *Pittsburgh Sunday Post*, toured Harmony and called it a "delightful spot." However, he wondered how long physical reminders of its history would remain. Forty years later, a *Pittsburgh Press* writer expressed concern that the Harmony Society cemetery "lies half-hidden and neglected." On a positive note, he learned that the Harmony Volunteer Fire Company had recently purchased the "great house" at Mercer and Main Streets and hoped to restore it and establish a museum there. The local historical society was reported to be inactive and without funds. On June 25, 1955, the fire company opened the Harmony Museum. In the mid-1960s, interest in the museum was revived and the Harmonist Historic and Memorial Association (later renamed Historic Harmony), founded in 1943, reorganized. The fire company transferred museum operation to Historic Harmony in 1967, and volunteers opened the museum to the public on a regular basis.

The Harmony Borough Council enacted a local historic zoning ordinance in 1986 to protect properties in the landmark district and later expanded the district. In 2004, the Harmony Borough Council received the second annual Pennsylvania State Association of Boroughs Historic Preservation Award for implementing a comprehensive historic preservation program with its continued emphasis on economic and community revitalization.

Today Harmony's tradition of service and volunteer effort is evident. The town diamond is a center of activity. The fire company, headquartered nearby, is marking its 135th year. A number of Harmony Society properties are still in use as homes and for businesses including two music studios and a dance school. The 1882 Harmony School houses borough offices and the post office. The borough council participates in regional activities with other municipalities while joining community groups and businesses in sponsoring concerts and other public events in Harmony. Historic Harmony volunteers offer tours year-round, and the museum's Doc Stewart Hall is used for museum exhibits, public meetings, and social activities. One of the borough council's most recent efforts is Silvester, a New Year's Eve celebration scheduled on German time, reflecting the community's heritage. Family oriented entertainment precedes a lighted ball drop and fireworks that ring in the new year at 6:00 p.m., which is midnight in Germany. Such innovative "traditions with a twist" bring visitors from around the world to catch a glimpse of the past and see what is on the horizon for Harmony.

One

Native American Settlements and Washington's Trail

Among the first Native Americans on western Pennsylvania land were Delawares who established a small settlement known as Murdering Town at or near present-day Harmony.

Maj. George Washington followed the Logstown Path to the village where he spent the night of November 30, 1753, on his way to Fort LeBoeuf near Erie. There he delivered an ultimatum from Lt. Gov. Robert Dinwiddie of Virginia that the French withdraw from British territory. The French responded by demanding the British get out of New France, assuring war between the two nations.

On his return trip to Williamsburg, Washington and his guide, Christopher Gist, met a Native American who fired on them. Washington documented the experience in his journal: "Just after we had passed a place called Murdering town where we intended to quit the path and steer across the country for Shanapin's town, we fell in with a party of French Indians, who had laid in wait for us. One of them fired at Mr. Gist or me, not fifteen steps off, but fortunately missed. We took this fellow into custody, and kept him until about nine o'clock at night, then let him go, and walked all the remaining part of night without making any stop, that we might get the start, so far as to be out of the reach of their pursuit the next day, since we were well assured they would follow our track as soon as it was light."

Gist recorded in his journal, "The Indian made a stop, turned about; the Major saw him point his gun towards us and fire. Said the Major, 'Are you shot?' 'No,' said I. Upon which the Indian run (sic) forward to a big standing white oak, and to loading his gun (sic); but we were soon with him. I would have killed him, but the Major would not suffer me to kill him."

Local historians consider the shooting on December 27, 1753, as the opening shot of the French and Indian War that expanded into the first worldwide conflict known as the Seven Years' War.

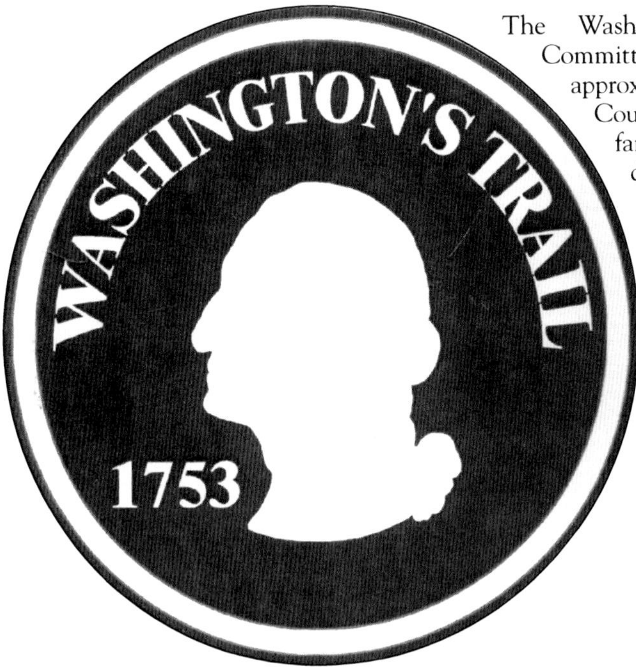

The Washington 1753 Commemoration Committee marked Washington's approximate route through Butler County with 150 signs bearing his famous profile. The first signs were dedicated in 2003 in the Harmony national historic landmark district, Moraine State Park, and at the Old Stone House. Other counties are adopting the design to mark Washington's path through their areas.

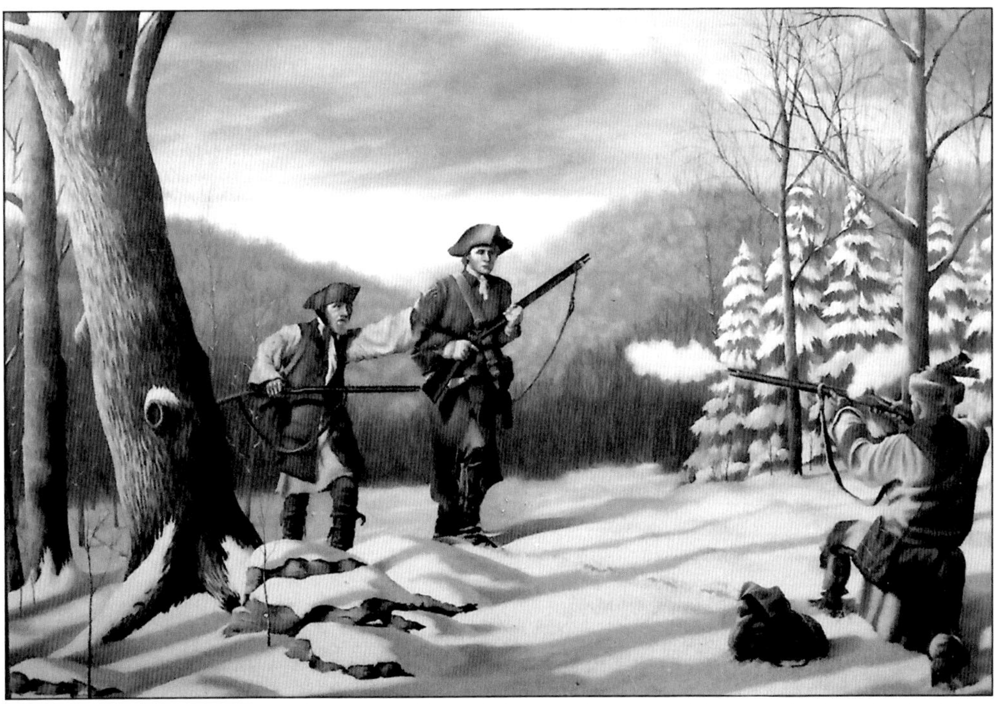

The First Shot, painted in oil by artist Deac Mong of Venango County, depicts the incident on December 27, 1753, when a Native American fired on Maj. George Washington and his guide, Christopher Gist. The painting, commissioned by retired Butler County Judge Martin J. O'Brien, was unveiled on April 10, 2008, at the Sen. John Heinz History Center in Pittsburgh. O'Brien chairs the committee that marked Washington's trek through Butler County. (Courtesy of Martin J. O'Brien.)

Two

THE HARMONY SOCIETY

Four years after Washington's near-fatal encounter near Harmony, Johann Georg Rapp was born in Iptingen, Wurttemberg, Germany. By the 1780s, dissatisfied with the duchy's Lutheran Church, he began conducting his own services and drew thousands of followers. Rapp was investigated by the church council and briefly imprisoned for refusing to attend church and for working on Sunday. Seeking to live a simpler form of Christianity, he and his followers came to America and settled Harmonie, the original spelling, in 1804. Early the next year, they created the Harmony Society, patterned on the life of Christ and His disciples. Rapp, called "father" by his followers, was involved in all aspects of the group's daily life. Visitors reported that the Harmonists appeared to be happy and sang as they walked to work in the fields. Although their interest was in eternity, the Harmonists' work ethic quickly made their community nearly self-sufficient with excess products to sell. Samuel Hambleton, who served as Oliver Hazard Perry's purser on the U.S. Brig *Lawrence*, visited Harmony in 1814 and noted two contrasting landmarks: the meetinghouse tower clock that he heard had cost $1,000 and the simple grotto in the labyrinth across the creek from town. He noted in his diary, "They [the Harmonists] have many shops and factories such as smiths, saddlers, shoemakers, curriers and wheelwrights. They have an excellent inn and retail store. From the fleeces of their own sheep they make good broadcloth and are beginning to press wine from their own vineyard." At the time, the society's wool cloth was selling for as much as $10 a yard.

Despite their success, the Harmonists were preparing to abandon their town. They had selected land in southwest Indiana and were offering Harmony for sale. Their reasons are still debated. Some historians believe they wanted more land away from encroaching development, while others focus on the effect of the war on the pacifist group. The Harmonists founded two more towns and endured for a century. The society's demise was related to the practice of celibacy, adopted in 1807 during a revival in Harmony.

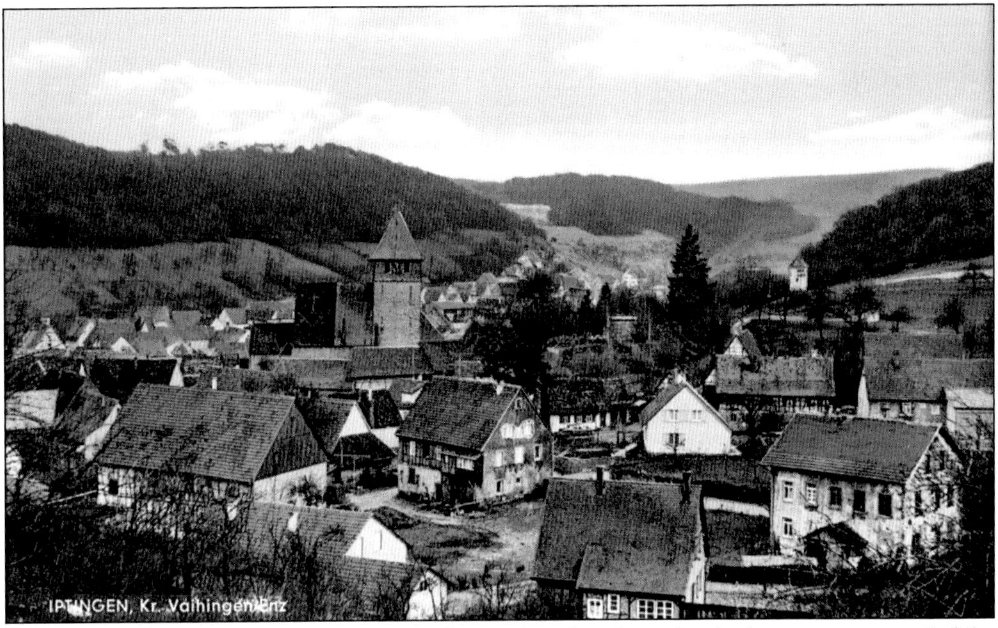

A vintage view of Iptingen, Germany, shows the church with clock tower surrounded by steep-roofed houses. This picture was taken from a hill covered with vineyards. Johann Georg Rapp, called George Rapp in America, was born in Iptingen where he attended the Lutheran Church, worked as a vinedresser and weaver, married, and had two children. He and his followers built their first American home on the pattern of Iptingen.

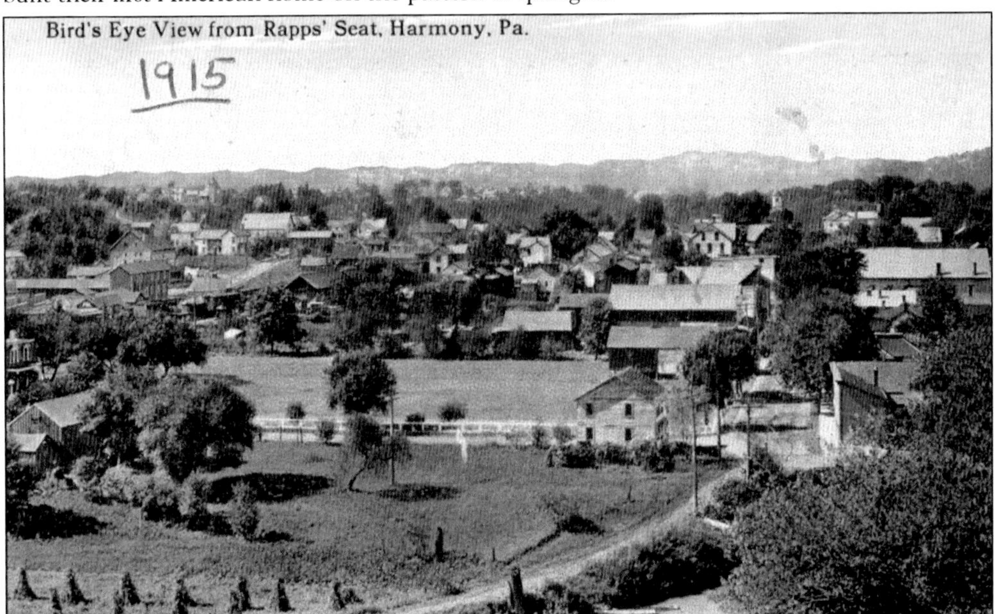

A photographer snapped this 1915 shot of Harmony from Rapp's Seat, named for the Harmony Society leader who was known to sit on a bench carved from a rock outcropping. Harmony, like Rapp's native Iptingen, Germany, is situated along a creek below a hillside that in the Harmonists' time was covered with vineyards. The society's first buildings surrounded the town diamond dominated by their church with a one-handed tower clock.

Rapp, the charismatic leader of the Harmony Society, came under investigation in his native Germany for conducting private worship services. Called before a church council, he stated, "I am a prophet and am called to be one." He and fellow separatists from the Lutheran Church came to Pennsylvania for religious freedom. They founded Harmony in 1804 and organized their millennial brotherhood the following year. The society numbered more than 800 by 1814 when they advertised Harmony for sale and moved to Indiana Territory to settle New Harmony.

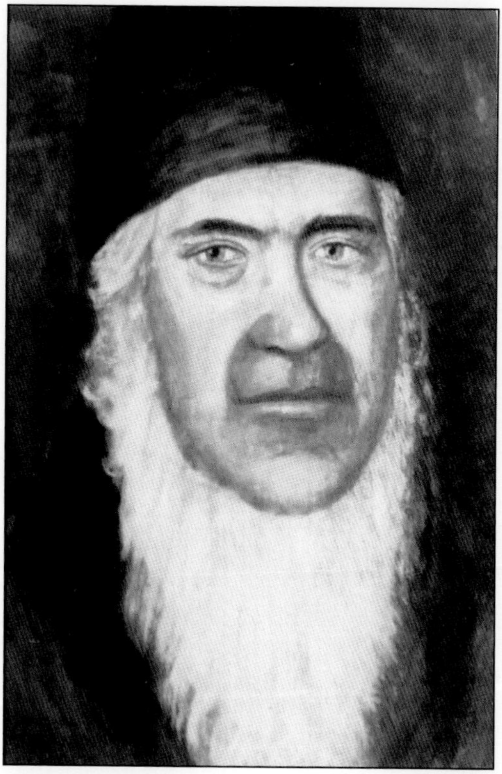

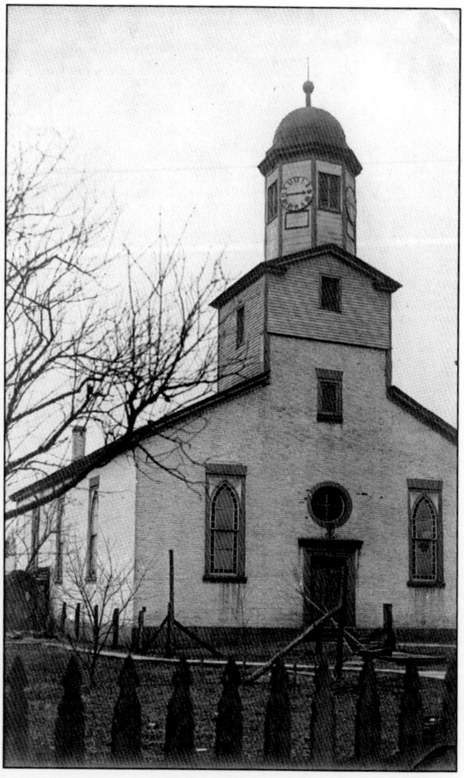

Society members attended morning and evening church services on Sunday and met for worship twice during the week. Both Rapp and his adopted son, Friedrich (Frederick) Reichert Rapp, preached in the meetinghouse and wrote hymns. Traveler John Melish observed in 1811, "The basis of the Society is religion . . . There is no instance of the church being neglected by those who are well and able to walk. It is their delight to attend it."

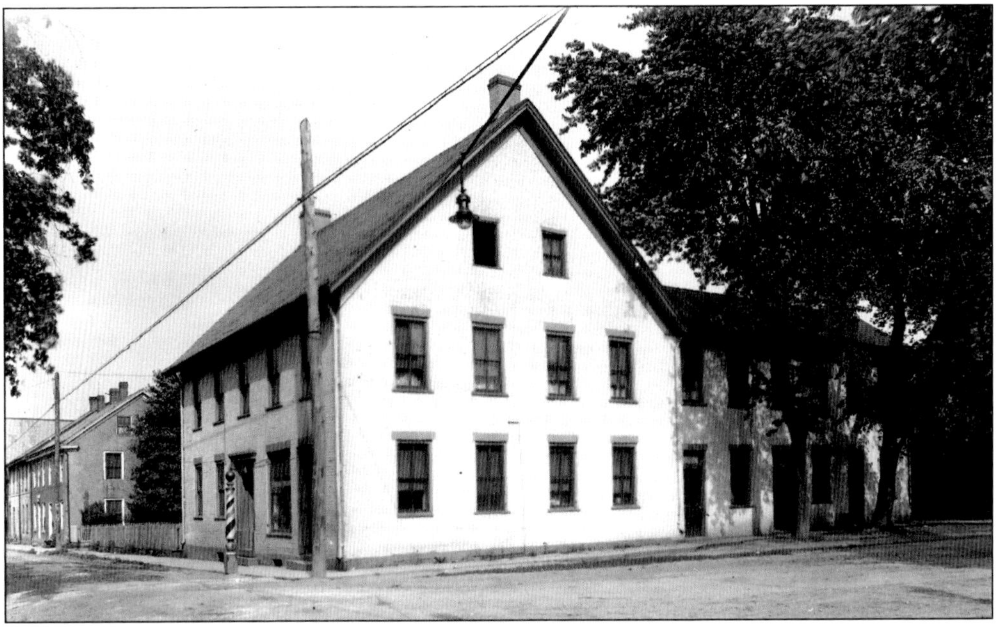

This view of upper Mercer Street from the diamond in the early 20th century shows three Harmony Society buildings: the warehouse, Wagner-Bentle house, and an 1811 structure. The pole in front advertises Melvin King's barbershop. The warehouse, today the Harmony Museum, has served as a multifamily dwelling, grocery store, candy shop, and car dealership. The rear portion, behind the trees, was added as a school for girls in 1817.

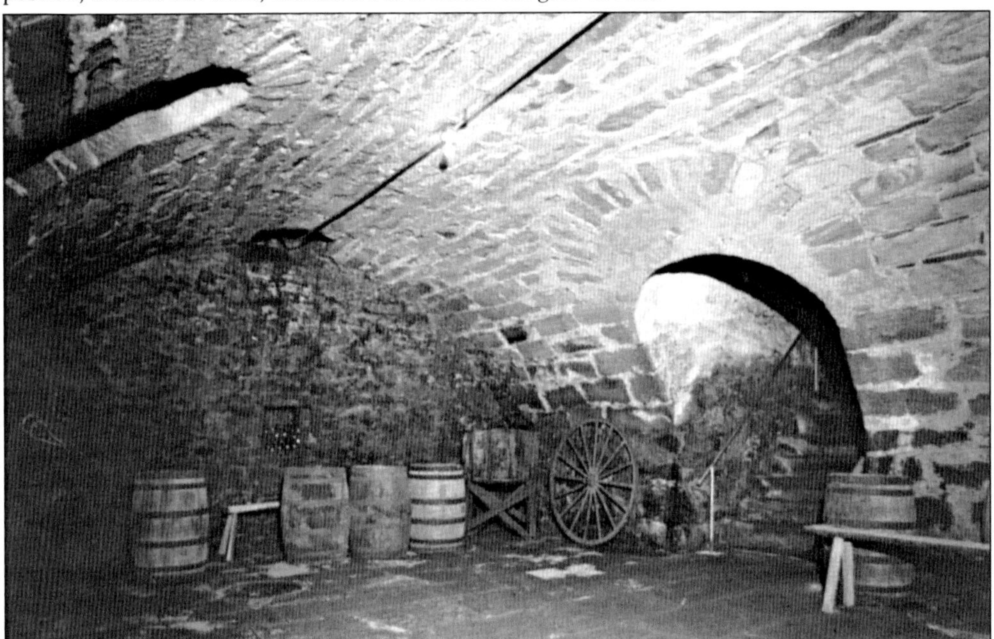

The Harmony Museum wine cellar looks much as it did when Harmonist workers constructed it in 1809. Stone for the floor was quarried from a hillside overlooking the Little Connoquenessing Creek in Jackson Township. The stone slabs were numbered and fitted together to provide a surface that has held up well for two centuries.

The stone door frame of the Harmony Society warehouse/granary (now the Harmony Museum) is capped by a carving of the Virgin Sophia, a spiritual symbol of wisdom. The rose and lily motif on the lintel is symbolic of Christ. The work was done by Frederick Reichert Rapp, an accomplished mason and architect who directed the society's building projects.

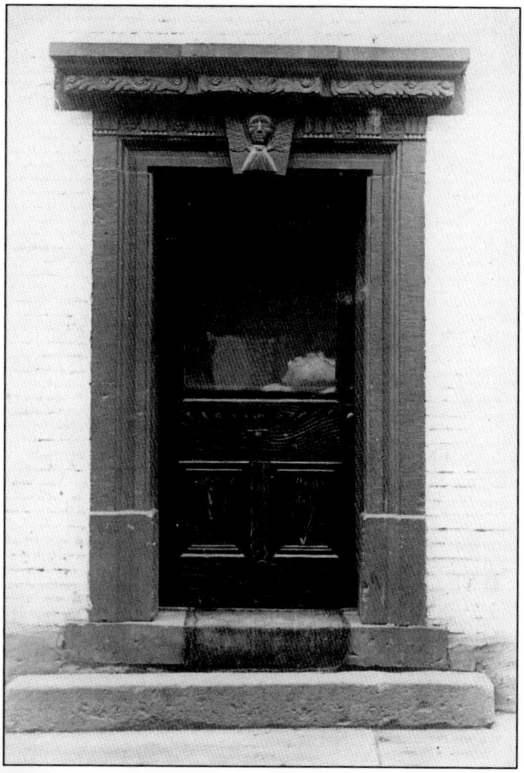

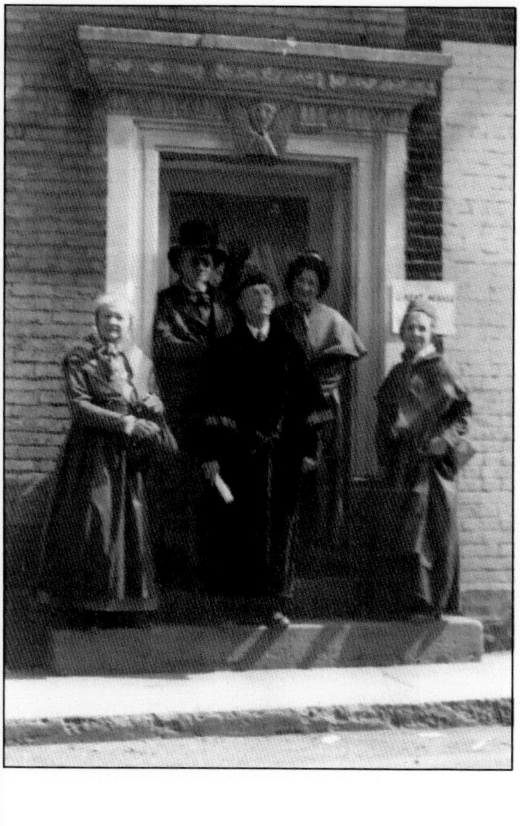

John Duss, one of the last Harmony Society trustees, poses at the society's warehouse in Harmony in 1937. He is wearing the robe of society leader George Rapp. The others are also clad in Harmonist clothing, including Christiana Kroll Knoedler (left) and Mary Truth (right), wearing silk material manufactured by society members who raised silkworms at Economy.

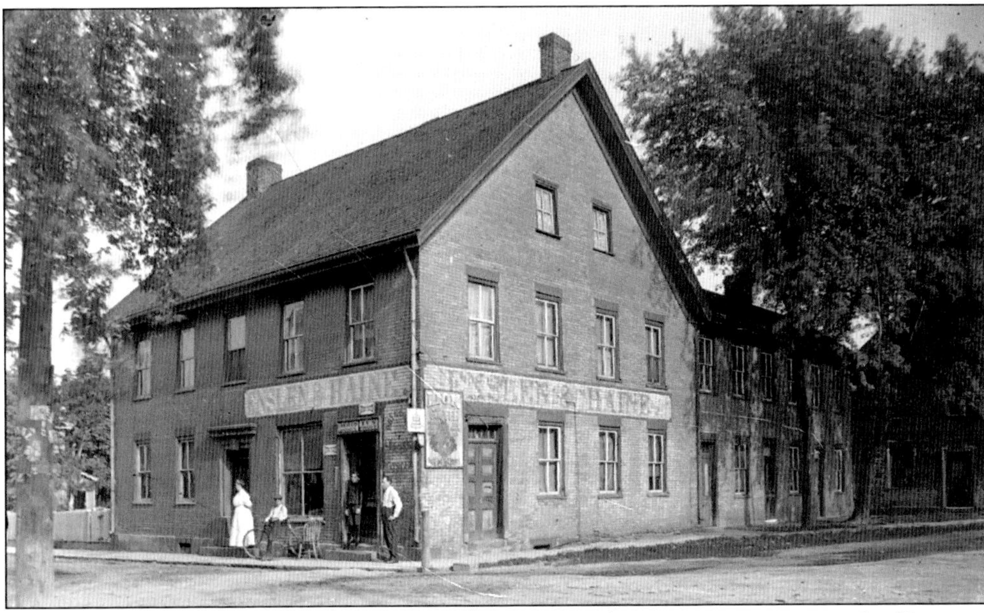

The Enslen and Haine store was one of several commercial enterprises occupying the Harmony Society warehouse over the years. One of the earliest tenants after the society departed was the Harmony Seminary for Young Ladies. Rev. Jacob Schnee, pastor of Smithfield Lutheran and Reformed Church in Pittsburgh, founded the boarding school in 1817. (Courtesy of the Pennsylvania Historical and Museum Commission/Old Economy Village.)

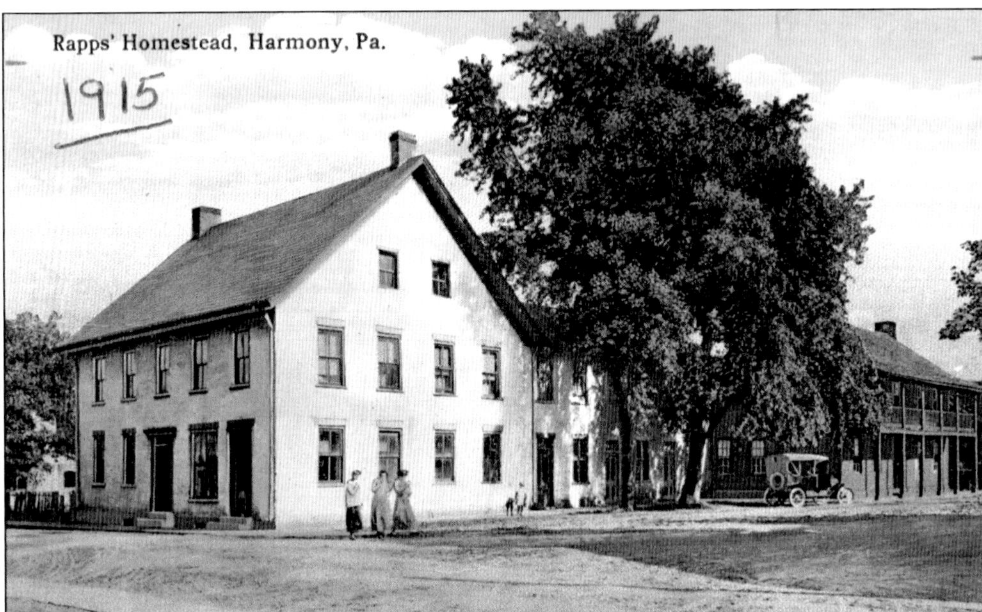

The Harmony Society warehouse is identified as Rapp's Homestead on this 1915 postcard, although George Rapp lived in a house north of the market diamond. This view shows the Langenbacher house with a double porch and brick walls that later were covered with stucco. The warehouse is now the Harmony Museum and the Langenbacher house is the Bottlebrush Art Gallery.

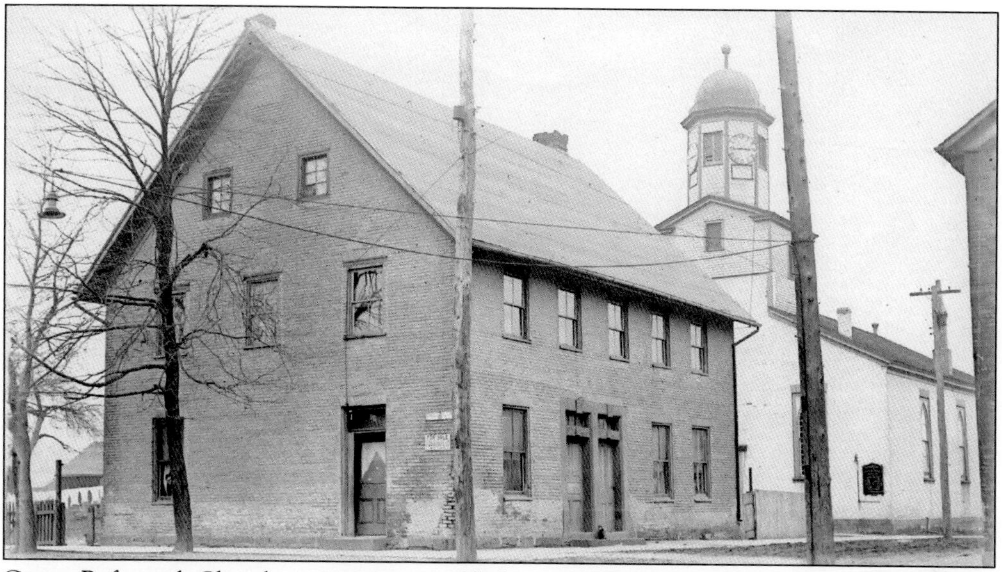

Grace Reformed Church congregation added a new sanctuary to the Harmony Society meetinghouse in 1929. The brick house in the foreground and another Harmonist building were removed. The double doorways with carved stone lintels, below, were part of the house shown above. The dated keystone lintel was incorporated in the new church addition. The other, depicting a lotus motif, was placed in a wall at the John L. Wise farm along Mercer Road and is now preserved at the Harmony Museum. (Courtesy of the Pennsylvania Historical and Museum Commission/Old Economy Village.)

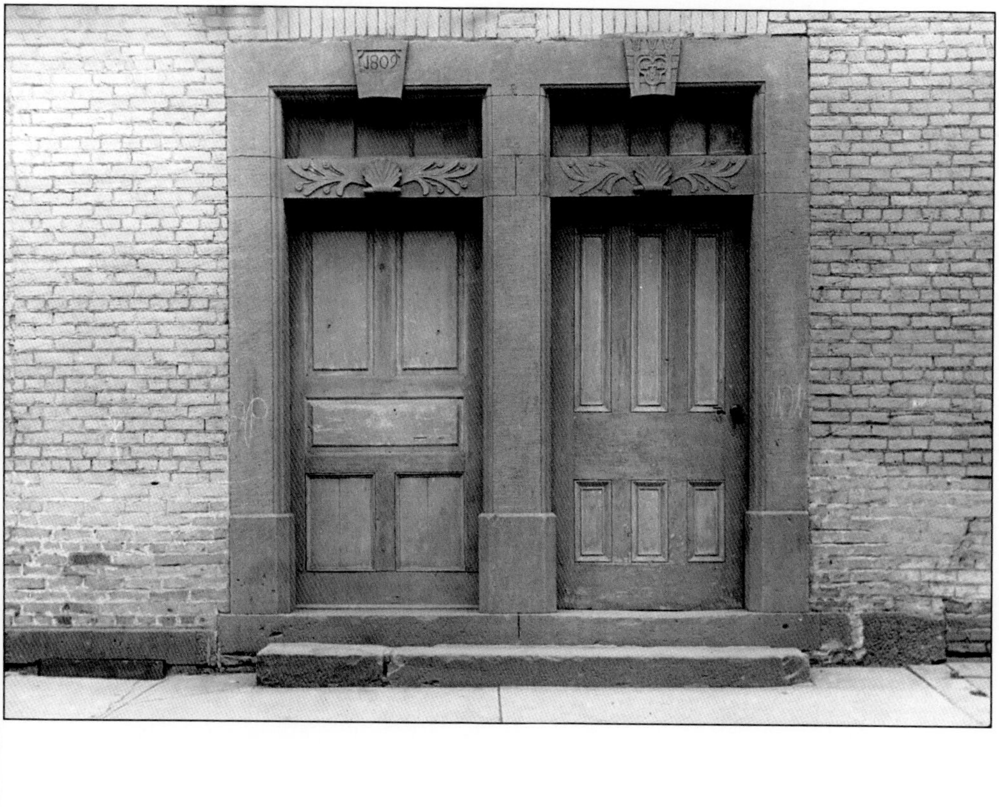

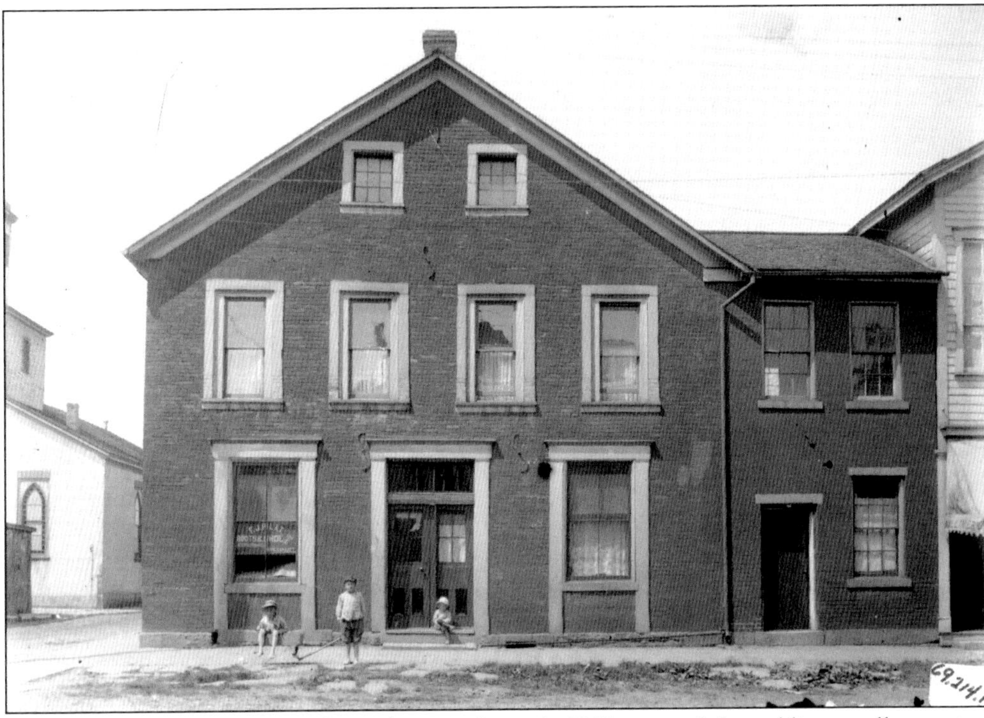

The Harmony Society's store, shown here in the early 1900s, served the public as well as society members. It contains an arched wine cellar similar to the cellar in the society's warehouse and an intricately carved stone door frame. The building is being restored with replica casement windows matching the one original Harmonist casement window that remains.

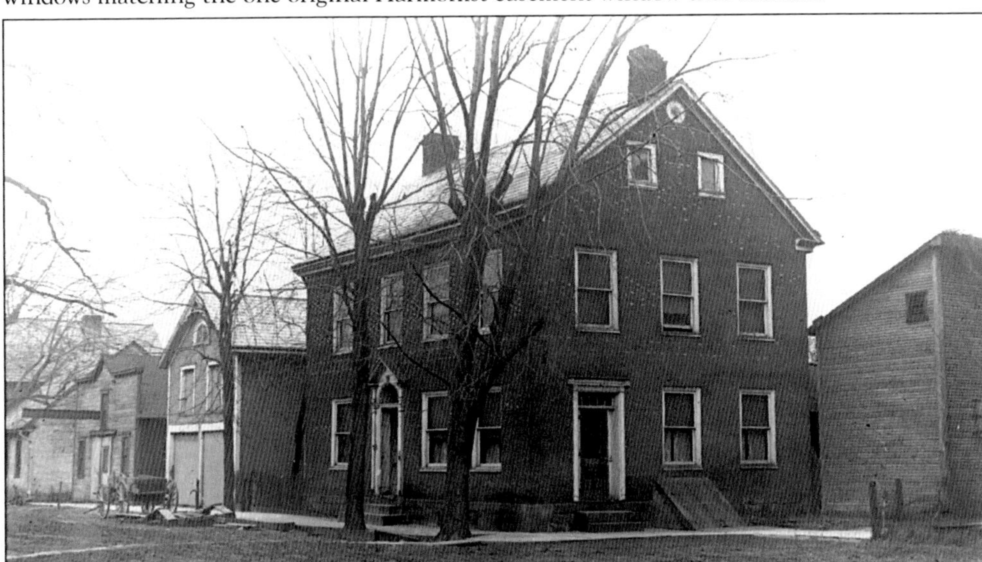

This Philadelphia Federal structure in the northeast corner of the diamond was the largest Harmonist single-family home and the only one with decorative exterior brickwork. It was built for Frederick Reichert Rapp opposite George Rapp's house. Frederick, the society's business agent, stonemason, and architect, coordinated the relocation of George's followers from Wurttemberg. (Courtesy of the Pennsylvania Historical and Museum Commission/Old Economy Village.)

The Harmony Society's one-handed clock was made by John Eberman Jr. and his son Joseph of Lancaster. In 1810, Frederick Reichert Rapp commissioned Eberman to supply a clock for the church tower. It was delivered to Harmony in May 1811 and installed later that year. The clock is displayed in the Harmony Museum. Only one of the original three faces survives. It is said that the Harmonists' clock had only one hand because they had no need to know the exact time; however, their night watchman called the time at intervals during the night: "Again a day is past and a step made nearer to our end; our time runs away and the joys of heaven are our reward." Below is a view of the handmade clockworks.

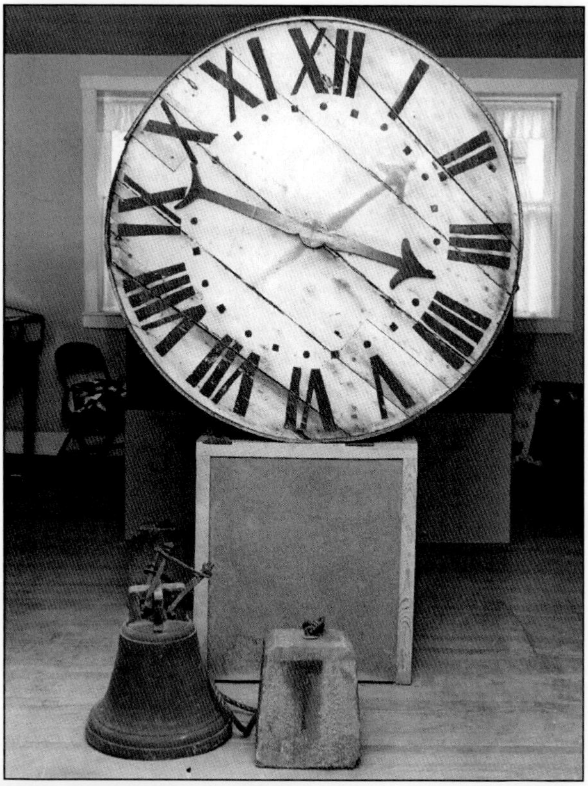

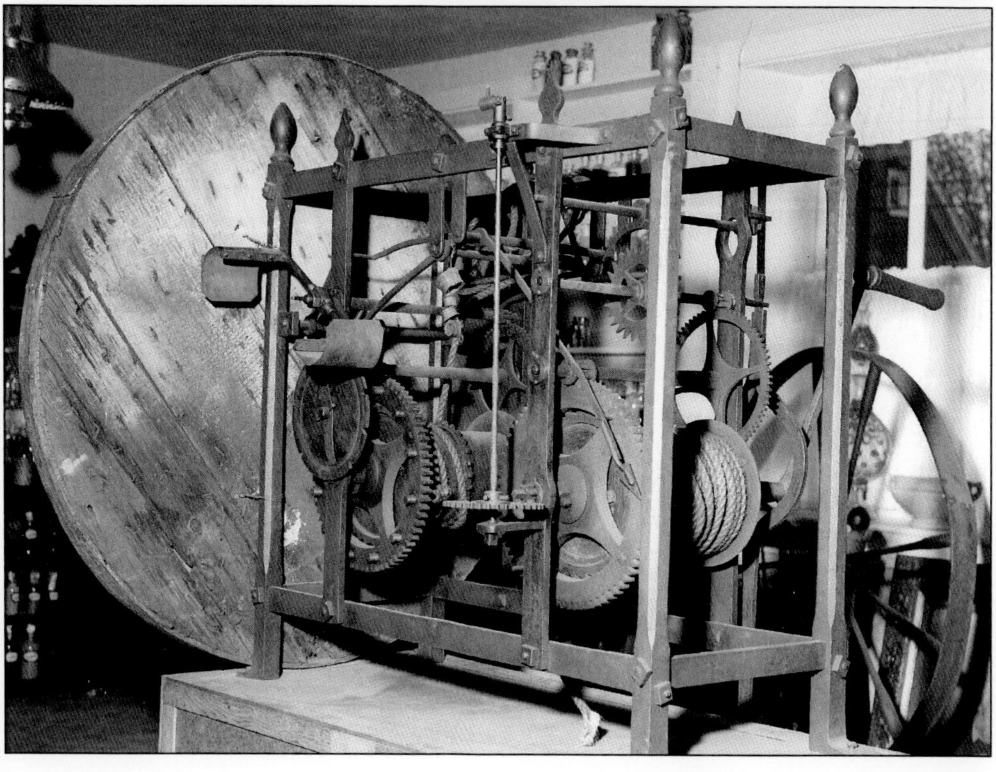

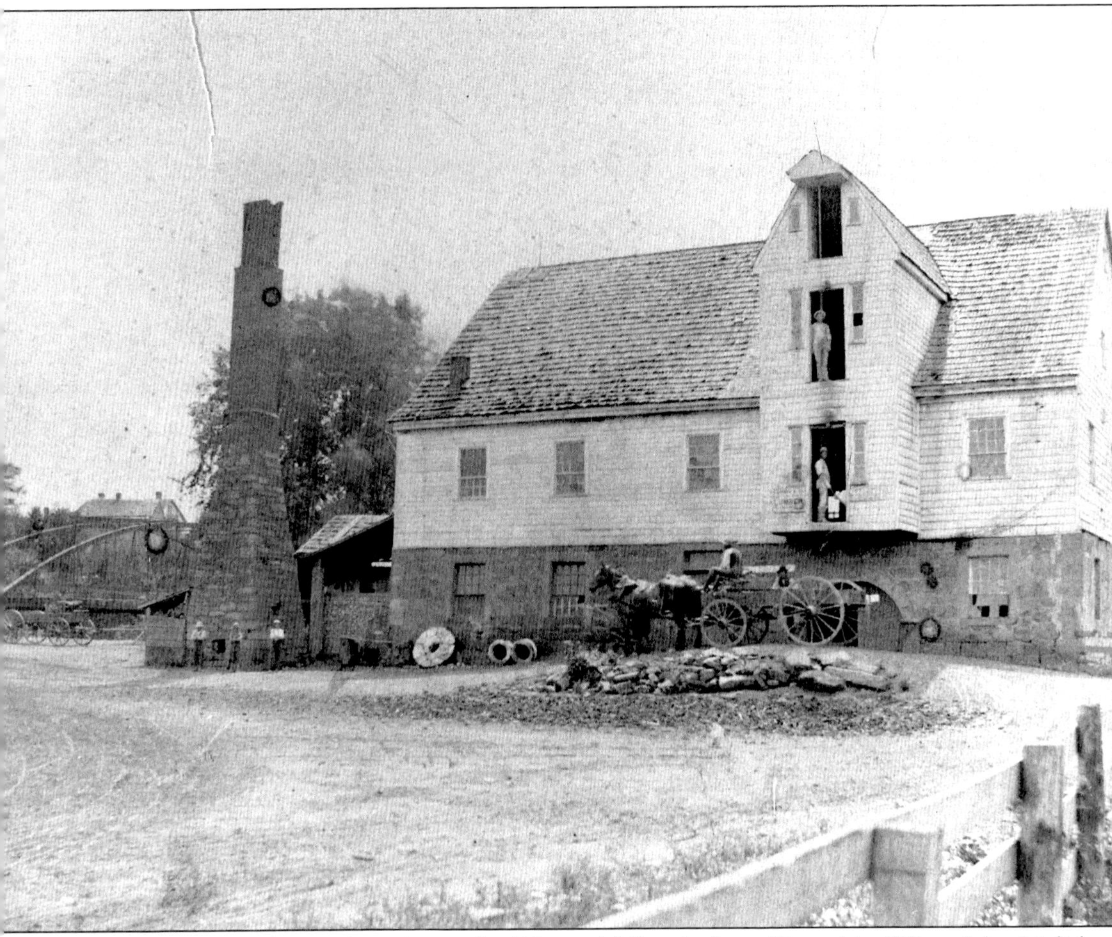

Workers pause during their day at the Edenau Mill in Jackson Township. When John Melish toured Harmony, he observed the Harmonists building a large mill on the Connoquenessing Creek in their village of Edenau (now Harmony Junction). "It is impossible to convey any adequate idea of the diligent industry and perseverance of this extraordinary people," he wrote. The mill later caught fire but was rebuilt and remained in business as the Ziegler Mill and Edenau Roller Mill. It was torn down in the early 20th century. The beaded stone archway with the 1811 keystone that capped the entrance to the original mill is displayed at the Harmony Museum. (Courtesy of Delsa White.)

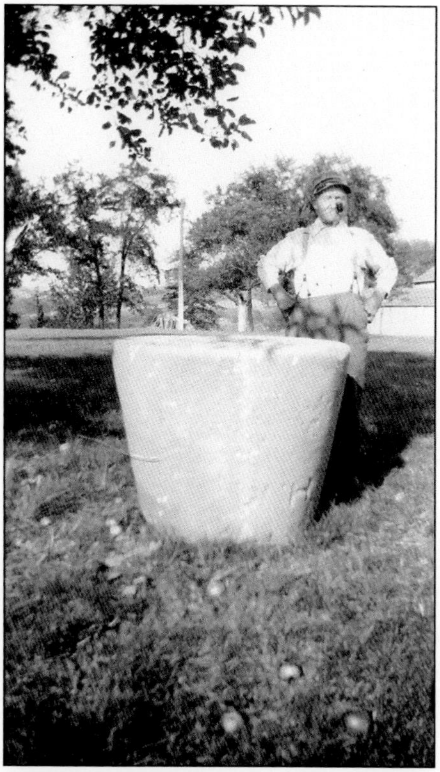

Melish saw a stone house east of town containing a gristmill and a hemp mill, an oil mill, and a fulling mill for processing cloth. The area is behind Evergreen Nursing Center, the former Knights of Pythias home, along Evergreen Mill Road. In this 1934 photograph at right, by Dr. Arthur Stewart, Davy Davis stands beside an oil grinding stone that was pulled from the Little Connoquenessing Creek behind the Pythian home. Below, his companions inspect a round millstone found in the creek. Harmonist mills produced oil from flax, pumpkin seeds, poppies, and peach pits.

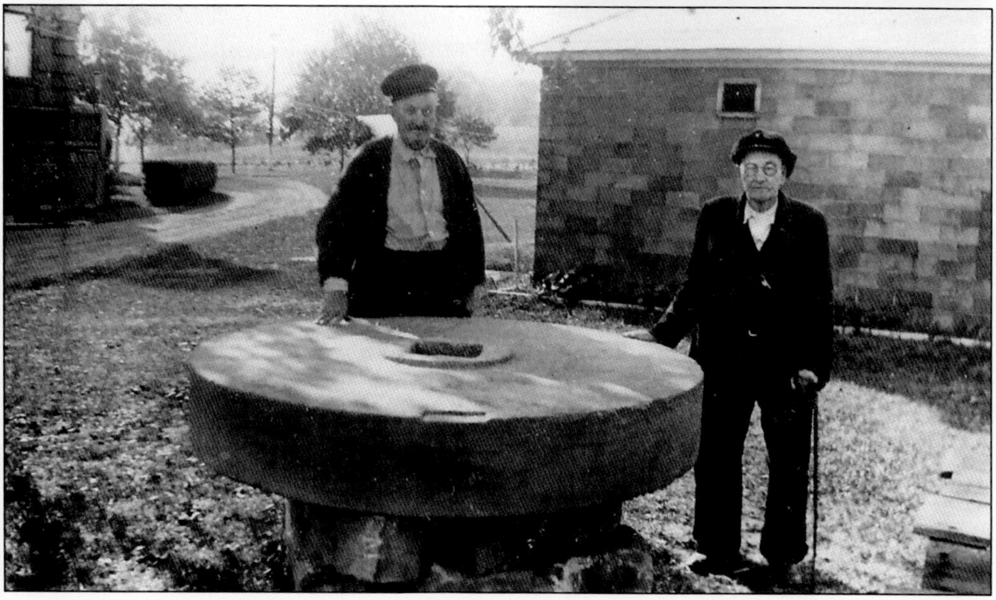

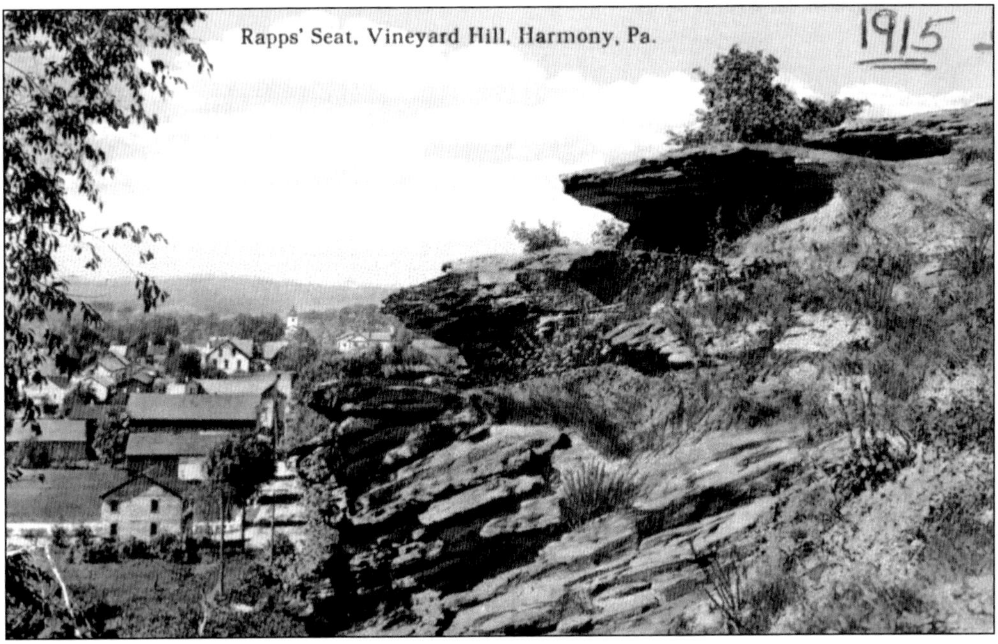

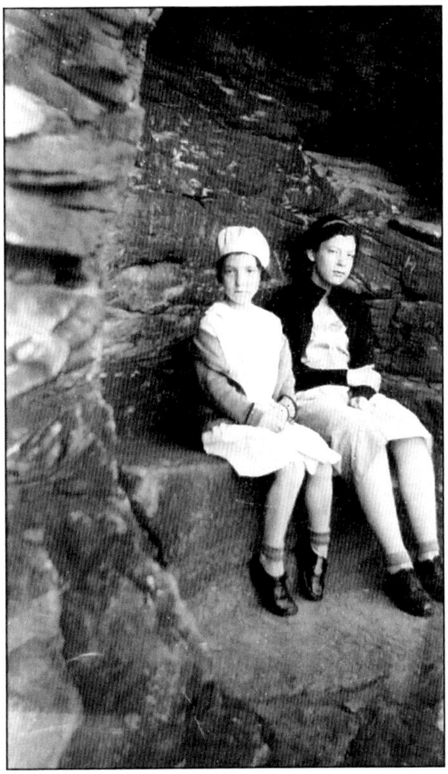

The view above shows Rapp's Seat on Vineyard Hill before trees covered the slopes. Traveler John Melish described his visit to the spot: "On our way we passed through one of the vineyards which is situated on the face of a steep hill, on the north side of the creek, and is converted into a number of terraces, supported by walls of stone in the manner that they cultivate the hills in China. We ascended by a regular flight of 137 steps; and from the top we had a fine view of the whole settlement, and of the country round." Rebekah (left) and Jane Stewart sit on Rapp's Seat for a photograph taken by their father, Dr. Arthur Stewart, in 1934.

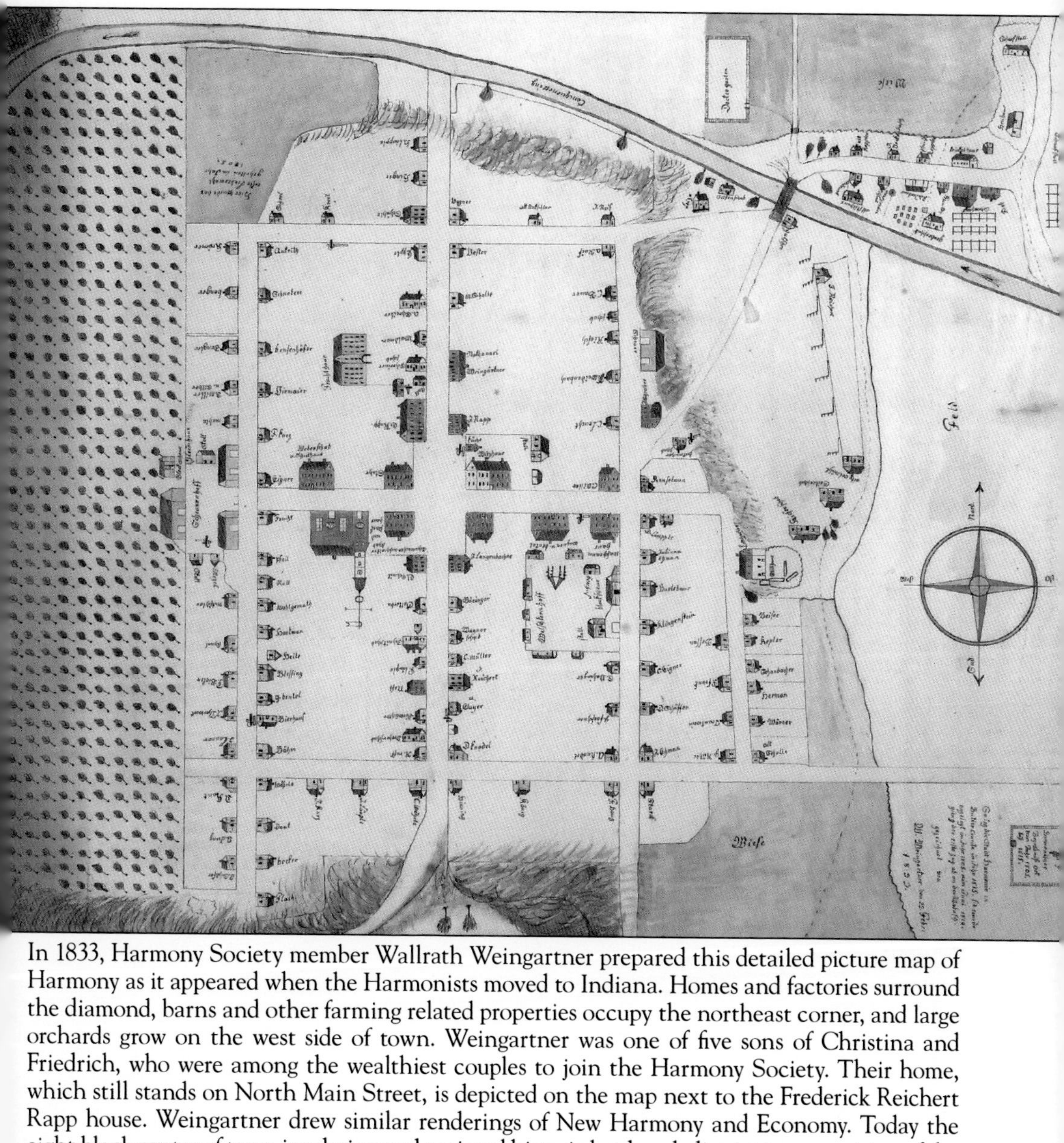

In 1833, Harmony Society member Wallrath Weingartner prepared this detailed picture map of Harmony as it appeared when the Harmonists moved to Indiana. Homes and factories surround the diamond, barns and other farming related properties occupy the northeast corner, and large orchards grow on the west side of town. Weingartner was one of five sons of Christina and Friedrich, who were among the wealthiest couples to join the Harmony Society. Their home, which still stands on North Main Street, is depicted on the map next to the Frederick Reichert Rapp house. Weingartner drew similar renderings of New Harmony and Economy. Today the eight-block center of town is a designated national historic landmark district in recognition of the cultural and architectural heritage of the founding Harmony Society. (Courtesy of Pennsylvania Historical and Museum Commission/Old Economy Village.)

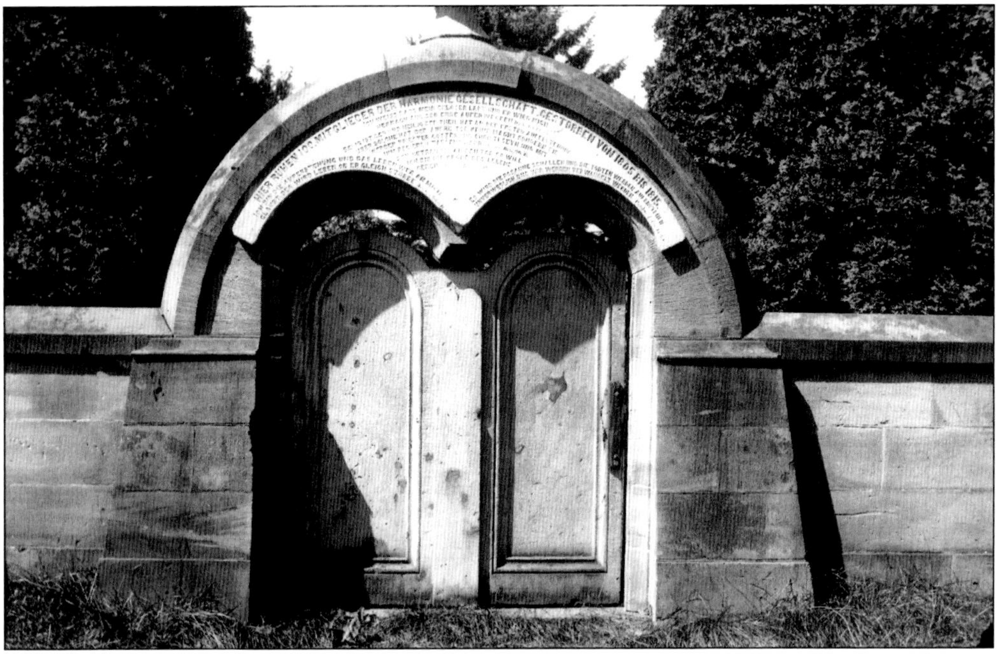

This stone wall with revolving gate surrounds the Harmonist Cemetery in Jackson Township at the edge of Harmony. Society members were buried here in unmarked graves, symbolizing their equality in the communal group. Five decades later, the society commissioned Elias Ziegler to supervise construction of the wall at a cost of $7,000.

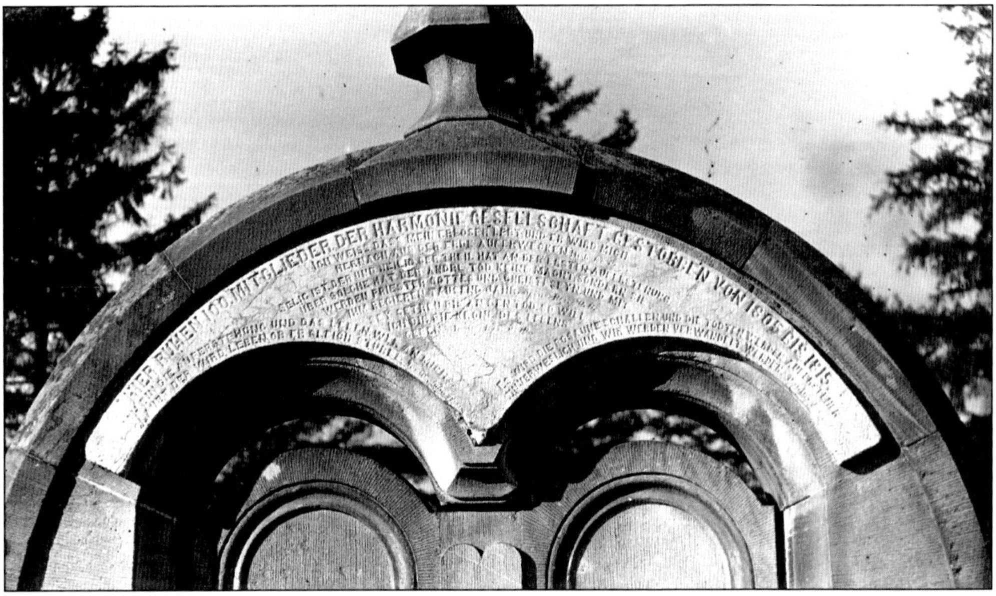

The cemetery gateway, representative of the Mosaic tablets, is carved from a solid stone slab weighing more than a ton. German inscriptions above the gate read, "Here rest 100 members of the Harmony Society who died from the years 1805 to 1815," followed by five Bible verses. The letters have been eroded by the elements, but the gate still swings easily with the push of a hand.

Three

THE MENNONITES

Mennonite Abraham Ziegler of Lehigh County agreed to buy the Harmony Society's entire holdings for $100,000. He signed the sales agreement with society business manager Frederick Reichert Rapp on May 16, 1815. Economic times grew harder, and Ziegler was unable to pay the full amount. As the Harmonists' wealth increased in Indiana, they eventually reduced the price and allowed Ziegler to make some payments in wool and other goods. He hired Jacob Swain, Samuel Swain, John Schwartz, and David Stauffer to raise sheep, paid the society with wool from the sheep, and paid the sheepherders with land.

Other Mennonites, most descendants of German and Swiss immigrants who settled in eastern Pennsylvania, followed Ziegler to Harmony. Among them were the Moyer, Boyer, Wise, and Rice families. With the Zieglers, they became known as the "First Five Families." Other early families were the Stauffers and Shontzs. Many of them built substantial houses and established farms in neighboring Connoquenessing Township (today's Jackson, Lancaster, Forward, and Connoquenessing Townships). The Harmony Farm Company organized and conducted a banking business until 1818. Shareholders were Abraham and John Ziegler, Jacob Stauffer, Henry Buchle, David Stauffer, and John Boyer. Abraham Ziegler became the town banker, storekeeper, miller, and brewer. He lacked sufficient workers to operate the industries established by the Harmonists and had to entice people of other faiths to settle in town. The Mennonites completed their meetinghouse in 1825 and conducted regular worship services there until the dawn of the 20th century. The active Mennonite membership dwindled as young people married into other faiths, and the congregation closed the meetinghouse in 1902. Local descendants of Mennonites have continued to hold reunions. A 1939 reunion of the five pioneer families lasted a week and featured five men representing each family, including Clyde R. Rice, a farmer in Lancaster Township; John L. Wise, a scientific farmer at Harmony; C. Glenn Moyer, chairman of the reunion committee; Edward F. Boyer, justice of the peace at Harmony; and Ferd Ziegler, tinner and proprietor of the Ziegler Sheet Metal Shop. It was noted that John L. Wise and his brother Paul were related to all five families.

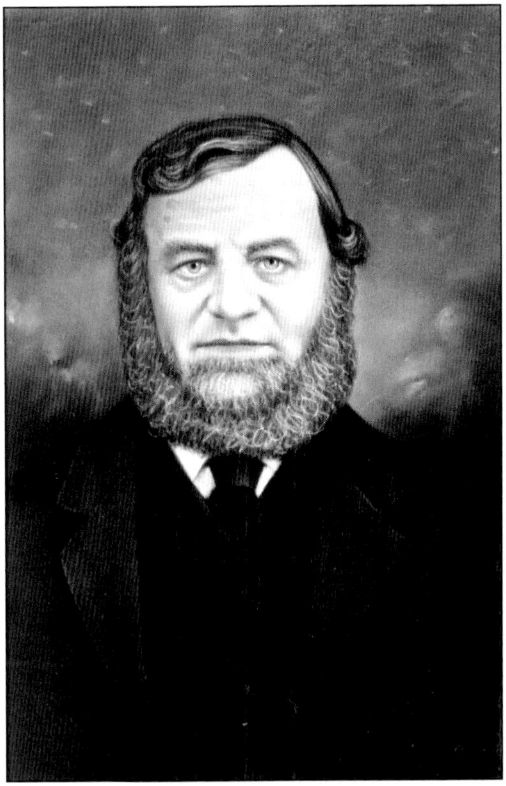

Abraham Ziegler was a 41-year-old Mennonite blacksmith from Lehigh County when he agreed to buy the Harmony Society's extensive properties, including the town of Harmony, three villages, and 9,000 acres. Ziegler and his family moved into the Langenbacher house where he died in 1836. The house, seen below, originally was the home of Harmonist Johannes Langenbacher.

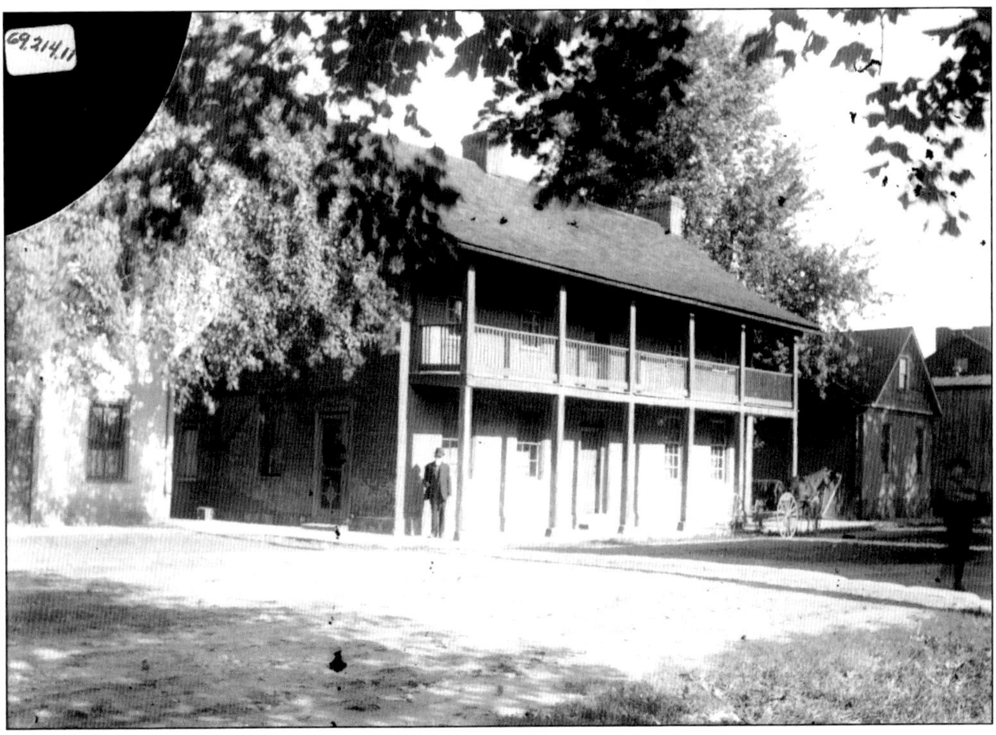

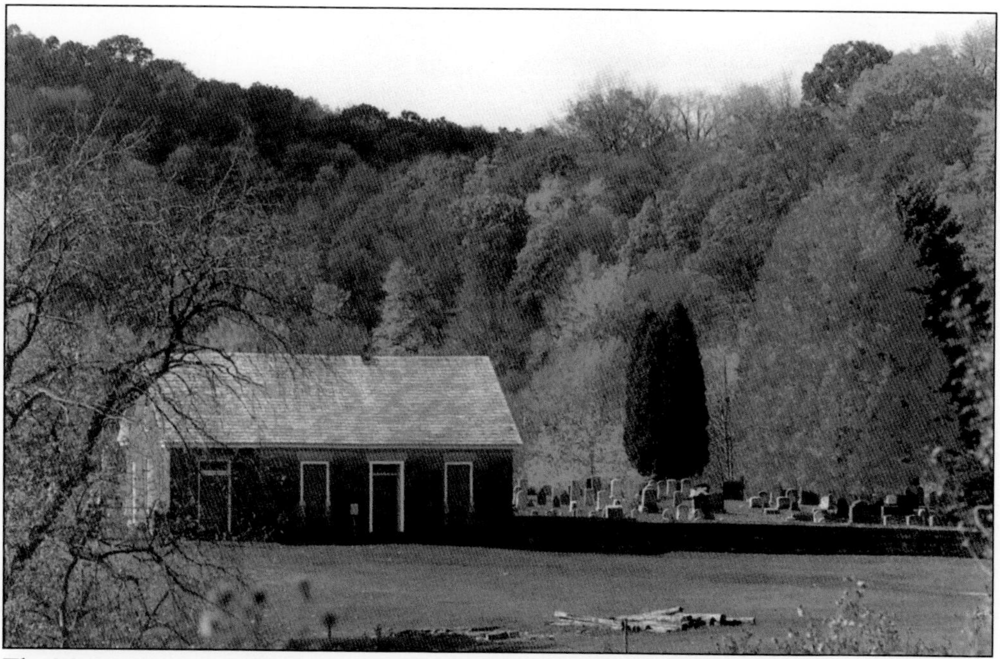

The Mennonite meetinghouse was built of stone on a hillside north of Harmony in 1825. The congregation selected the site in Jackson Township to accommodate farm families living outside of town. A brick section was later added. The Mennonites held their last regular worship service here in 1902. Historic Harmony owns and maintains the building.

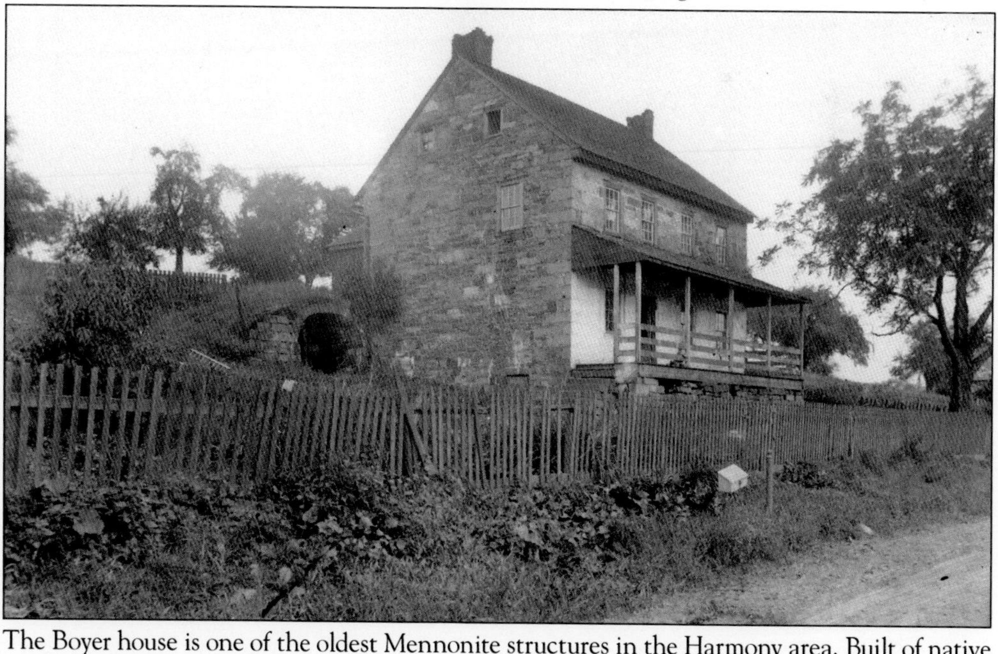

The Boyer house is one of the oldest Mennonite structures in the Harmony area. Built of native stone in 1816, it stands along U.S. Route 19 in Jackson Township north of town. It was the home of John Boyer, the first bishop of the Harmony Mennonite congregation. Boyer was among the first Mennonites to join Ziegler in Harmony. By 1818, Boyer had purchased about 1,200 acres from Ziegler.

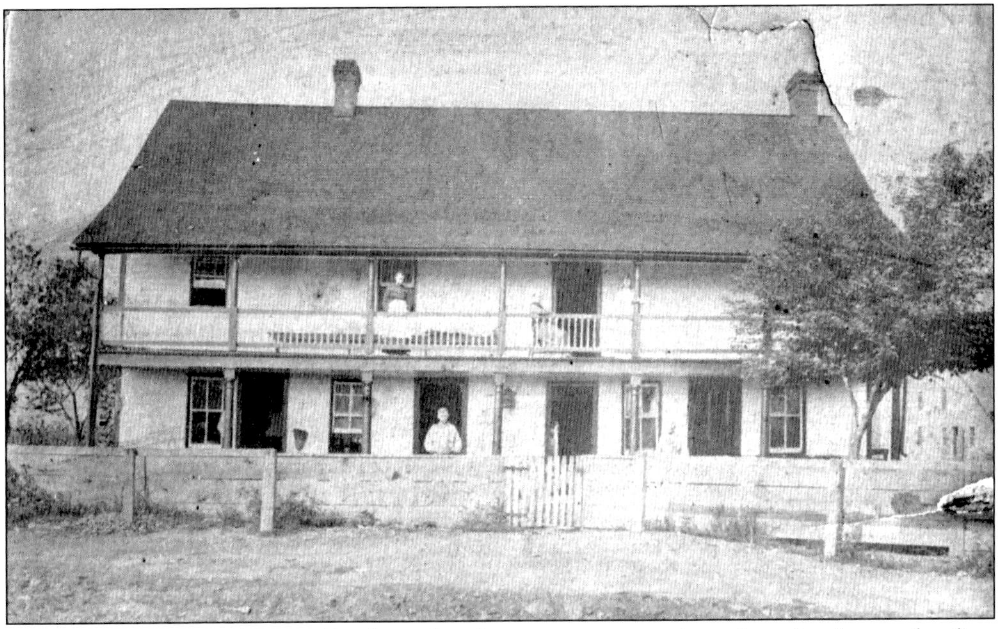

The Drover's Inn on Mercer Road north of town was a stopping place for drovers herding livestock to market in Pittsburgh. Under the ownership of Abraham Shontz, it was a popular watering spot, especially during Harmony Fair days. The Connoquenessing Valley Agricultural Association held a fair and race meet from 1874 to 1885 on 20 acres of the Shontz farm. The Wise family has owned the property since the late 1800s.

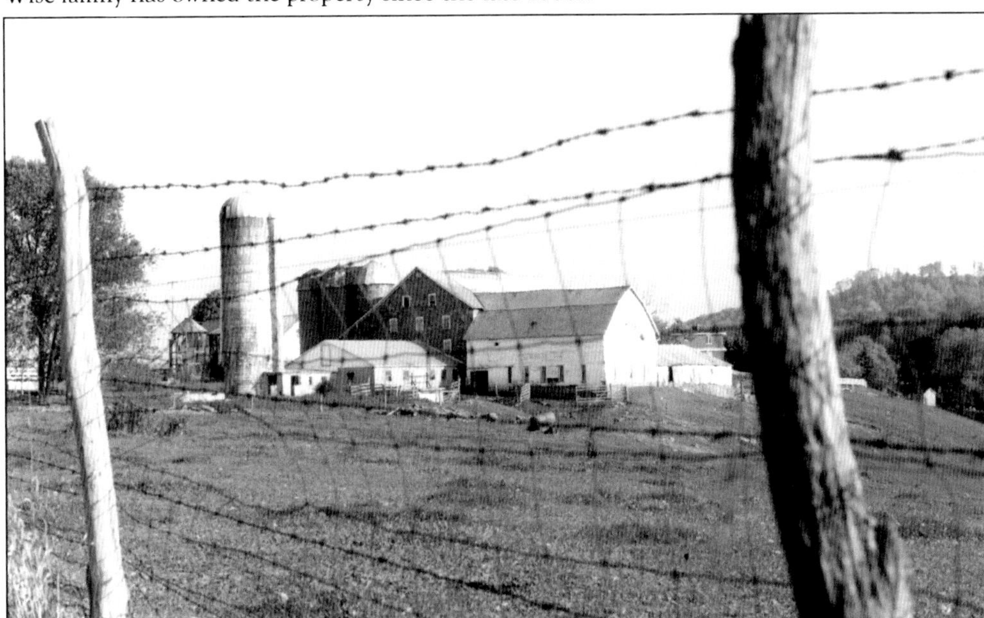

This view of Drover's Inn farm shows the stone barn built in 1835 by Aaron and Elizabeth Ziegler Shontz. John L. Wise, born on the farm in 1892, recalled the days when the farm sprouted oil rigs and coal was mined from hillsides near the Mennonite meetinghouse. His uncle Levi Wise used his profits from coal mining to pay for law school, became an attorney, and bought the *Butler Eagle* newspaper. (Courtesy of Sally Jones Rodgers.)

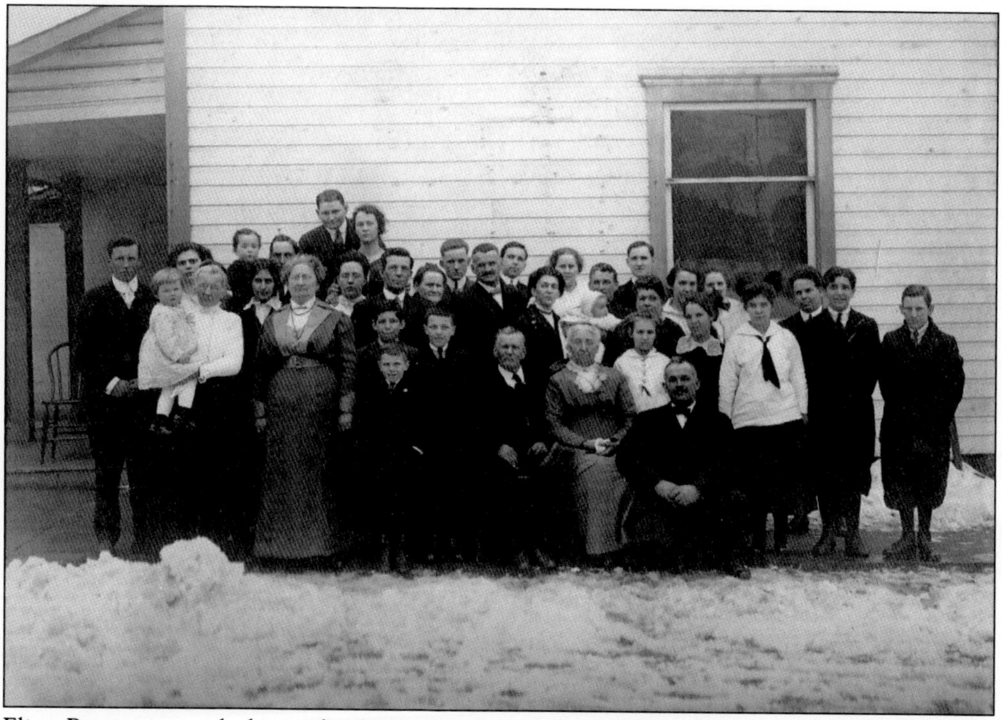

Elias Boyer sits with his wife, Susan Lambert Boyer (front, center) and family in their snow-covered yard at Liberty and German Streets. Their son Charles C. Boyer (with baby) and wife, Salome "Sadie" Schnauffer Boyer to his right, stand behind his parents. The Boyers purchased the property in February 1904 and moved to Harmony from Lancaster Township. Elias was a descendant of Rev. John Boyer. (Courtesy of Marsha Moser Huba.)

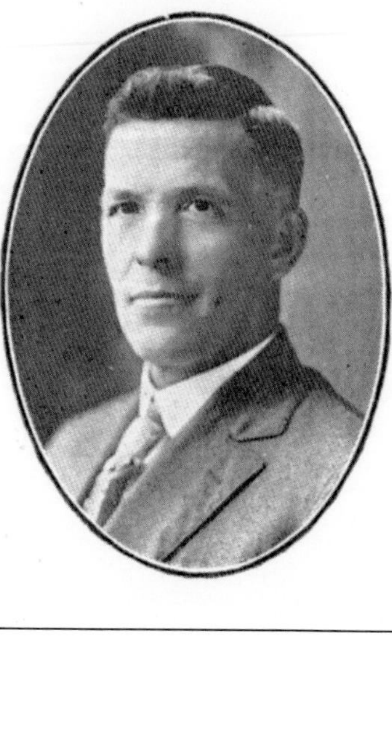

FOR

COUNTY COMMISSIONER

Edward F. Boyer

Of Harmony Borough
Formerly Lancaster Twp.

Your Vote and Influence Solicited

Taught in the Common Schools; 24 years a farmer on 200 acre farm in Lancaster township; rig builder.

Republican Primary September 18, 1923

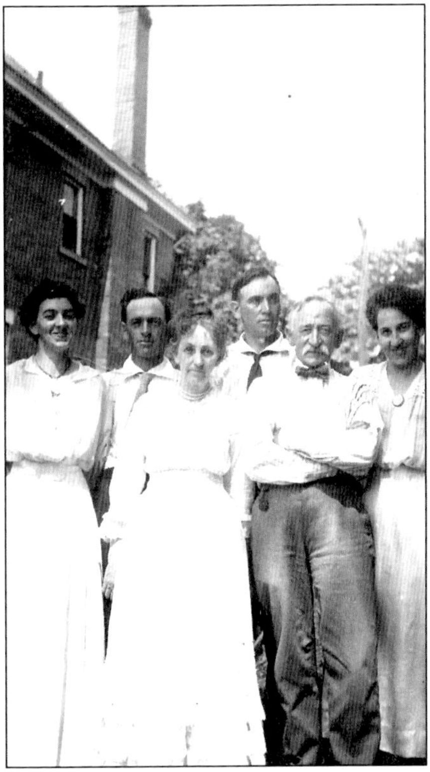

Gottlieb Zeigler, a descendant of the pioneer Abraham Ziegler, is shown with his wife, Ida Dambaugh Randolph Zeigler, and their children, from left to right, Emma Zeigler Zehner, Clarence Zeigler, Walter Zeigler, and Virginia Zeigler Kelly. The photograph was taken in 1920. (Courtesy of May Zeigler Lutz.)

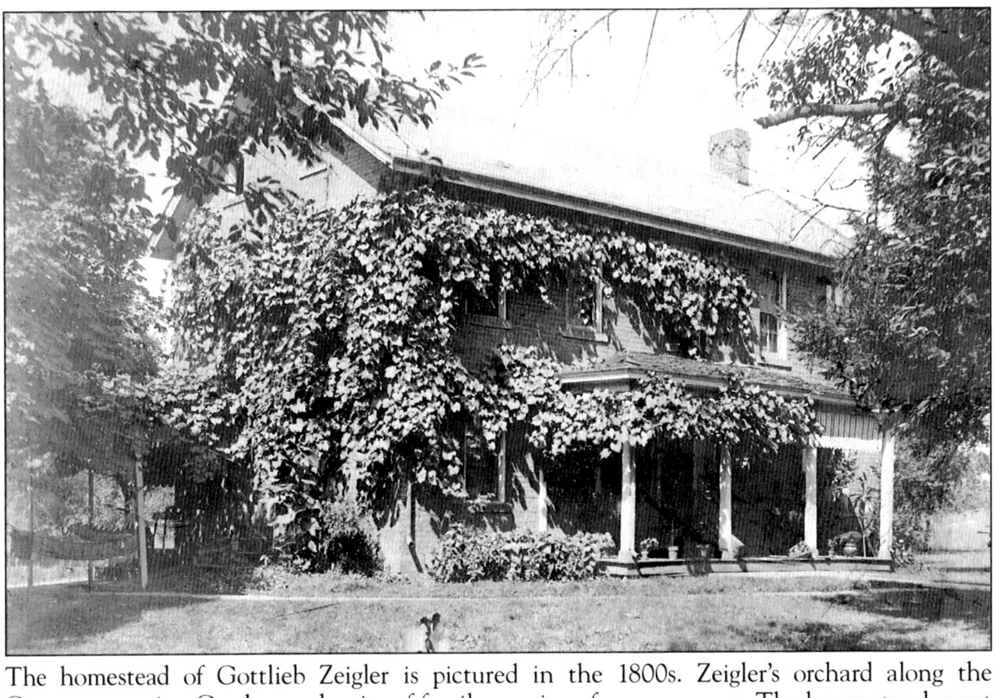

The homestead of Gottlieb Zeigler is pictured in the 1800s. Zeigler's orchard along the Connoquenessing Creek was the site of family reunions for many years. The house stands next to the creek north of the Mercer Road bridge. The porch has been removed, and the house is now painted white. (Courtesy of Bruce Randolph Zeigler.)

Walter Randolph Zeigler stands at the door of the Harmony Post Office, the former Harmonist Wagner-Bentle house, where he served as postmaster. The son of Gottlieb and Ida Zeigler, Walter died at the age of 43 in 1924, leaving his widow, Katherine Shaffer Shaner Zeigler, and three young children. (Courtesy of May Zeigler Lutz.)

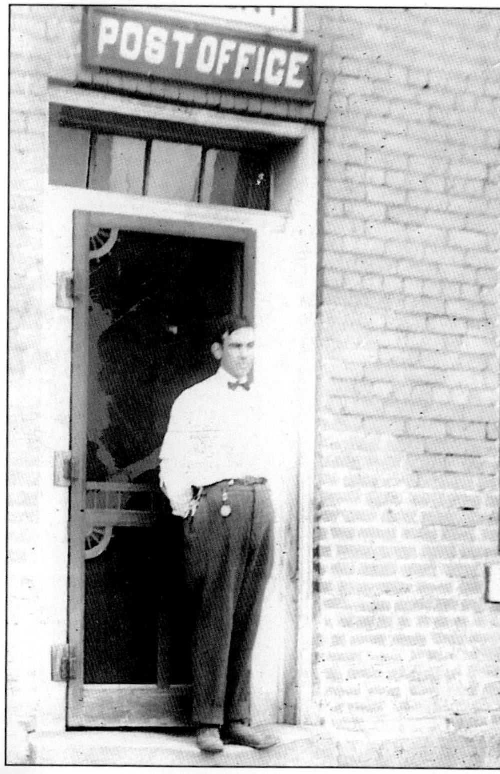

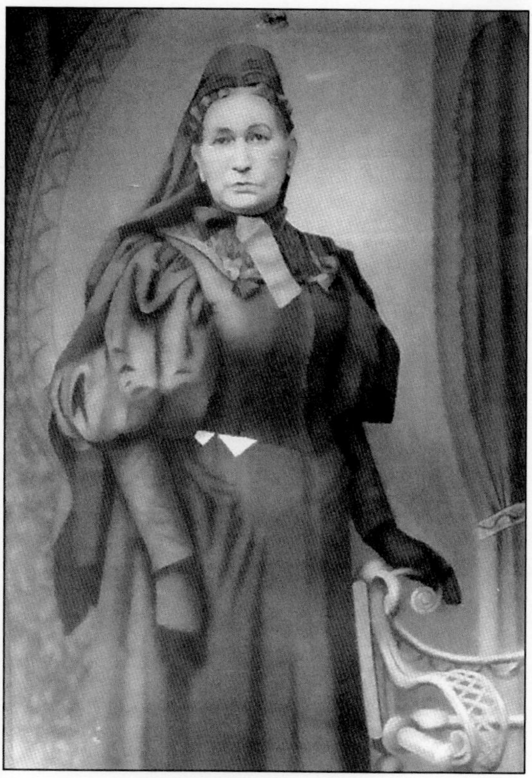

Artist Gertrude Ziegler (1874–1963) was the daughter of Elias and Melissa Goehring Fiedler Ziegler and a descendant of the Mennonite pioneer. She was well known for her artistic talent, creativity, free spirit, and unconventional dress. After her father's death, she created this portrait in charcoal of her mother dressed in "widow's weeds" as black mourning clothes commonly were called. The portrait hangs in the Harmony Museum.

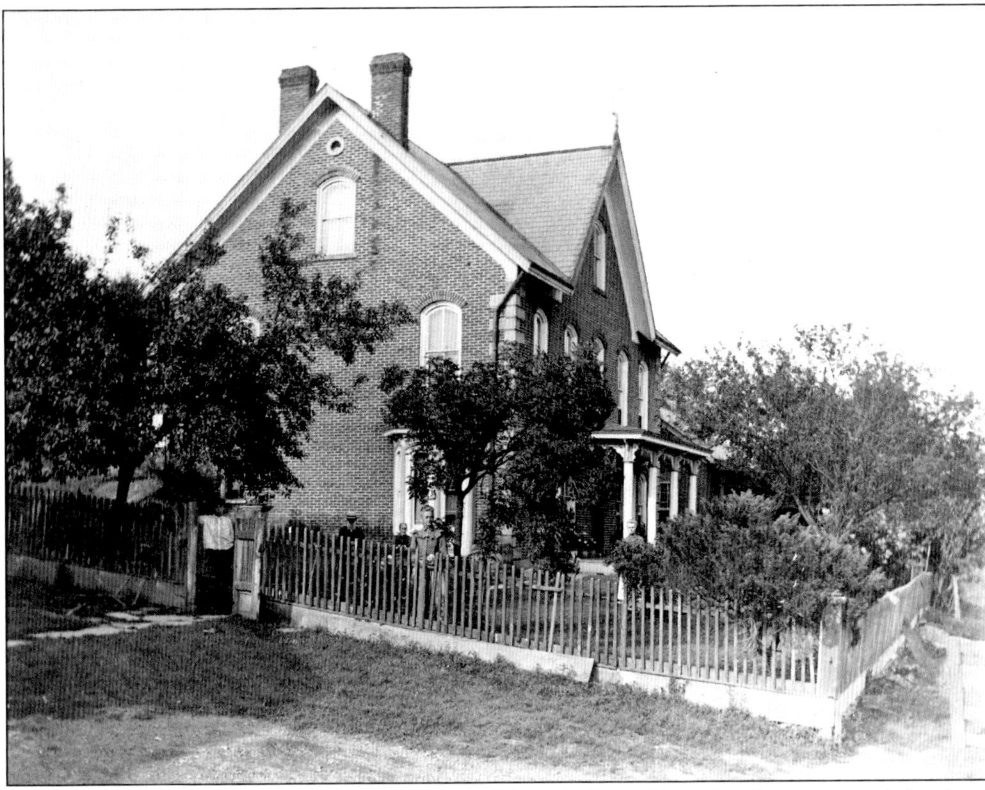

The Martin Sitler family is shown in the yard of their Jackson Township home around the dawn of the 20th century. From left to right are Maxwell Sitler (grandson of the Sitlers), Martin Sitler, his wife, Fanny Zeigler Sitler, and their daughters Lorraine Sitler Gallagher and Elizabeth Sitler Goehring. The 160-acre Brashear Camp for Pittsburgh children operated on the Sitler farm from 1930 until the early 1980s. The property is now privately owned. Below, a young boy stands at the entrance to the Sitler wine cellar in 1934.

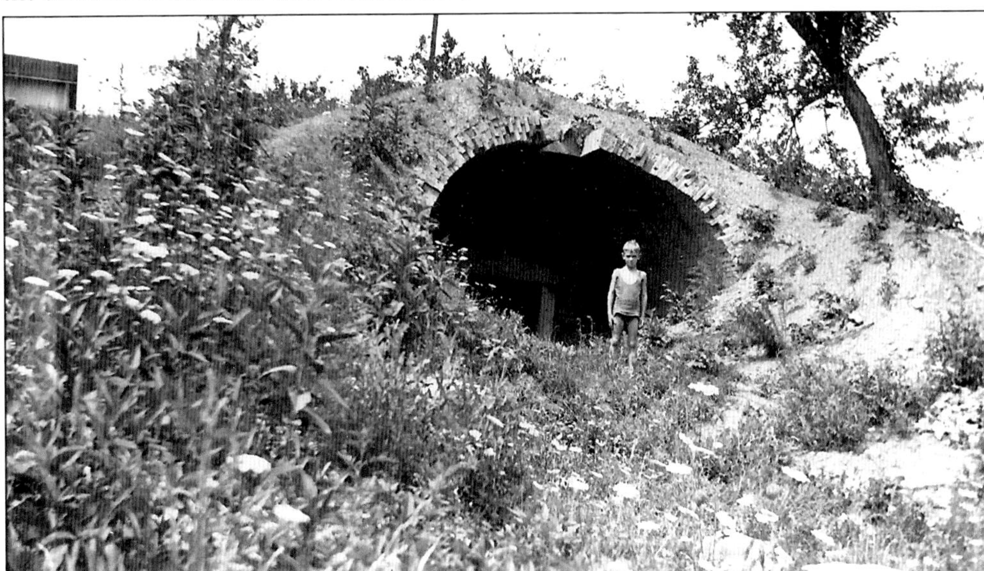

Sec. 562, P. L. & R.
U. S. Postage
PAID
Zelienople, Pa.
Permit No. 11

THE ZIEGLER

CENQUATENNIAL CELEBRATION

AUGUST 6 TO 12, 1939 HARMONY, PA.

An entire week of celebrations in honor of the Five Family Pioneers since 1804 in the Harmony - Zelienople Community.

Rice - Wise - Moyer - Boyer - Ziegler

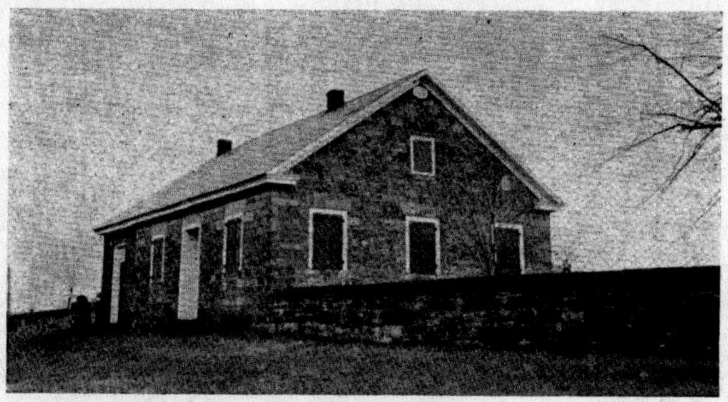

THE HISTORIC MENNONITE CHURCH, HARMONY, PA.

WELCOME TO SPECIAL SERVICES IN THIS CHURCH
AT 2 P. M., SUNDAY, AUGUST 6, 1939
This Service Marks The Initial Event in the Celebration

Spend Your Vacation In Harmony

ATTEND THIS CENQUATENNIAL CELEBRATION
IN HONOR OF

The Five Famliy Pioneers

Keep This Valuable Souvenir Program — Bring It With You

This Ziegler Cenquatennial Celebration program invites descendants of Harmony's "First Five Families" of Mennonite descent to a weeklong celebration.

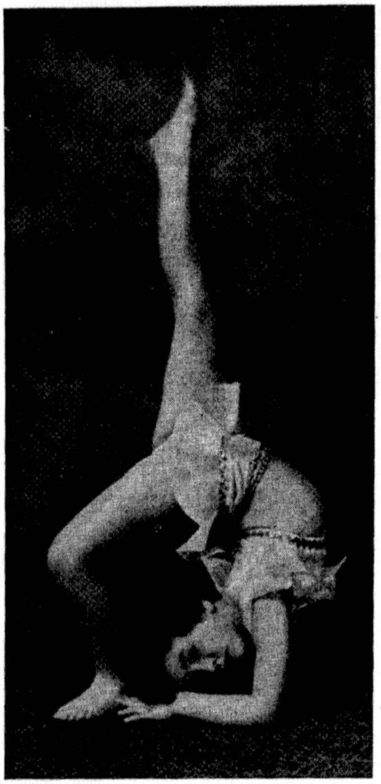

MISS DOLORES CLAYTON

Dolores Clayton is an acrobatic dancer of delightful charm and accomplishment. She is eight years old and lives at Harmony, Pa. She is a pupil of the Jack Barry Studios at Pittsburgh, Pa. Together with her brother, Billy, she will appear on the program of the Celebration alternate nights.

SPECIAL ATTRACTIONS OF CENQUATENNIAL CELEBRATION

The Mennonite Church service on Sunday afternoon at 2 o'clock.

Special entertainment programs each night at Rapp park on the grand stand in front of the bleachers.

Band music each night.

Boxing bouts Monday and Wednesday nights; finals Friday night.

Mushball games each afternoon in the meadow formerly known as the Harmonite Orchards, just north of the Rapp Park along the Connoquenessing.

Childrens pet parade for all youth Thursday at 2 p. m.

Museum of pioneer relics of the Five Famoly early settlers.

American Indians of the Mohawk Tribe in full tribal costume will camp here all week and display genuine Indian wares.

Model Airplane flying contes Wednesday at 2 p. m. Prizes given.

Five Family Public Wedding Ceremony, Monday through Friday.

Historic tours of Harmony and vicinity.

Carnival events each night at Rapp Park.

THE FIVE FAMILY REUNION ALL DAY SATURDAY AT RAPP PARK.

Read detailed description of these events on following pages.

NO INTOXICATING LIQUOR PERMITTED ON THE GROUNDS DURING THE CELEBRATION

Shown here is the second page of the Ziegler Cenquatennial Celebration program.

THE ZIEGLER CENQUATENNIAL CELEBRATION

Calendar of events, Sunday, August 6, through August 12, 1939

All events on Eastern Standard Time.

Each Evening—A Wedding, Carnival Events and Entertainment Program

SUNDAY, AUG. 6 2 P. M.—Religious services in the Historic Mennonite church at Harmony, featuring addresses by Hon. Judge John H. Wilson and Rev. A. G. Steiner. Chorus and quartet from Ohio.

MONDAY, AUG. 7—Band Music, Dolores Clayton acrobatic dancing, Boxing bouts 10 P. M.Mushball game 2 P. M.

TUESDAY, AUG. 8—Evans City Band, Indians in tribal costume, Mushball game.

HON. JUDGE JOHN H. WILSON

President Judge of Butler County. Judge Wilson was born and lived in Harmony, attending public school here. He became a school teaceher, advanced his education and became an attorney. He was elected district attorney and later judge. His interest in local history and clean government has won him a wide honor. Two years ago he published a history of Harmony depicting the days of his boyhood here.

He will speak at the services in the Mennonite church at 2 P. M., Sunday. August 6.

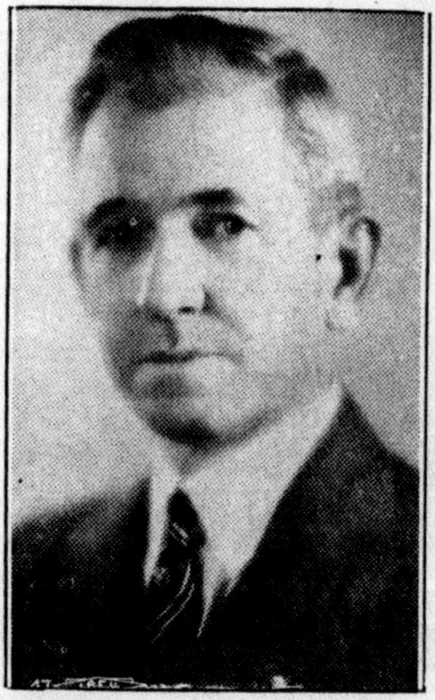

WEDNESDAY. AUG. 8—Model airplane flying contest, 2 P. M., Rapp park. Dolores Clayton; Boxing bouts 11 P. M.

THURSDAY, AUG. 9—Kiddies pet parade 2 P. M. Mushball game 3 P. M. Evening Zelienople high school band; John S. Duss and Harmonite costume display.

FRIDAY, AUG 10—Harmony band concert, finals in boxing matches, acrobatic dancing.

SATURDAY, AUG. 12—ALL DAY—FIVE FAMILY REUNION AT

RAPP PARK, HARMONY

This is page three of the Ziegler program.

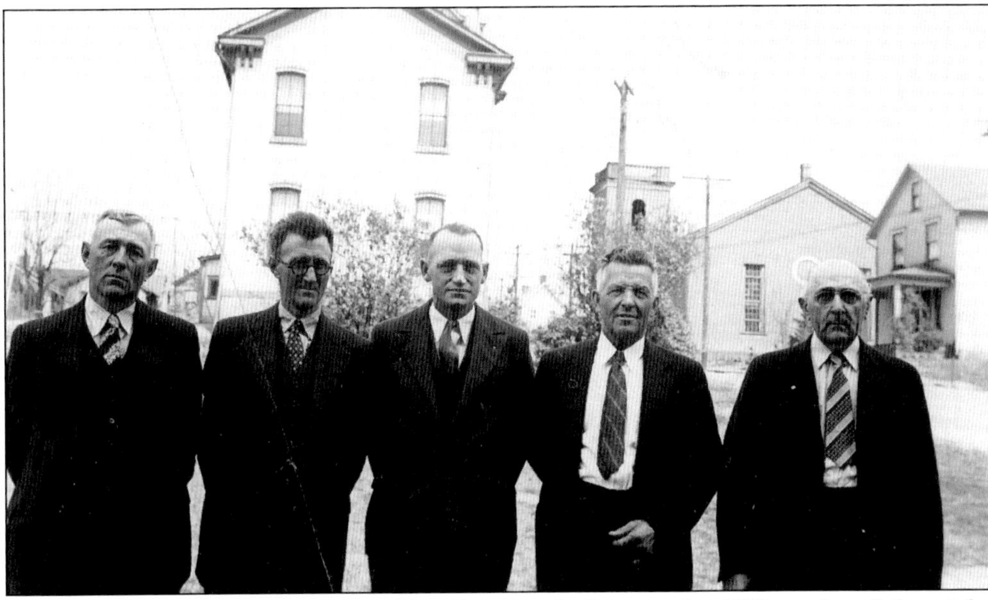

Descendants of Harmony Mennonite "First Five Families" pictured in 1939 are, from left to right, Clyde R. Rice, John L. Wise, C. Glenn Moyer, Edward F. Boyer, and Ferd Ziegler. (Courtesy of Ruth Werner, photograph by Dr. Arthur Stewart.)

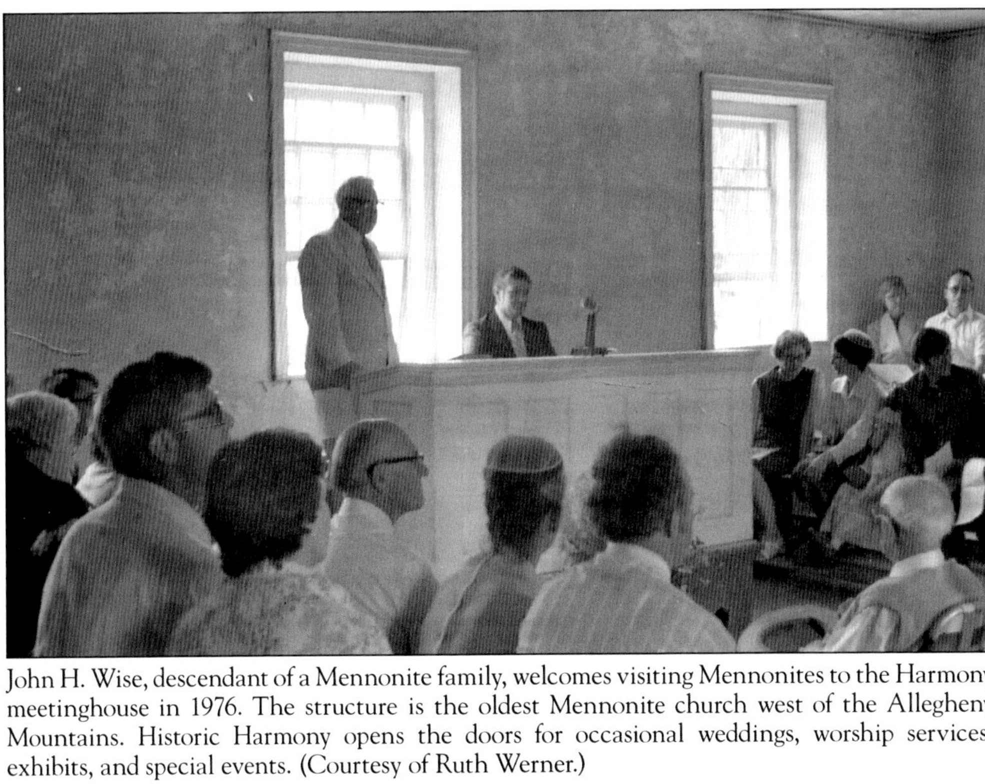

John H. Wise, descendant of a Mennonite family, welcomes visiting Mennonites to the Harmony meetinghouse in 1976. The structure is the oldest Mennonite church west of the Allegheny Mountains. Historic Harmony opens the doors for occasional weddings, worship services, exhibits, and special events. (Courtesy of Ruth Werner.)

Four

RELIGION AND EDUCATION

Freedom to worship in their own way brought the Harmonists to America, and their spiritual life was the binding force that kept their society alive for a century. Their brick meetinghouse became famous for the one-handed clock with three faces mounted on its tower.

Harmony's first Mennonite families also worshipped there until 1825 when they constructed a stone meetinghouse adjacent to their cemetery north of town. The next year, Abraham Ziegler sold the Harmonist meetinghouse to the German Evangelical and Reformed congregation. Its name evolved to Grace Evangelical and Reformed Church and is now Grace Church of Harmony. Forerunners of the Harmony-Zelienople United Methodist and Calvin Presbyterian Churches were founded in Harmony. In Lancaster Township, St. John's Evangelical Lutheran "Stone" Church was organized in 1806, and the Zion Lutheran congregation in Middle Lancaster was formed in 1842.

The Harmony Society opened the first school in town. Although the Harmonists spoke German, they taught their children English along with writing and arithmetic. After the Harmonists left, subscription schools were offered. An early teacher was John Fleming, poet and post master who founded Flemingsburg between Harmony and Zelienople.

Rev. Jacob Schnee, pastor of Pittsburgh's Smithfield Lutheran Church, established the Harmony Seminary for Young Ladies in 1817 in the former Harmony Society warehouse. Among trustees were prominent western Pennsylvanians Christian Buhl and Philipp Passavant, both of Zelienople, and Pittsburghers William Wilkins, James Ross, Henry Baldwin, and Walter Forward.

The Harmony Collegiate Institute was located in the old society weaver shop on Mercer Street and was succeeded by a public school. Future songwriter Stephen Collins Foster attended classes there while his family boarded at the Benjamin Franklin Otto home (now Harmony Moose Lodge), according to Otto family members. Major League Baseball player George "Rube" Waddell also attended school in Harmony.

A two-room brick schoolhouse was built on the town commons in 1852. Thirty years later, it was replaced by a larger brick structure on Mercer Street that served both elementary and high school grades. Harmony High School operated until 1932. Professor Vickerman and Raymond Gibb served as principals.

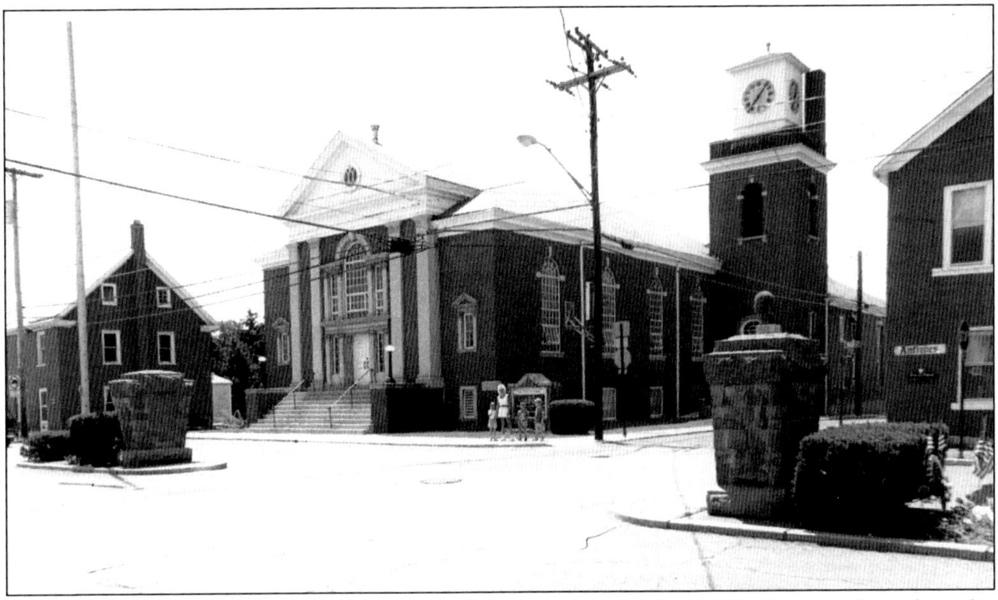

The Grace Church building on the diamond incorporates the town's first house of worship, the Harmony Society's brick meetinghouse. Construction of a new sanctuary extended the church to Main Street. The 19th-century section contains classrooms and meeting areas. An electrified tower clock was added in 1953 to replace the original Harmonist clock. George Otto presented the clock to the church in memory of his brother, Thomas Peter Otto. (Courtesy of the Butler Eagle, photograph by Ray Thompson.)

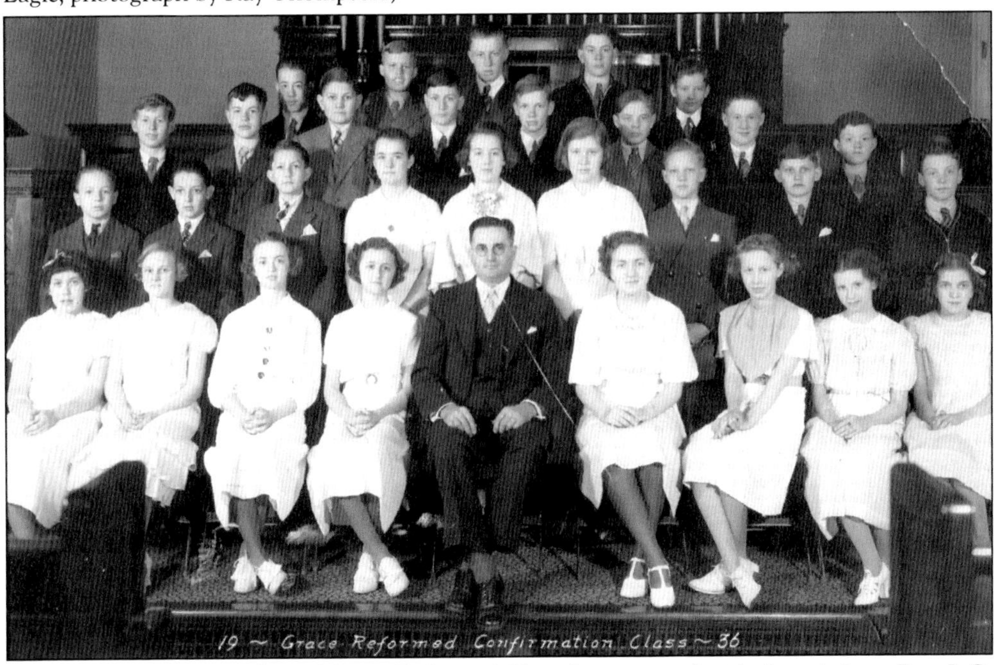

The 1936 confirmation class of Grace Reformed Church is pictured with the minister, Rev. J. O. Gilbert. When Harmony borough celebrated its centennial of incorporation two years later, Gilbert and Dr. Arthur Stewart compiled a history of the town. Others on the book committee were C. L. Druschel and J. W. Flinner. (Courtesy of Kathryn Ziegler Bauder.)

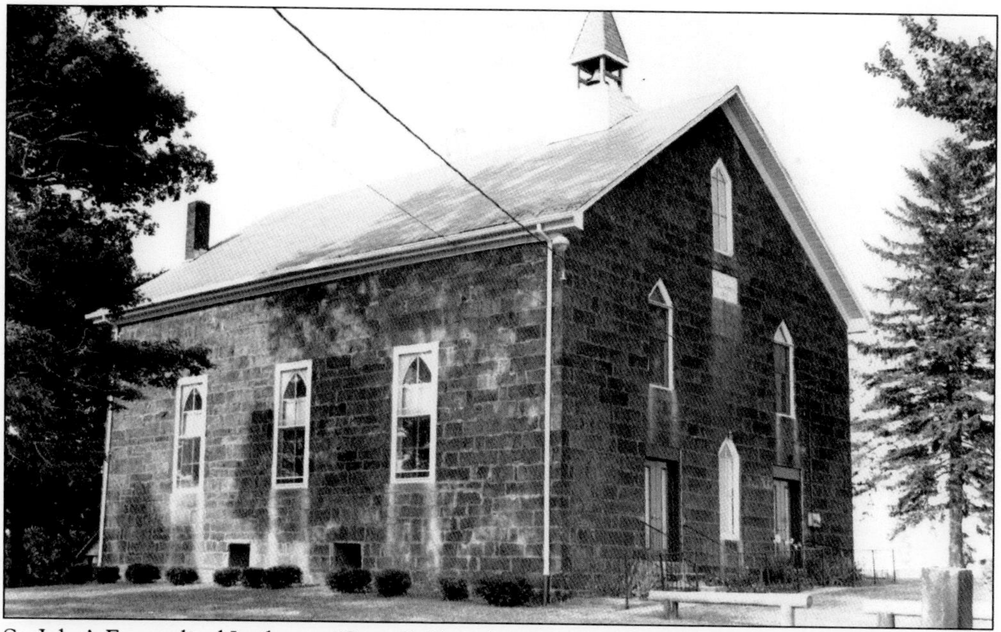

St. John's Evangelical Lutheran "Stone" Church in Lancaster Township dates to 1806 and is the oldest continuously worshiping congregation in the area. The church pastors once conducted both Lutheran and Reformed services in German and English. Church construction began in 1829, and the dedication was celebrated in 1831. The church received a Historic Harmony Heritage Award for preservation. (Courtesy of the Butler Eagle, photograph by Ray Thompson.)

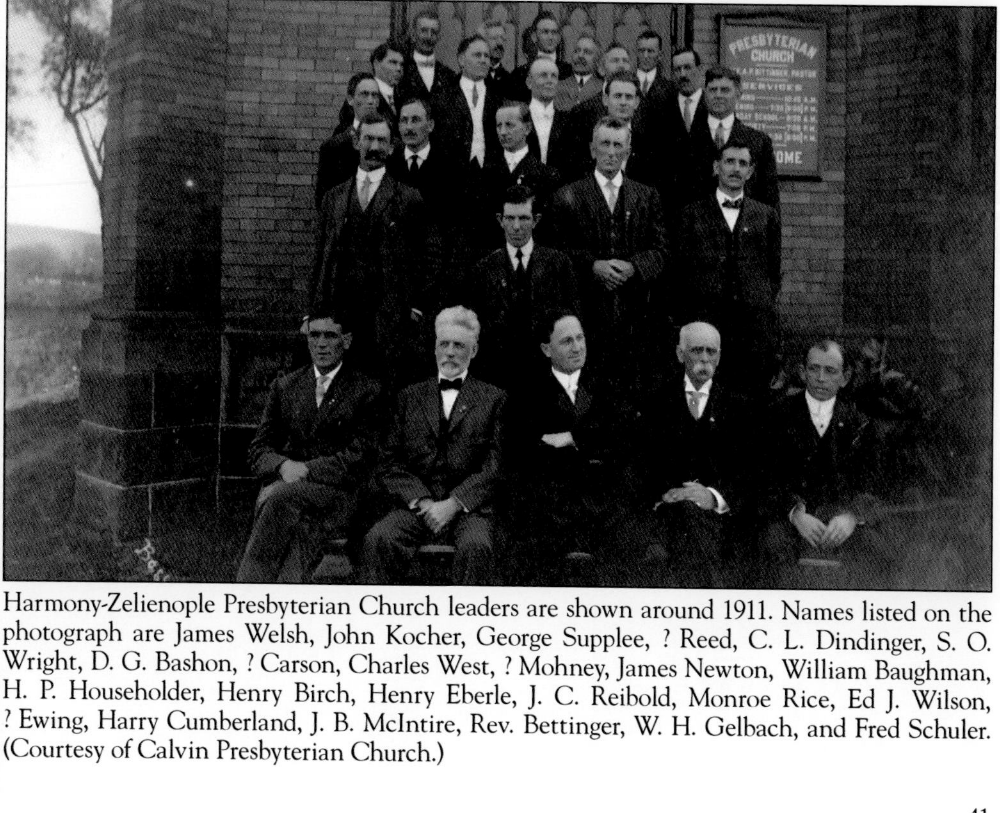

Harmony-Zelienople Presbyterian Church leaders are shown around 1911. Names listed on the photograph are James Welsh, John Kocher, George Supplee, ? Reed, C. L. Dindinger, S. O. Wright, D. G. Bashon, ? Carson, Charles West, ? Mohney, James Newton, William Baughman, H. P. Householder, Henry Birch, Henry Eberle, J. C. Reibold, Monroe Rice, Ed J. Wilson, ? Ewing, Harry Cumberland, J. B. McIntire, Rev. Bettinger, W. H. Gelbach, and Fred Schuler. (Courtesy of Calvin Presbyterian Church.)

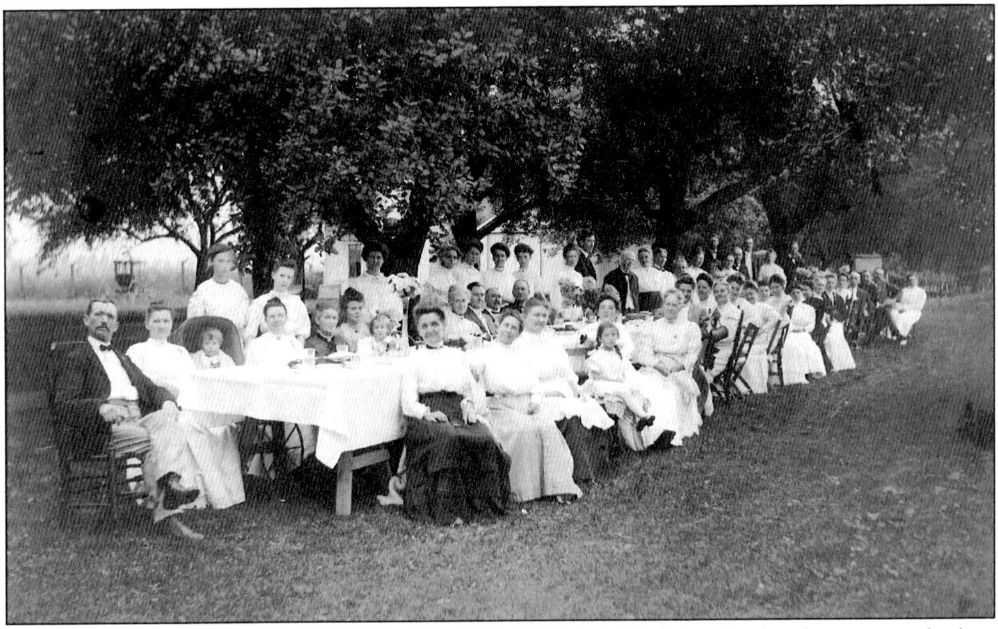

Members of Harmony-Zelienople Presbyterian Church enjoy a dinner under the trees in the late 1800s. The church on Grandview Avenue was renamed Calvin Presbyterian in 1959. Below, the Calvin Presbyterian congregation celebrates with a dinner on March 8, 1955, following the dedication of an addition for classrooms, meeting facilities, and a kitchen. (Courtesy of Calvin Presbyterian Church.)

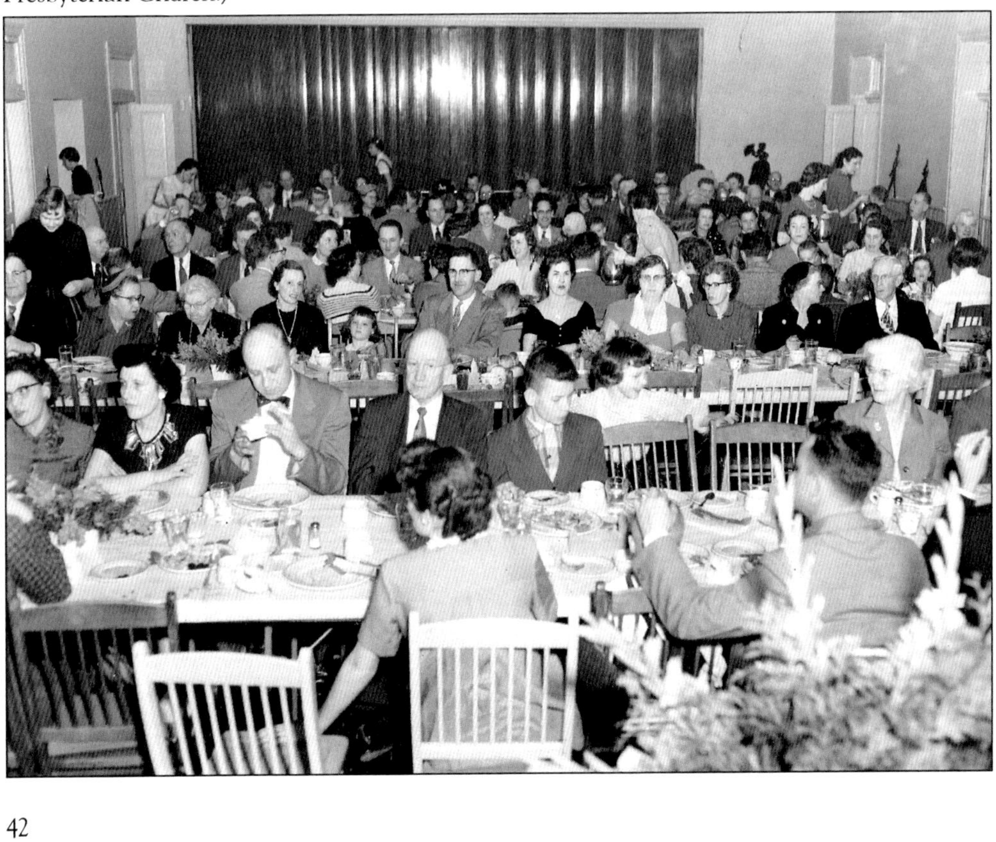

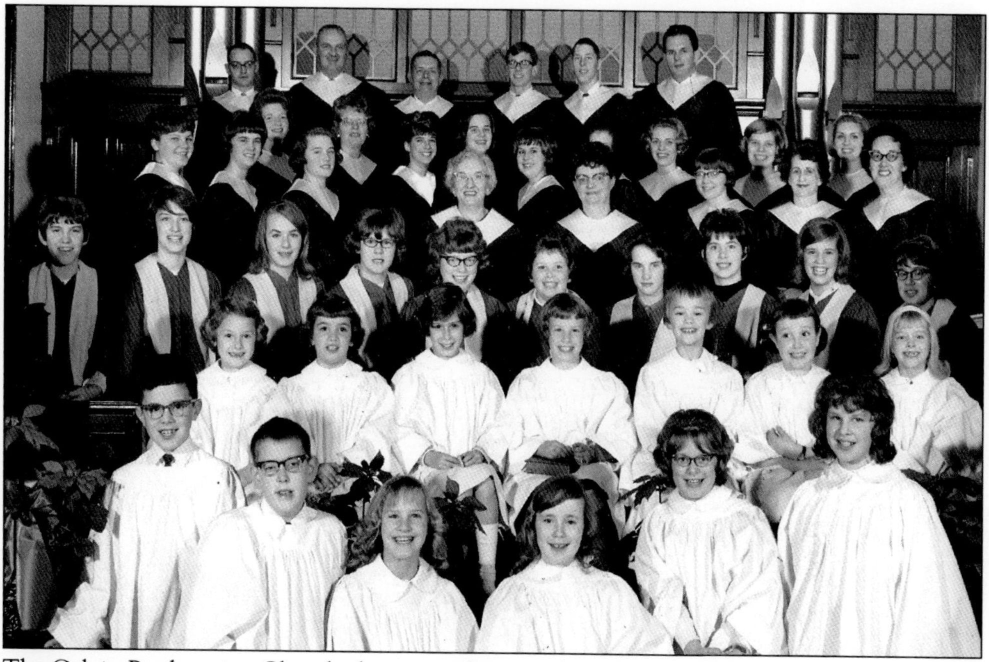

The Calvin Presbyterian Church choirs join for a worship service in the mid-1960s. The church sanctuary was built in 1901 to expand the original church that dates to 1854. A decade before raising the first building, the congregation was organized by local natives of Scottish descent who wanted worship services conducted in English. (Courtesy of Calvin Presbyterian Church.)

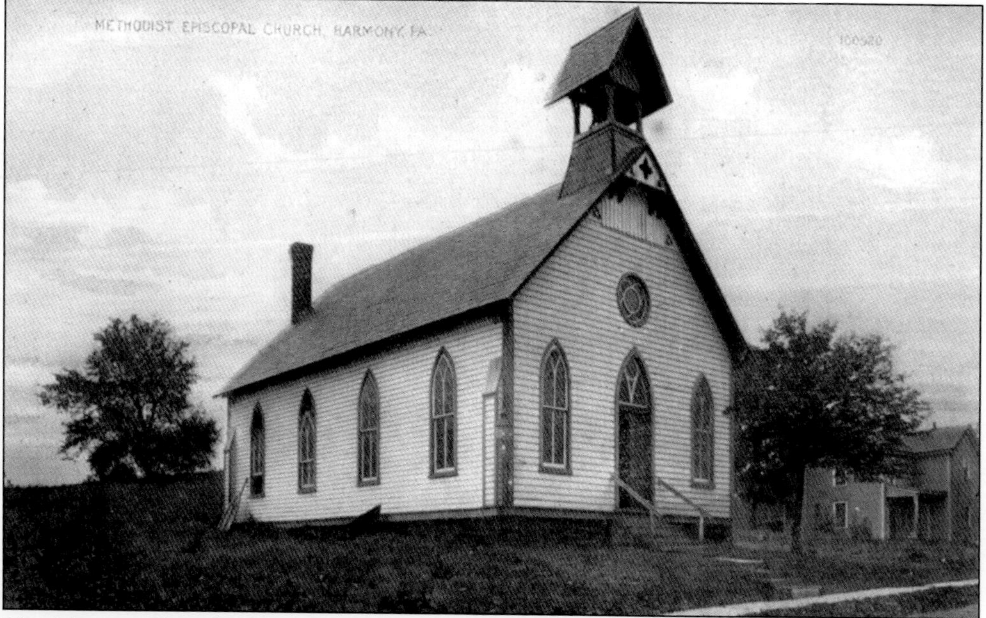

The Monroe Chapel of the Methodist Episcopal Church was organized in 1842, and in 1880, the congregation built a church on German Street. The church was rechartered as the Harmony Methodist Episcopal Church and later relocated. Harmony Veterans of Foreign Wars bought the old church and planned a New Year's Eve celebration in 1948. Fire broke out during the event and destroyed the building.

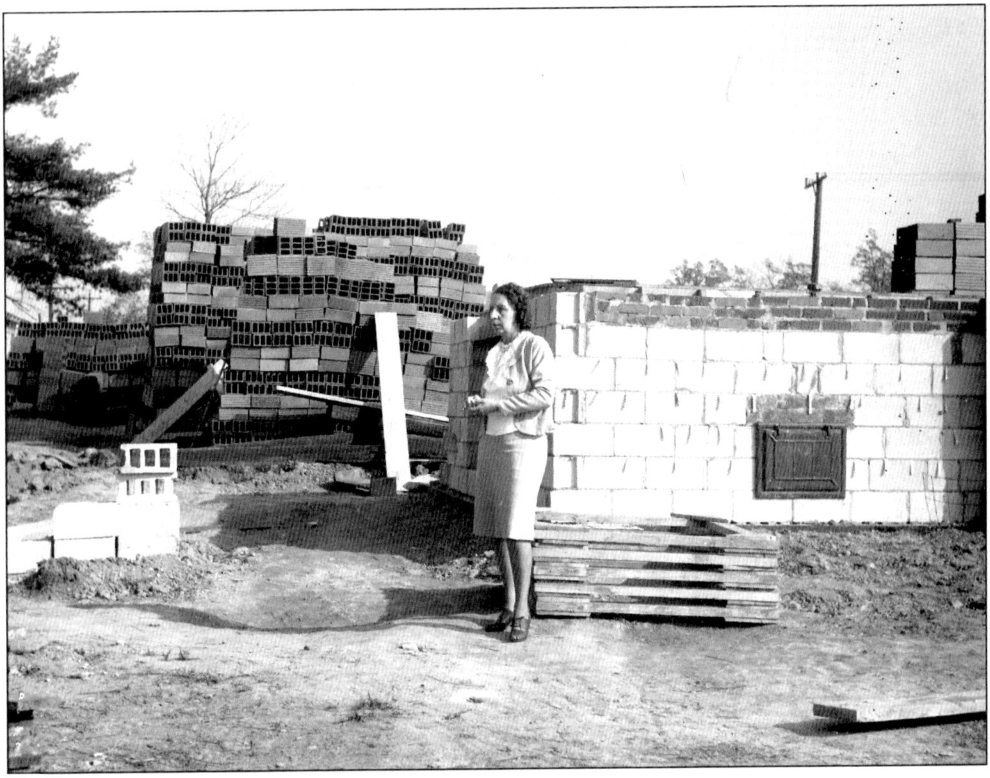

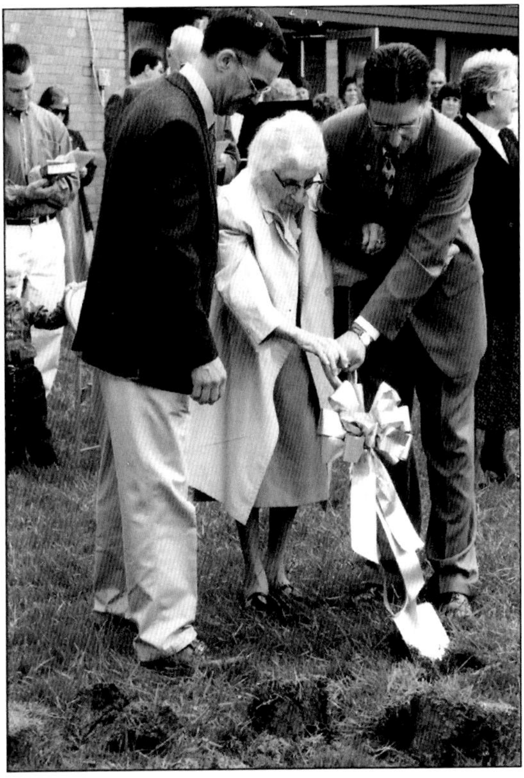

Harmony Methodist Episcopal Church merged with a Zelienople congregation to form the Harmony-Zelienople United Methodist Church and built a church on Pittsburgh Street. Above, Sunday school teacher Isabelle Wiser looks over the work site in 1947. At left, as the oldest active member of Harmony-Zelienople United Methodist Church, she helps break ground in 1998 for a new sanctuary addition. Lending a hand are church historian Sam Cooper (left) and Rev. John Seth. (Courtesy of Harmony-Zelienople United Methodist Church.)

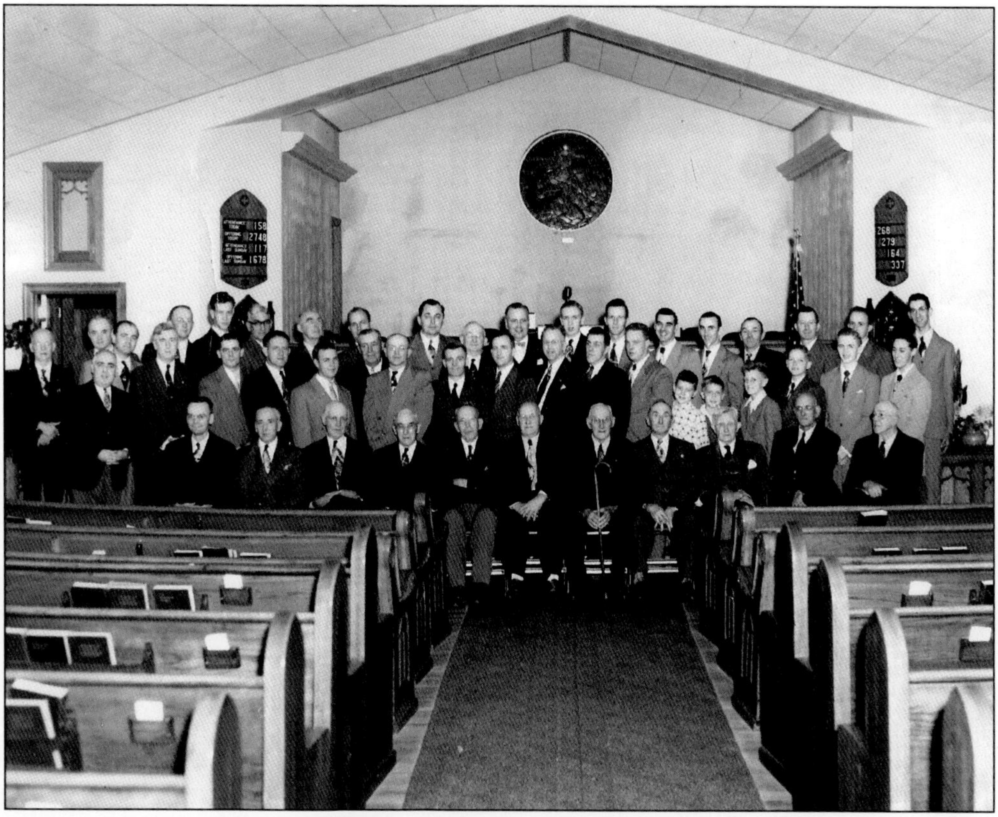

Men attending Sunday school classes at the Harmony-Zelienople United Methodist Church sat for a photograph in 1948. The new church on Pittsburgh Street had just been dedicated. (Courtesy of Harmony-Zelienople United Methodist Church.)

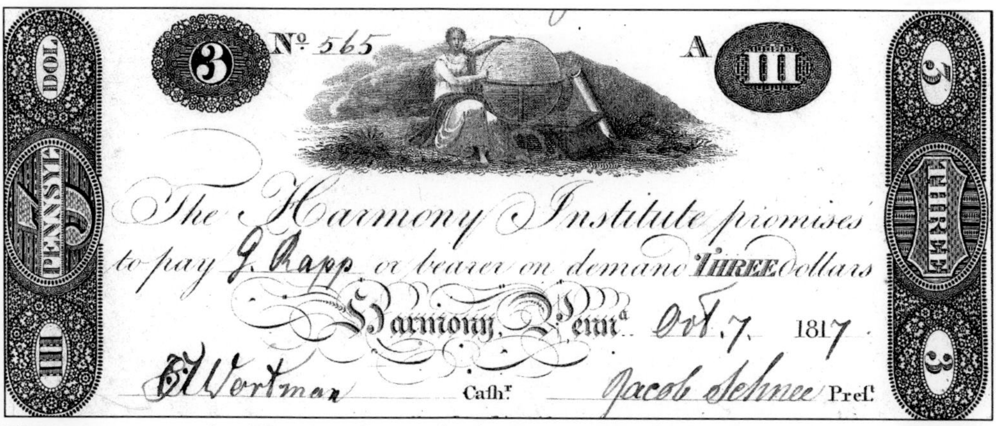

This note was issued to Harmony Society leader George Rapp by Rev. Jacob Schnee's Harmony Institute, a short-lived venture that funded the Harmony Seminary for Young Ladies. Schnee established the school in the former society warehouse to educate female children of privileged western Pennsylvania families. Tuition for the school year that ran from September to July was $150, including books, school supplies, board, and laundry service.

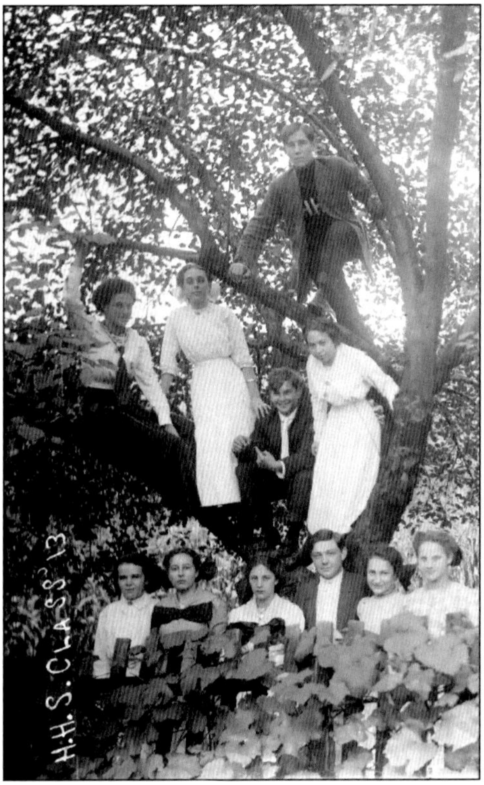

Harmony High School's 1913 graduates gather in a natural setting. From left to right in the tree are Tillie Powell, Annie Nolan, Art Weigel, Dora Schott, and Fritz Kaetzel (top); (standing) Alberta Eppinger, Deanie Kaetzel, Lettie Ziegler, Edward (Pud) Stauffer, Isabella Hardie, and Irene Burkett. The high school classes were discontinued in 1932, and Harmony students began attending Zelienople High School. (Courtesy of Nancy Wiser.)

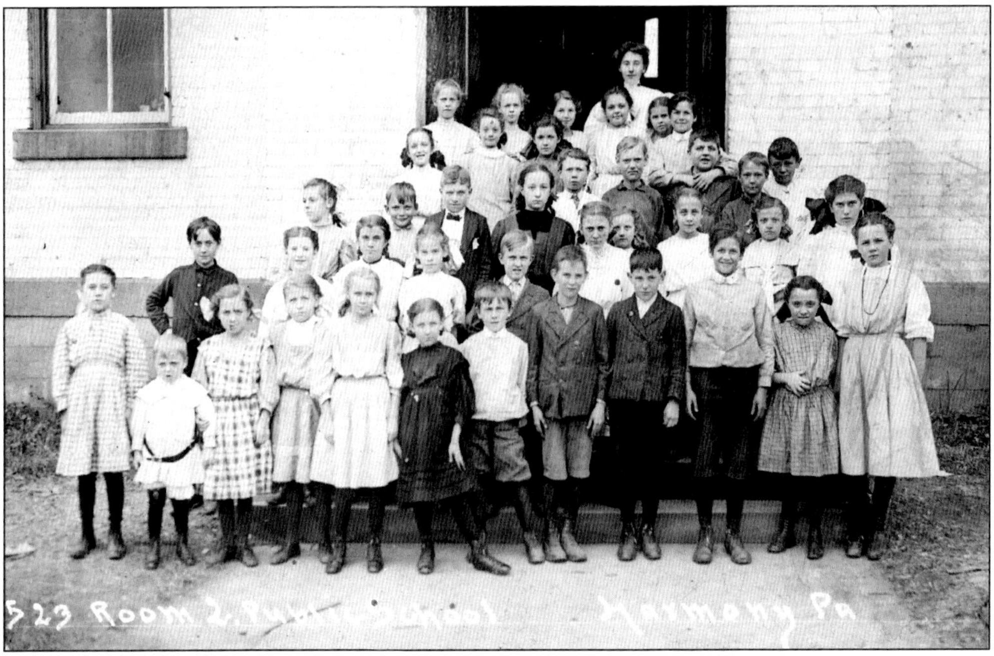

Harmony School pupils stand outside for the annual photograph in the early 1900s. The little guy in the front row must have been visiting. Teacher Elsie Wilds stands in the doorway.

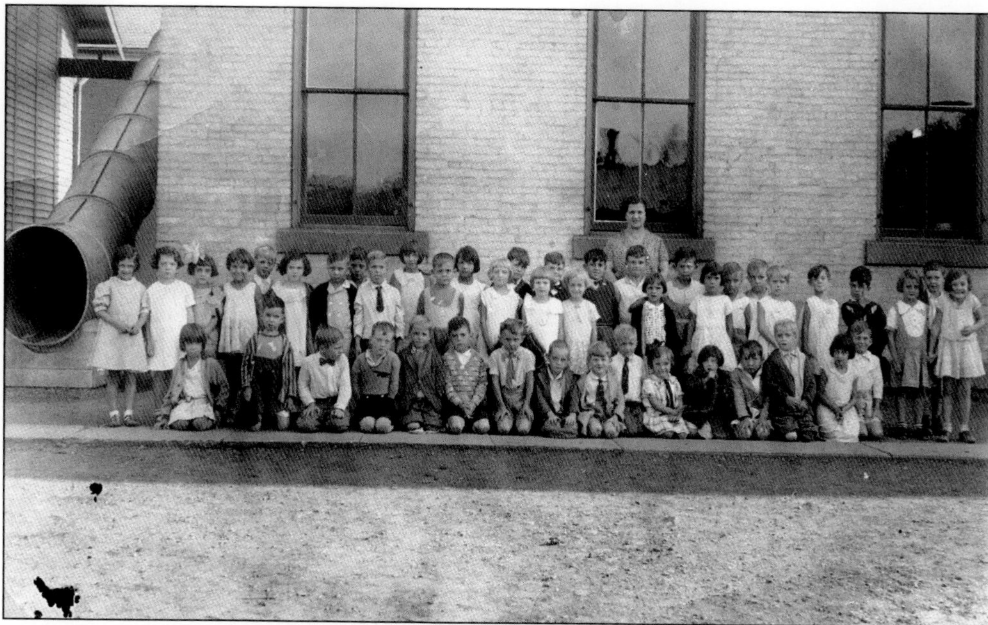

Harmony primary students line up with teacher Helen Wiser McQuistion in the early 1930s. At left is the fire escape tube attached to an upstairs room. McQuistion recalled, "We had fire drills and every child had to slide down that tube." She began teaching in the 1920s at Schiever School, walking three miles each day to work, and last taught in 1969 at Connoquenessing Valley Elementary in Harmony.

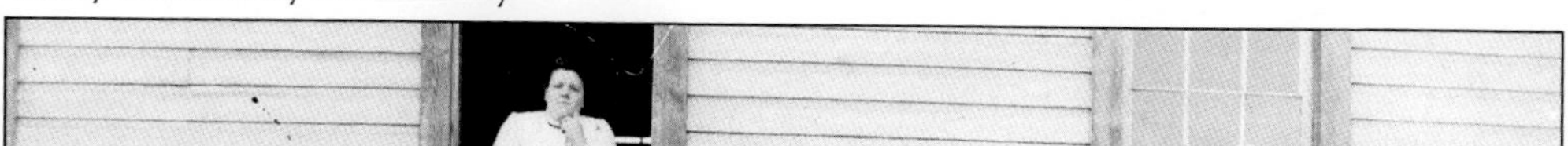

Seen here are pupils, parents, and teachers at the one-room Schiever School in Lancaster Township. Scott Brenner, who donated the photograph to the Harmony Museum, noted, "First year in school. Catharine Dindinger on my lap. Mother's in the window." Helen Wiser McQuistion, who taught there in the 1920s, recalled, "The children were so lovely to me. They even helped me sweep and dust. We had a wonderful time."

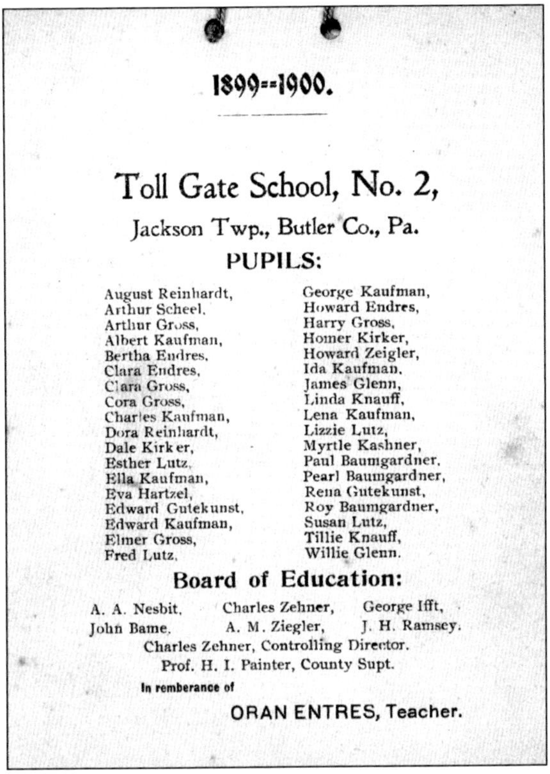

1899--1900.

Toll Gate School, No. 2,

Jackson Twp., Butler Co., Pa.

PUPILS:

August Reinhardt,	George Kaufman,
Arthur Scheel,	Howard Endres,
Arthur Gross,	Harry Gross,
Albert Kaufman,	Homer Kirker,
Bertha Endres,	Howard Zeigler,
Clara Endres,	Ida Kaufman,
Clara Gross,	James Glenn,
Cora Gross,	Linda Knauff,
Charles Kaufman,	Lena Kaufman,
Dora Reinhardt,	Lizzie Lutz,
Dale Kirker,	Myrtle Kashner,
Esther Lutz,	Paul Baumgardner,
Ella Kaufman,	Pearl Baumgardner,
Eva Hartzel,	Rena Gutekunst,
Edward Gutekunst,	Roy Baumgardner,
Edward Kaufman,	Susan Lutz,
Elmer Gross,	Tillie Knauff,
Fred Lutz,	Willie Glenn.

Board of Education:

A. A. Nesbit, Charles Zehner, George Ifft,
John Bame, A. M. Ziegler, J. H. Ramsey.
Charles Zehner, Controlling Director.
Prof. H. I. Painter, County Supt.

In remberance of

ORAN ENTRES, Teacher.

The names of students who attended the Toll Gate School in Jackson Township at the dawn of the 20th century are listed in this souvenir card.

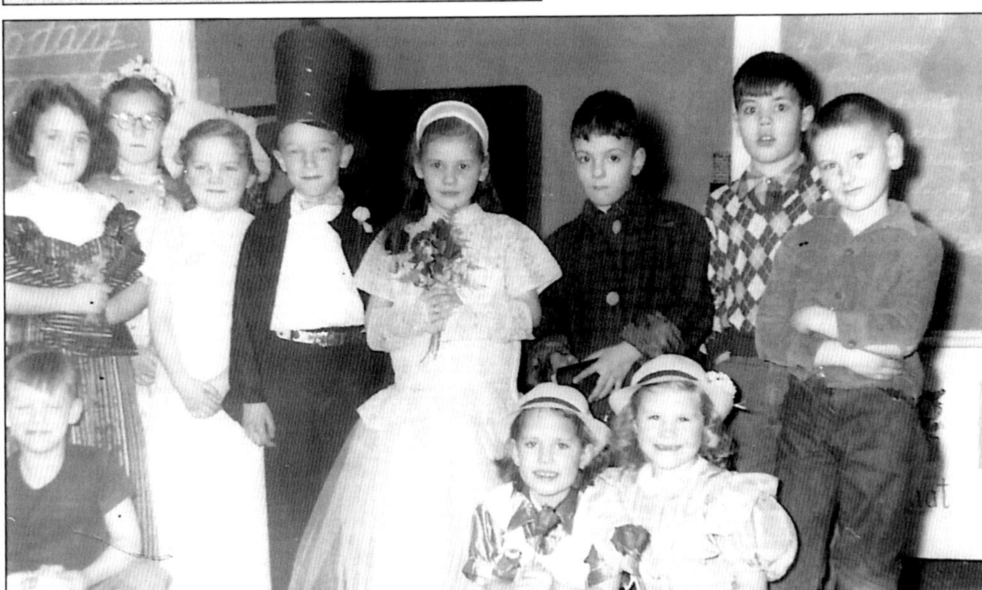

Harmony second graders in Evelyn Rodemoyer's class took part in this Tom Thumb wedding about 1955 or 1956. The class met upstairs in the Langenbacher house on Main Street. From left to right are (first row) unidentified, flower girl Marcy Luek, and flower girl Mary Mulvey Johnson; (second row) Linda Curry Nye, Linda Druschel Stowell, bridesmaid Gay Schiedemantle Wittmann, bridegroom Delmar Shever, bride Kathy Deemer Brown, preacher Bruce Rape, groomsman Ron Oswald, and unidentified. (Courtesy of Marcy Luek.)

Three workmen stand beside the one-handed clock atop the Harmony School in the late 1930s. The massive handmade timepiece crowned the communal Harmony Society's meetinghouse for more than a century and was removed when Grace Reformed Church enlarged the building. In 1938, the clock was moved across Mercer Street and installed on the school. A portable building that held extra classrooms stands at right.

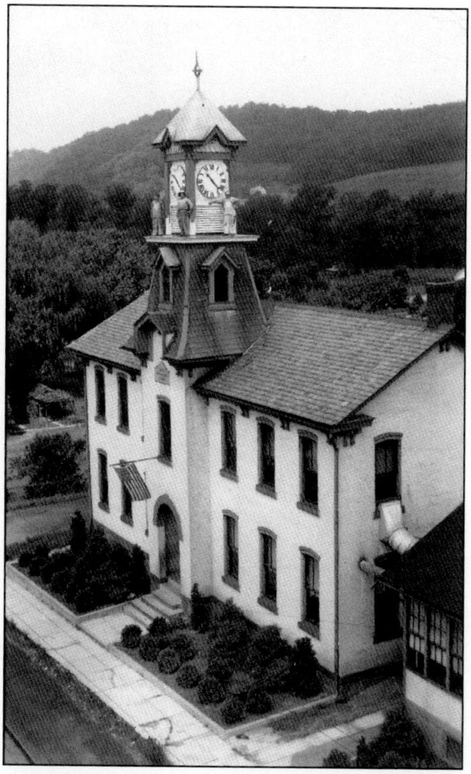

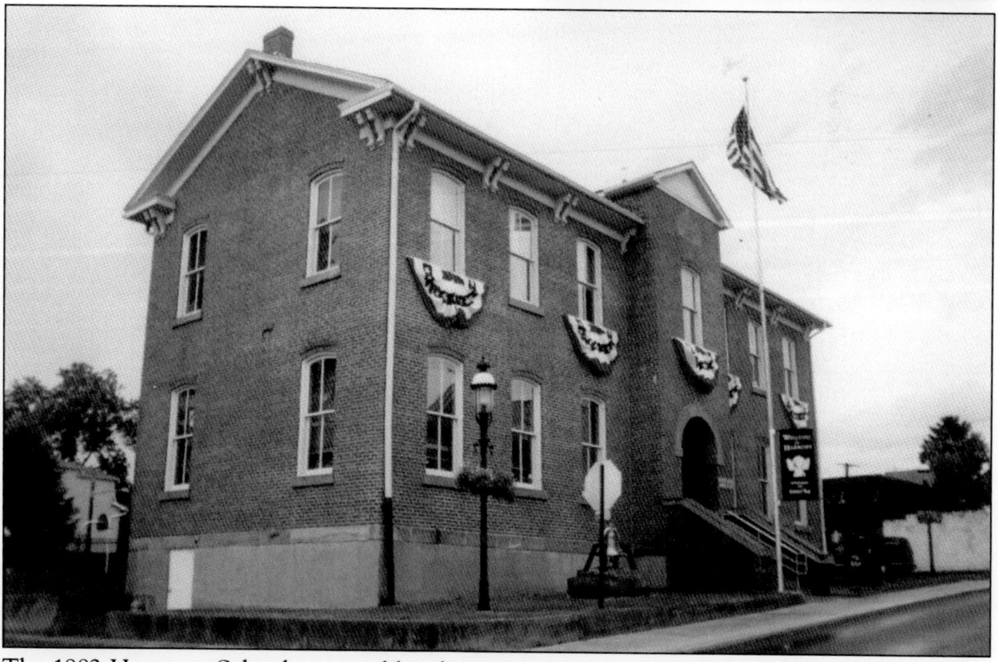

The 1882 Harmony School was used by elementary classes until the mid-20th century. It now houses borough offices and the Harmony Post Office. The borough council restored the exterior of the building by having paint removed from its brick walls and the mortar repaired. The council received a Historic Harmony Heritage Award for facade restoration in 1994.

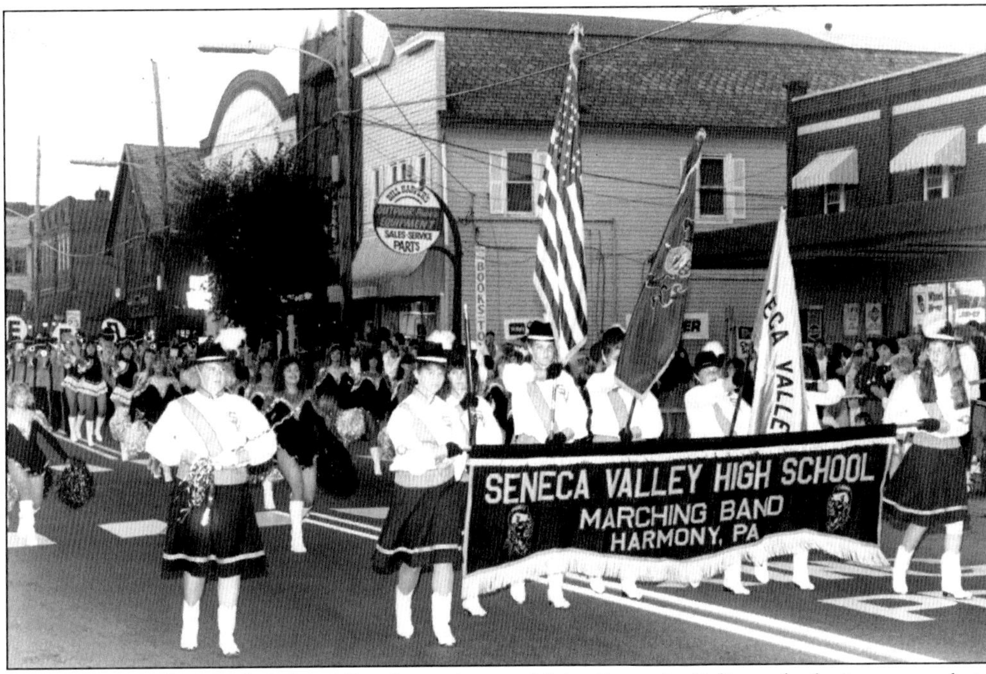

The Seneca Valley High School Band marches on Main Street in Zelienople during a parade in the 1980s. Instrumental and choral programs in all district schools keep the local musical tradition alive. Harmony area one-room schools remained open into the 1950s, but the educational system quickly changed as Butler County's population grew in the last half of the 20th century. The aerial view shows the Seneca Valley High School complex in Jackson Township. The district serves about 7,775 students in kindergarten through 12th grade in Callery, Evans City, Harmony, Seven Fields, and Zelienople Boroughs and Cranberry, Forward, Lancaster, and Jackson Townships. (Courtesy of the Butler Eagle, photographs by Ray Thompson.)

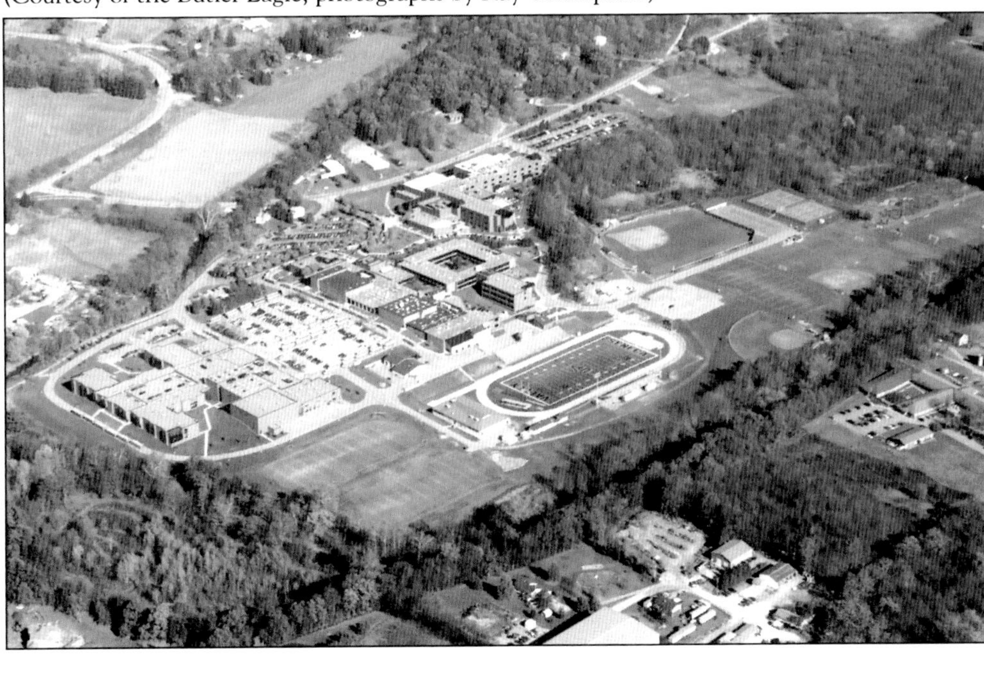

Five

Transportation

The first roads across the region were Native American trails, including the Logstown Path that Gen. George Washington followed in 1753. The few rutted roads leading to Harmony in the early 19th century were little more than paths, yet the Harmony Society successfully exported products by hauling them to the confluence of the Ohio and Beaver Rivers in Beaver County. During the War of 1812, soldiers and supply carriers followed the main north–south track through Harmony to Oliver Hazard Perry's fleet at Erie. The rough trail became U.S. Route 19, known as the Perry Highway.

Two road problems were solved in the 1850s by "the cut," an 18-foot-deep excavation on Main Street between German and Division Streets. The project eliminated a steep grade and provided fill that was spread over a swamp on East Mercer Street, raising the surface by about 16 feet.

The first train arrived in Harmony in 1879, and the Pittsburgh, Harmony, Butler, and New Castle Railway's electric interurban Harmony line opened in 1908. Rail company brochures tempted Pittsburghers to travel by describing rural pleasures to the north: "Out from the bustle and hum of the greatest industrial city in the world, away from this clanging, jarring, smoke-dimmed hive of ceaseless energy and toiling, tired humanity—come with us for a little time, out into the glorious shining land of blue skies, of rolling sun-flecked meadows, come and smell once again the cool, subtle perfume of the deep-shaded valley." The interurban era was exciting but short-lived. Financial tangles forced the company out of business, and the last car ran on August 15, 1931. The Harmony Short Line bus fleet went into service, continuing until 1961. U.S. Route 19 was diverted in 1936 over a new bridge north from Zelienople's Main Street and on through Jackson and Lancaster Townships, leaving Harmony off the beaten path for the first time in 130 years.

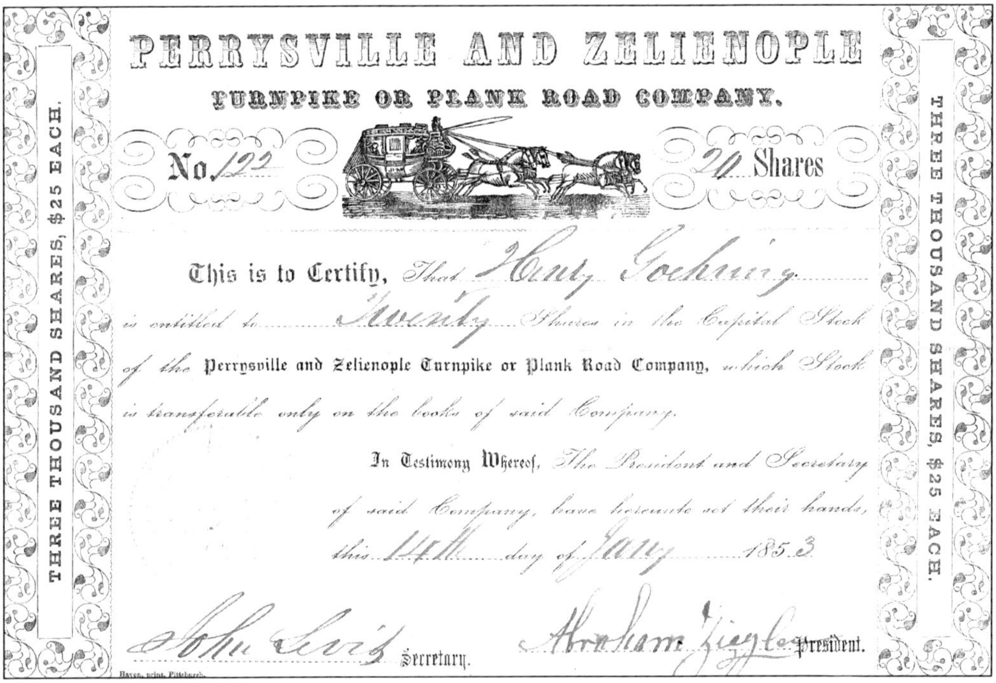

PERRYSVILLE AND ZELIENOPLE

TURNPIKE OR PLANK ROAD COMPANY.

THREE THOUSAND SHARES, $25 EACH.

No. 122 — 20 Shares

This is to Certify, That Henry Goehring is entitled to Twenty Shares in the Capital Stock of the Perrysville and Zelienople Turnpike or Plank Road Company, which Stock is transferable only on the books of said Company.

In Testimony Whereof, The President and Secretary of said Company, have hereunto set their hands, this 14th day of Jany 1853

John Levis Secretary. Abraham Ziegler President.

Haven, print, Pittsburgh.

This plank road stock certificate was signed by company president Abraham Ziegler Jr., son of the Mennonite pioneer. Ziegler tried to improve the roads by installing wooden planks and financing them with fees collected at tollhouses. Toll Gate Road that intersects U.S. Route 19 and Old Perry Highway in Jackson Township is a reminder of that era.

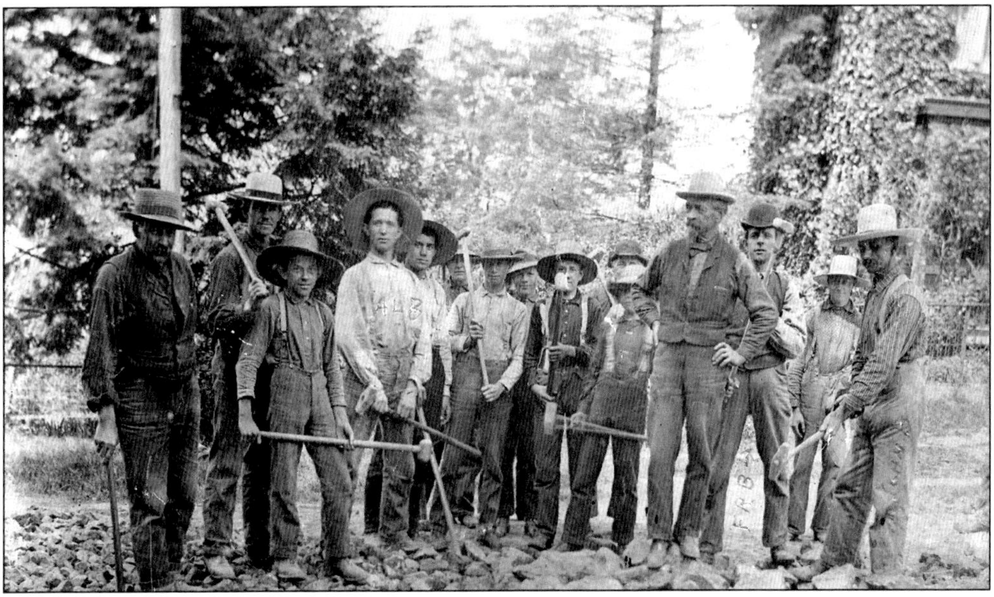

Road repair has been a constant concern around Harmony and Zelienople since the time of founders George Rapp and Dettmar Basse. This crew tackles a rocky job on the Perry Highway (U.S. Route 19) in Middle Lancaster in the days when men could do roadwork in place of paying their taxes. A. A. Brenner is fourth from left, and F. Brenner is third from right.

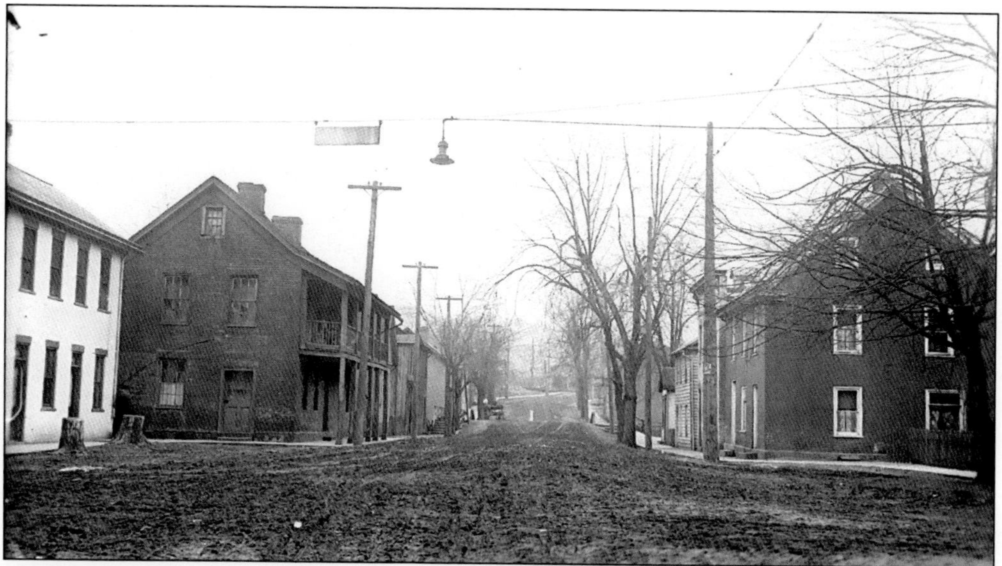

South Main Street was also part of U.S. Route 19, the primary route between Pittsburgh and Erie. On the left in this view from about 1912 are the Harmonist warehouse, the Langenbacher house, and two buildings that no longer exist. Near right are the Harmonist Schmidt House, now owned by Grace Church, and the Harmony National Bank that is gone. (Courtesy of Pennsylvania Historical and Museum Commission/Old Economy Village.)

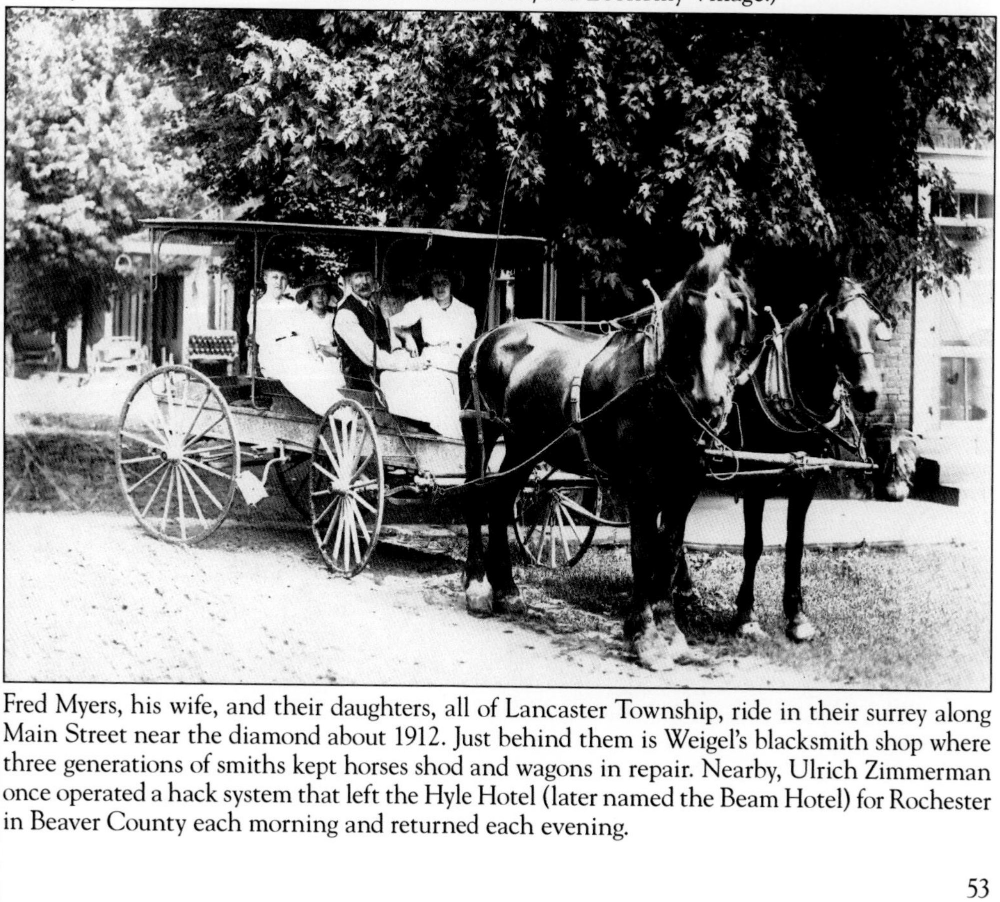

Fred Myers, his wife, and their daughters, all of Lancaster Township, ride in their surrey along Main Street near the diamond about 1912. Just behind them is Weigel's blacksmith shop where three generations of smiths kept horses shod and wagons in repair. Nearby, Ulrich Zimmerman once operated a hack system that left the Hyle Hotel (later named the Beam Hotel) for Rochester in Beaver County each morning and returned each evening.

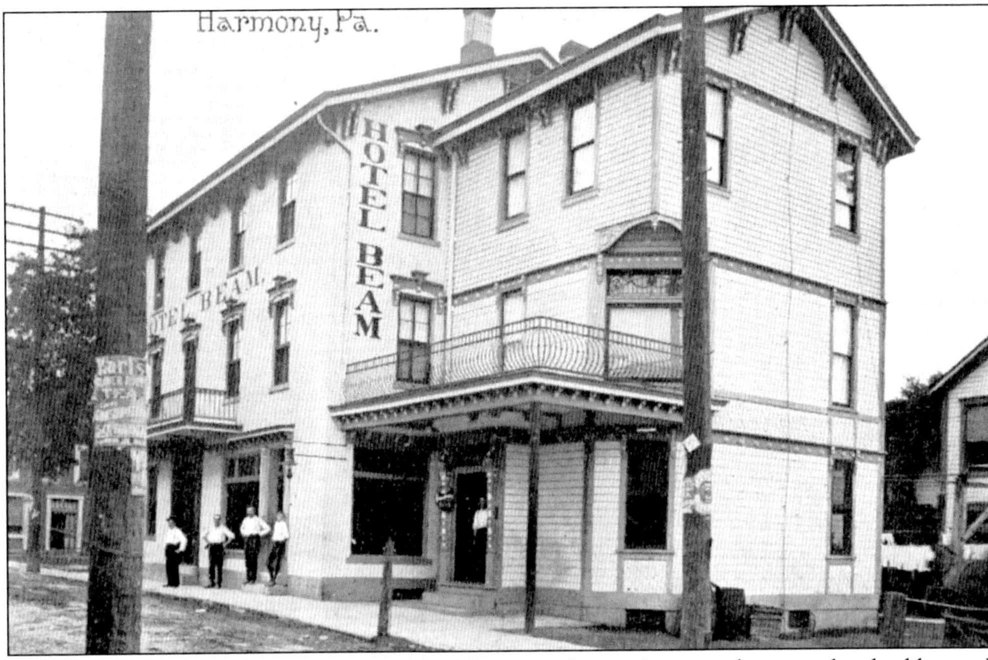

The Hyle Hotel was built on the site of the Harmony Society's inn and tavern that had burned. Samuel Beam bought the hotel in the 1880s and renamed it. It stayed in the Beam family for four generations under the management of George Beam, S. A. Beam, and Charles Beam. Their hotel had 22 sleeping rooms, a dining room, and bar. (Courtesy of Bernice Stamm Lewis.)

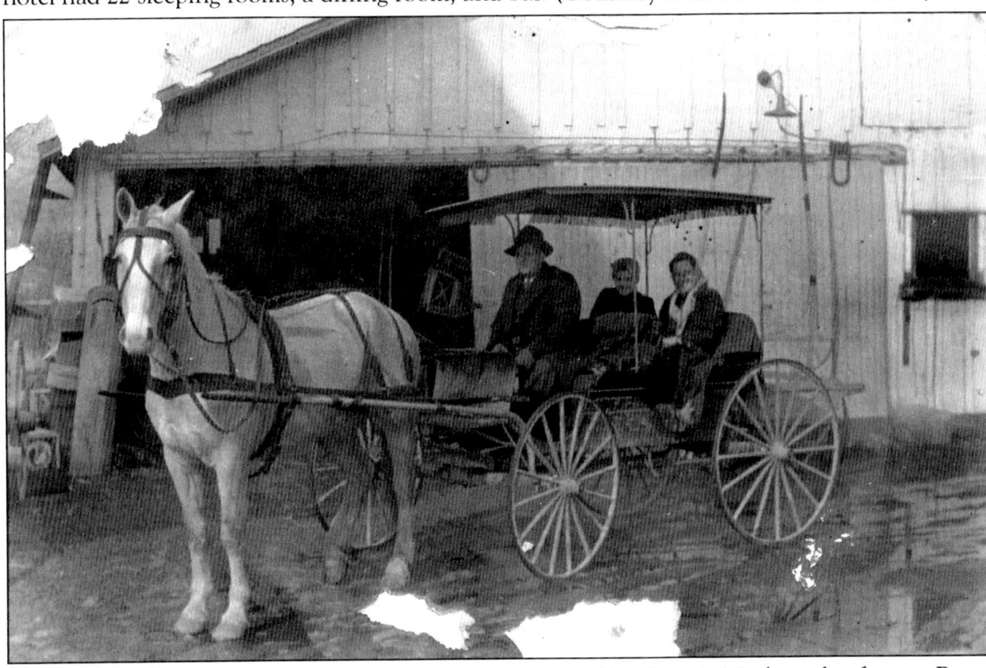

Joseph Sapienza Jr. hitches up his wagon in the yard of Sapienza's Market, the former Beam Hotel. In back are his daughter Gloria (left) and his wife, Lucy. A collector of ponies and antique horse-drawn vehicles, he seemed to enjoy traveling the old-fashioned way. (Courtesy of Nancy Wiser.)

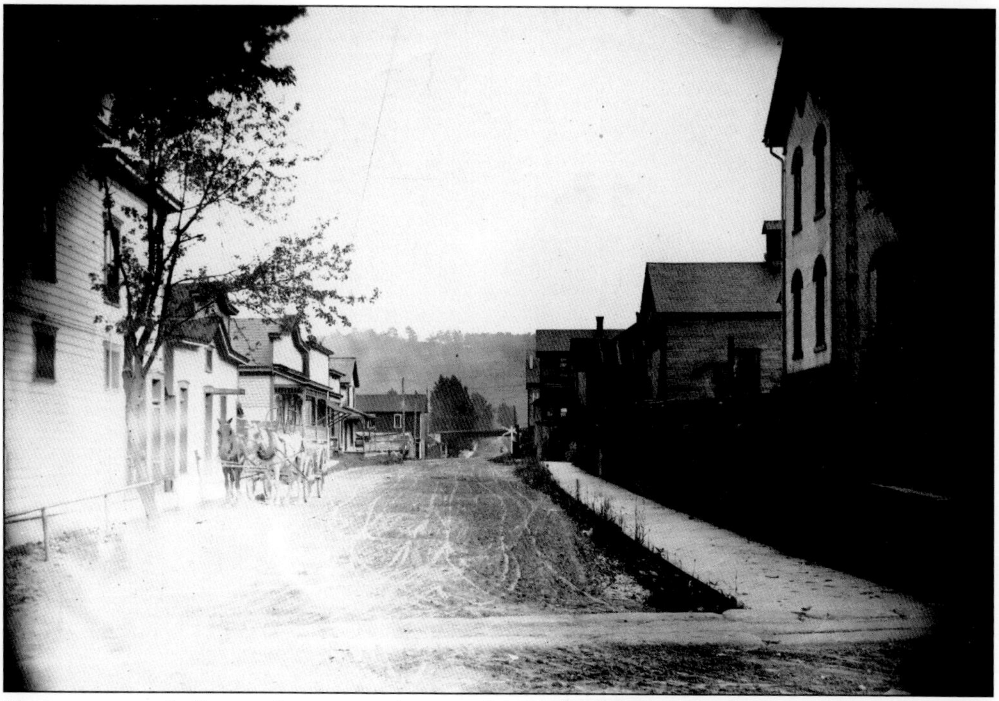

Horsepower and dirt roads were evident in this early 1900s view of Spring Street from the corner of Mercer Street. Milleman's Store can be seen at left and Dambach Lumber stands at Spring and German Streets in the distance. At right is the Hotel Ziegler. Directly behind the photographer was a necessary business in every town in those days, the livery. J. K. Scott Livery advertised livery, feed, and stable. The Sterling Store later opened here. (Courtesy of Bernice Stamm Lewis.)

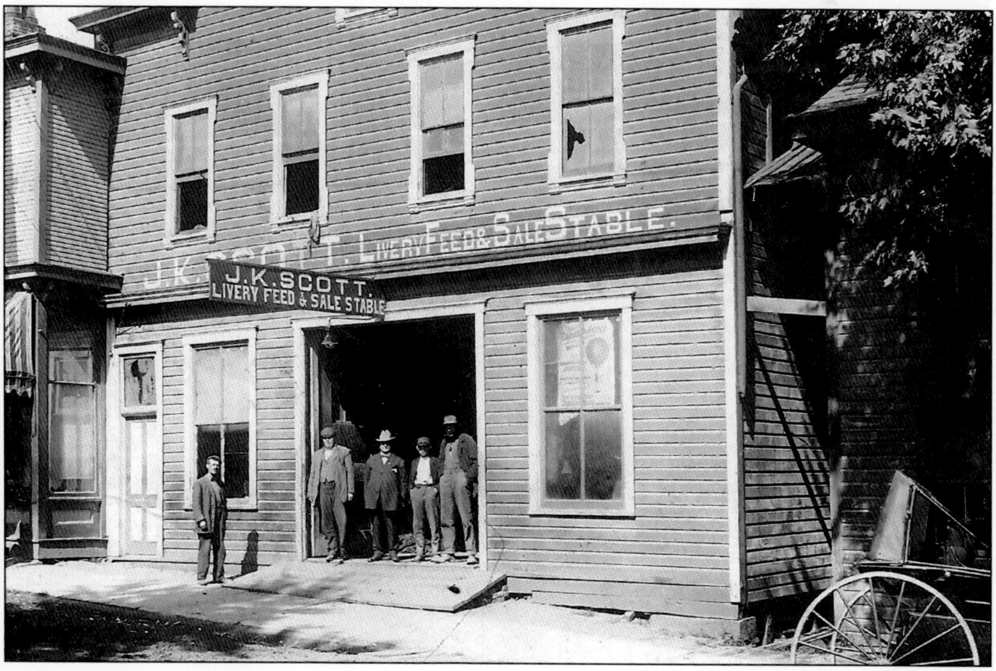

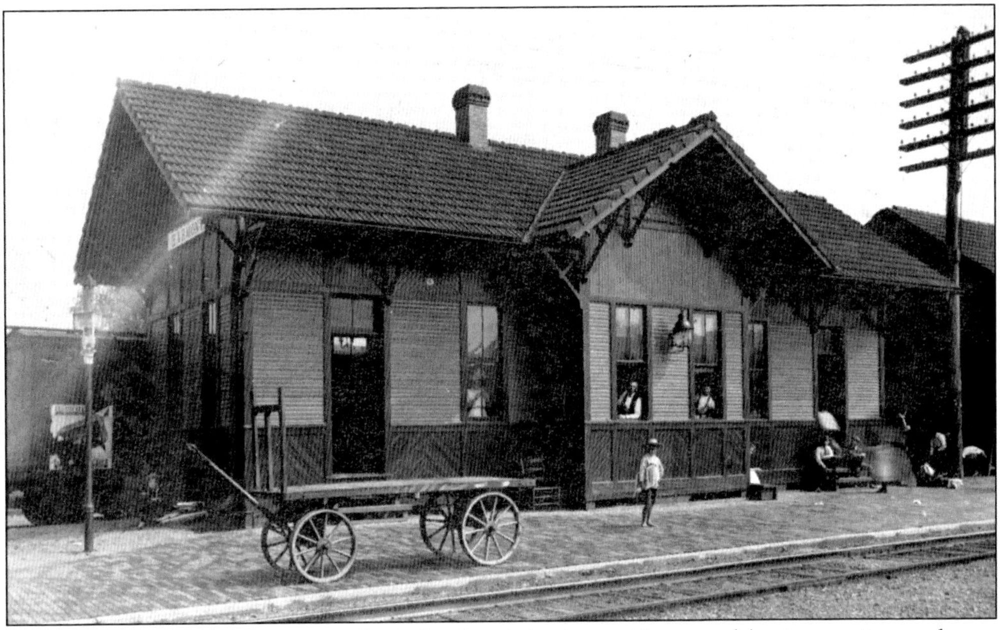

The Harmony train station was the hub of activity for residents and businesses in southwest Butler County. The first train arrived here in 1879. Butler County president Judge John H. Wilson, who grew up in Harmony, recalled that when oil was struck in the vicinity, the station did more passenger, freight, and telegraph business than any other station between the city of Allegheny (now North Side in Pittsburgh) and New Castle.

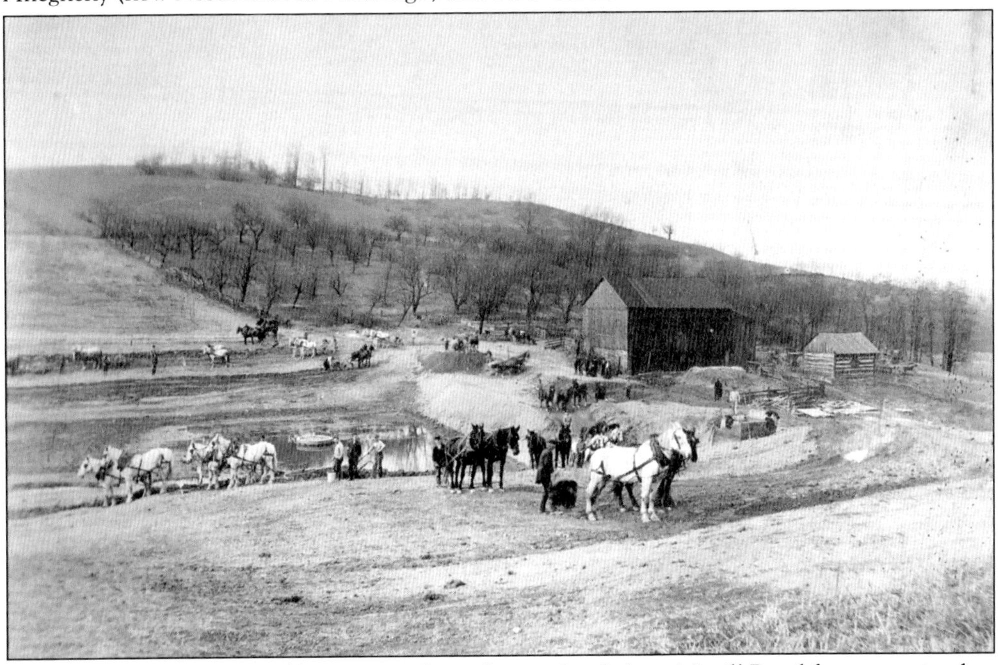

In the early 1900s, men and horses were busy digging land along Magill Road for reservoirs that supplied water to the electric plant at Harmony Junction. A Jackson Township mine furnished fuel for the plant. Shallow coal mining was conducted in the area throughout the 19th and early 20th centuries. (Courtesy of Bernice Stamm Lewis.)

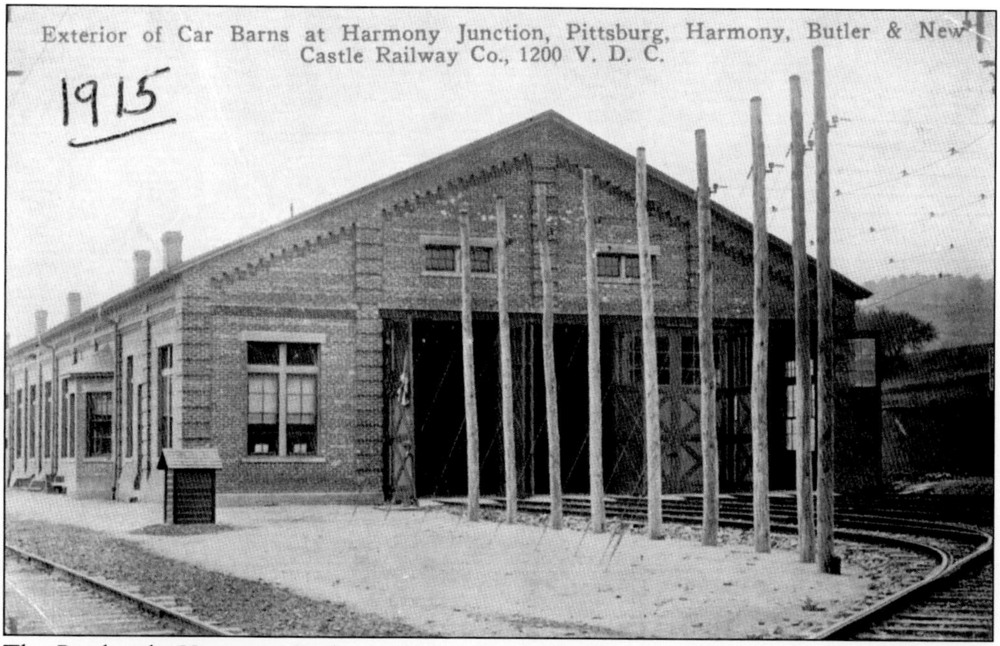

The Pittsburgh, Harmony, Butler and New Castle Railway Company built this carbarn and power plant along the Connoquenessing Creek in Jackson Township and the Harmonists' Edenau acquired a new name—Harmony Junction. The plant supplied electricity to power the interurban cars that made frequent stops at stations across Butler County.

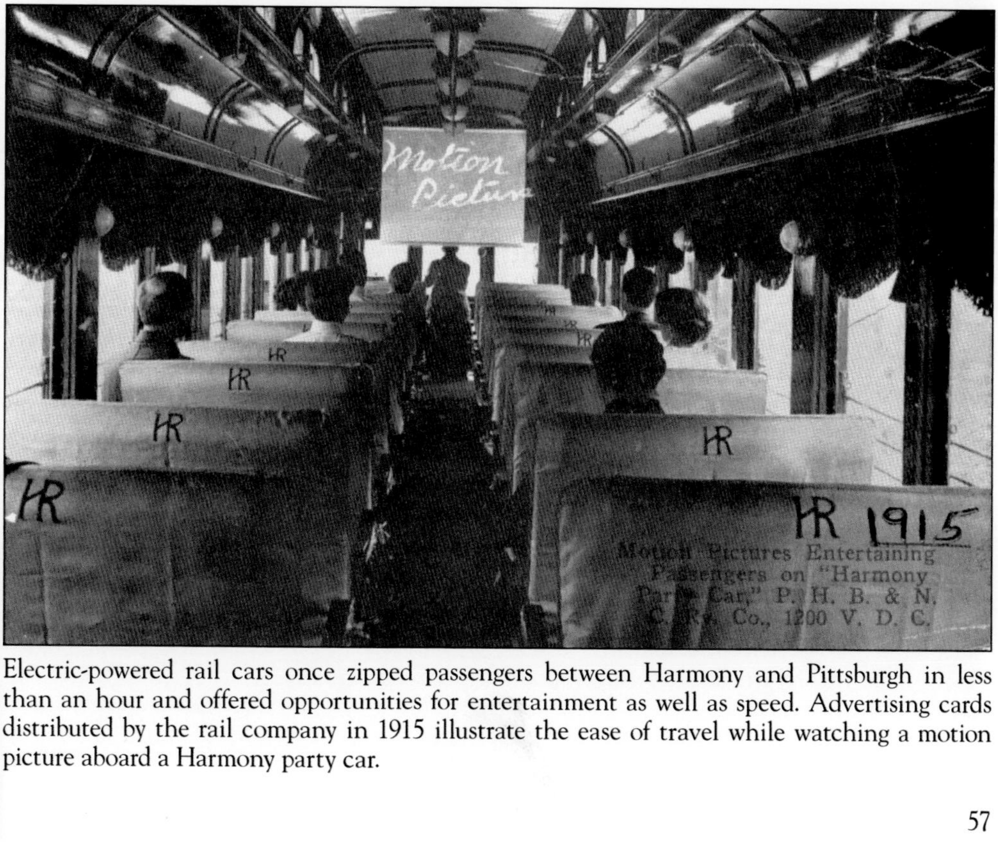

Electric-powered rail cars once zipped passengers between Harmony and Pittsburgh in less than an hour and offered opportunities for entertainment as well as speed. Advertising cards distributed by the rail company in 1915 illustrate the ease of travel while watching a motion picture aboard a Harmony party car.

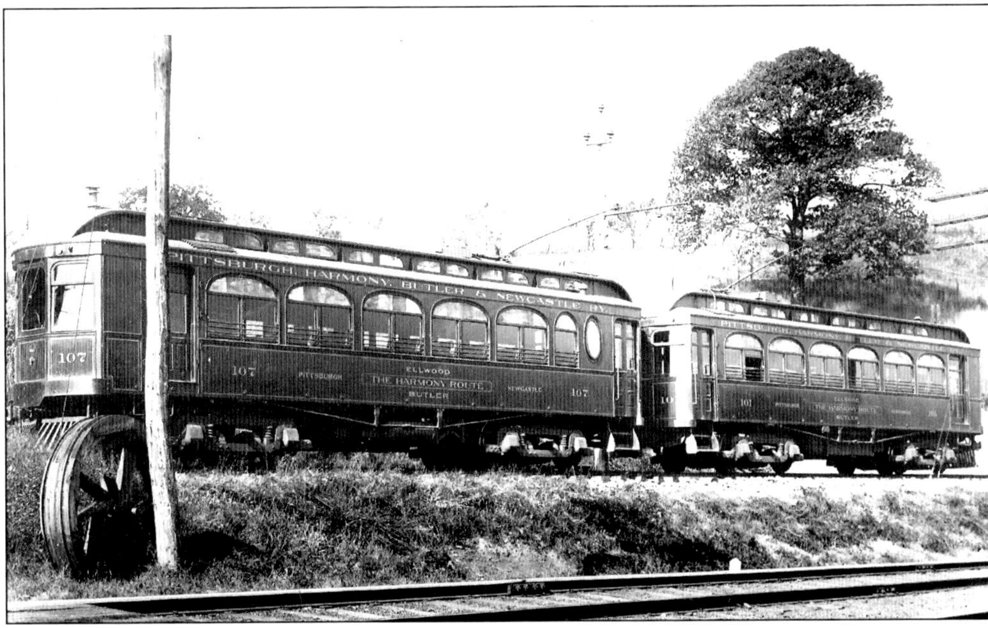

A Harmony route double car sits on the track near Harmony in the early 1900s. Commuting became convenient in 1908 when the Pittsburgh, Harmony, Butler and New Castle Railway Company launched its interurban line. The company folded in 1931; today little evidence remains of the mass-transit service. (Courtesy of Ray Thompson.)

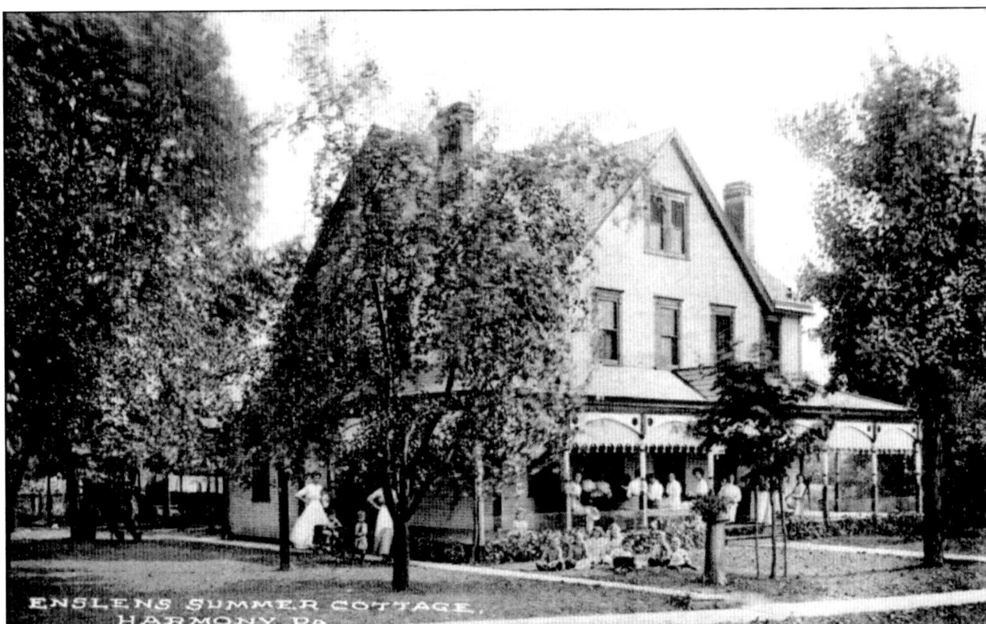

The interurbans boosted the summer population of Harmony, Evans City, Zelienople, and parts of Jackson Township. Creekside cottages sprang up and some residents, such as the Enslens on German Street, opened their doors to guests. Helen Wiser McQuistion, who was born there in 1906, said her grandmother Susan Fiedler Ziegler Enslen built an addition to her house to accommodate boarders.

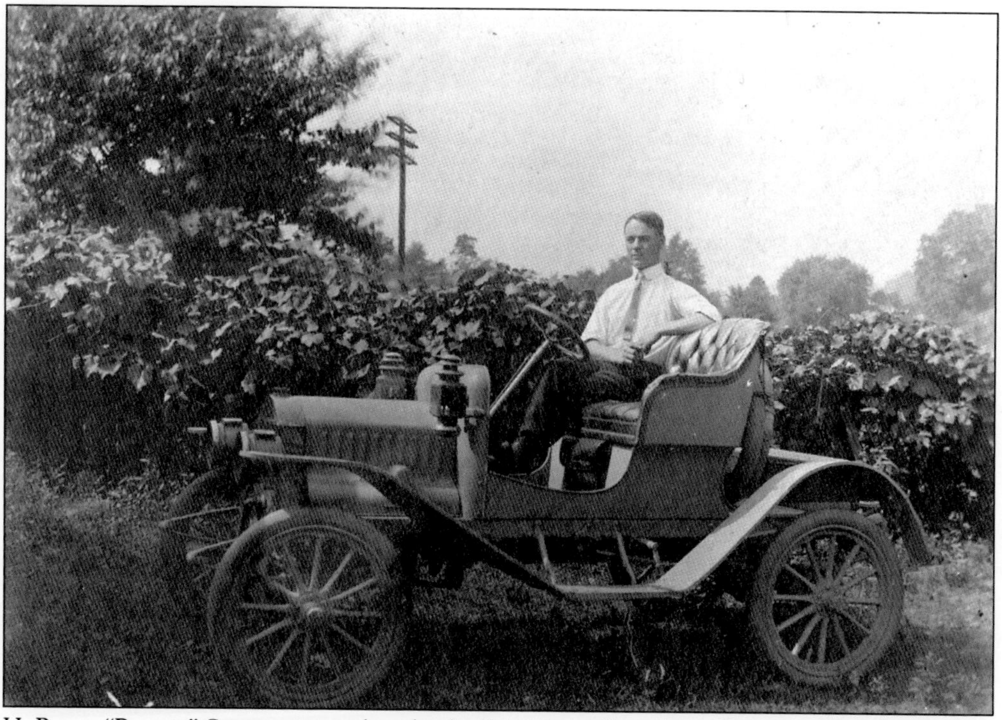

H. Byron "Barney" Stamm sits at the wheel of his Maxwell in the 1920s. As automobiles began to frequent Butler County roads, interurban use declined. It was the beginning of the shift away from mass transit to Americans in the driver's seat, which put many mass-transit enterprises out of business. (Courtesy of Bernice Stamm Lewis.)

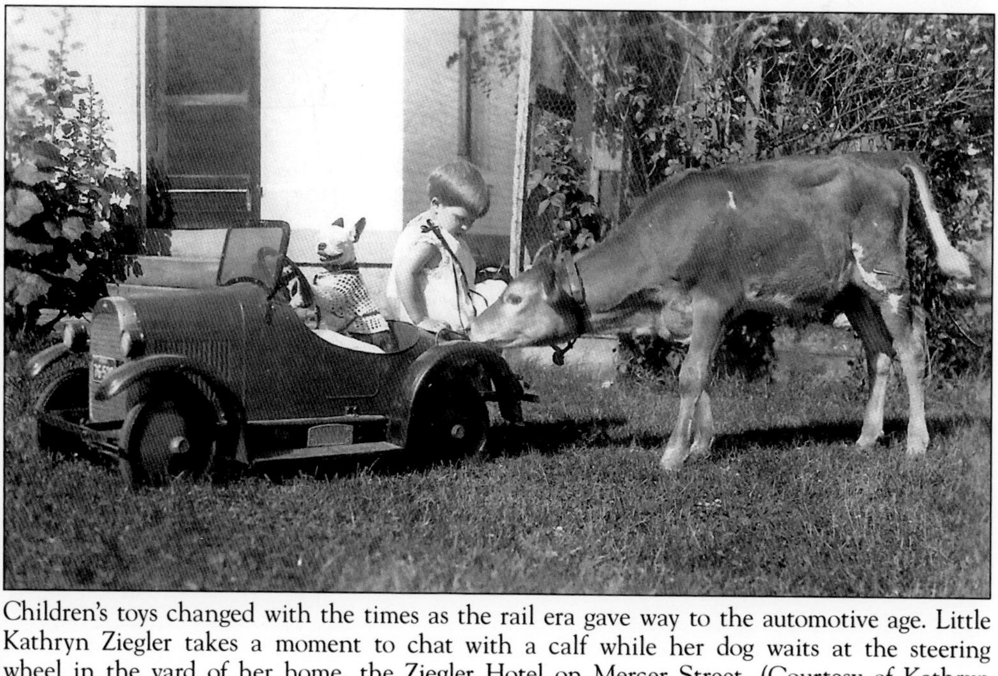

Children's toys changed with the times as the rail era gave way to the automotive age. Little Kathryn Ziegler takes a moment to chat with a calf while her dog waits at the steering wheel in the yard of her home, the Ziegler Hotel on Mercer Street. (Courtesy of Kathryn Ziegler Bauder.)

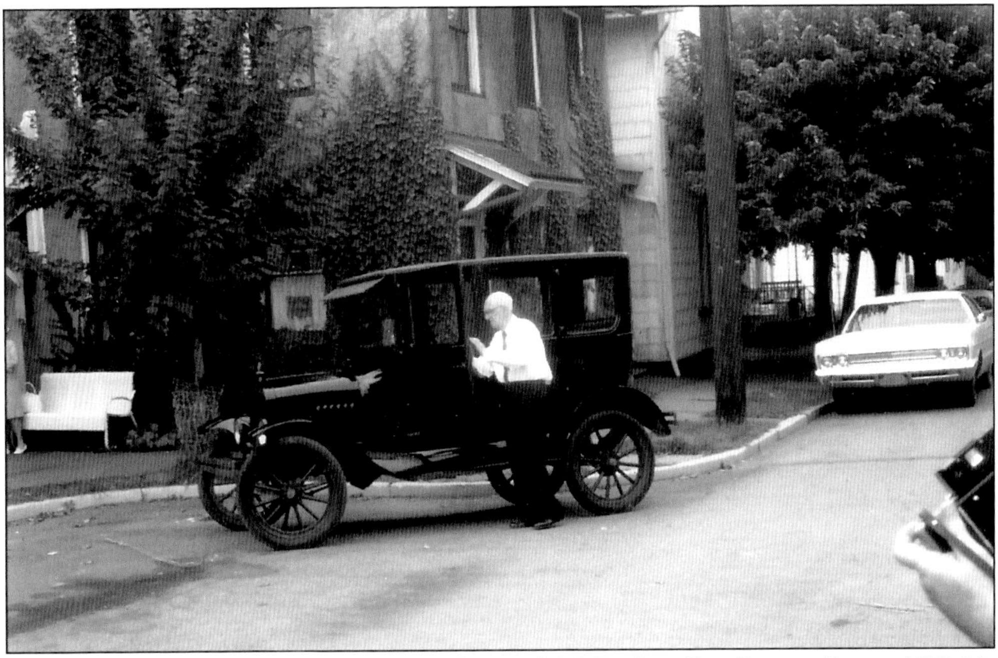

Dr. Arthur Stewart gets ready for a spin in his Model T Ford on Doc Stewart Day in 1970. He once drove the car to make house calls. During six decades as a country doctor, he employed other methods of reaching his patients, including walking, horseback, horse-drawn wagons, and farm tractors. (Courtesy of Ruth Werner, photograph by Robert Werner.)

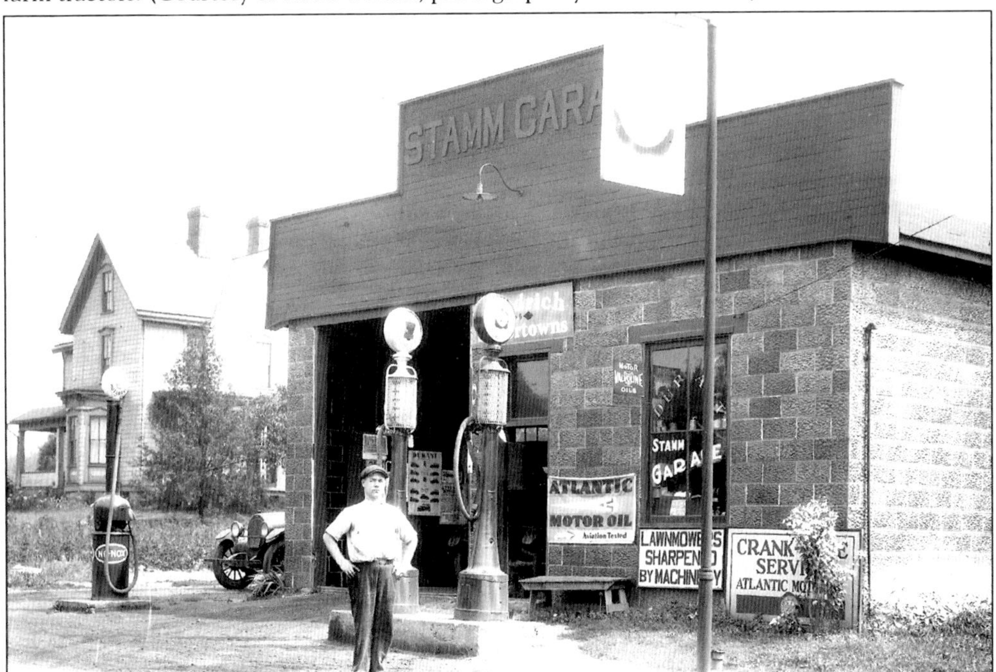

H. Byron "Barney" Stamm opened a garage on German Street in Harmony in the 1930s to service the growing number of cars and trucks in town. He and his wife, Esther, lived in the 1875 David Zeigler house seen in the background. (Courtesy of Bernice Stamm Lewis.)

The Harmony Short Line Motor Transportation Company was formed in 1922, mainly to carry freight. It added passenger service after the interurbans stopped running. Bus schedules such as this one from 1950 were issued, but as roads were improved and more people acquired cars, ridership declined. The bus service was discontinued on March 31, 1961. (Courtesy of Delsa White.)

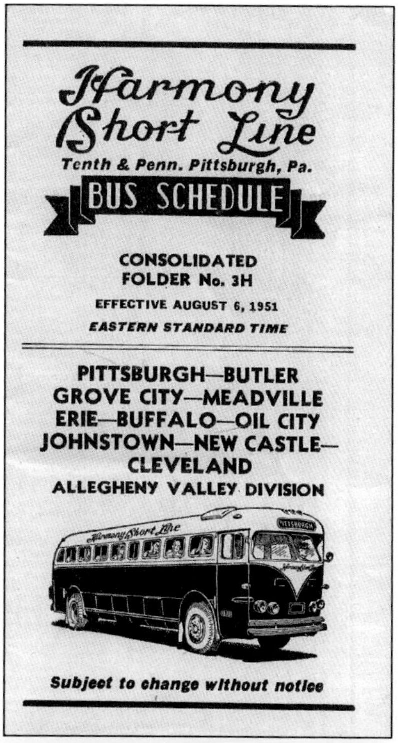
Harmony Short Line
Tenth & Penn. Pittsburgh, Pa.
BUS SCHEDULE
CONSOLIDATED
FOLDER No. 3H
EFFECTIVE AUGUST 6, 1951
EASTERN STANDARD TIME
PITTSBURGH—BUTLER
GROVE CITY—MEADVILLE
ERIE—BUFFALO—OIL CITY
JOHNSTOWN—NEW CASTLE—
CLEVELAND
ALLEGHENY VALLEY DIVISION
Subject to change without notice

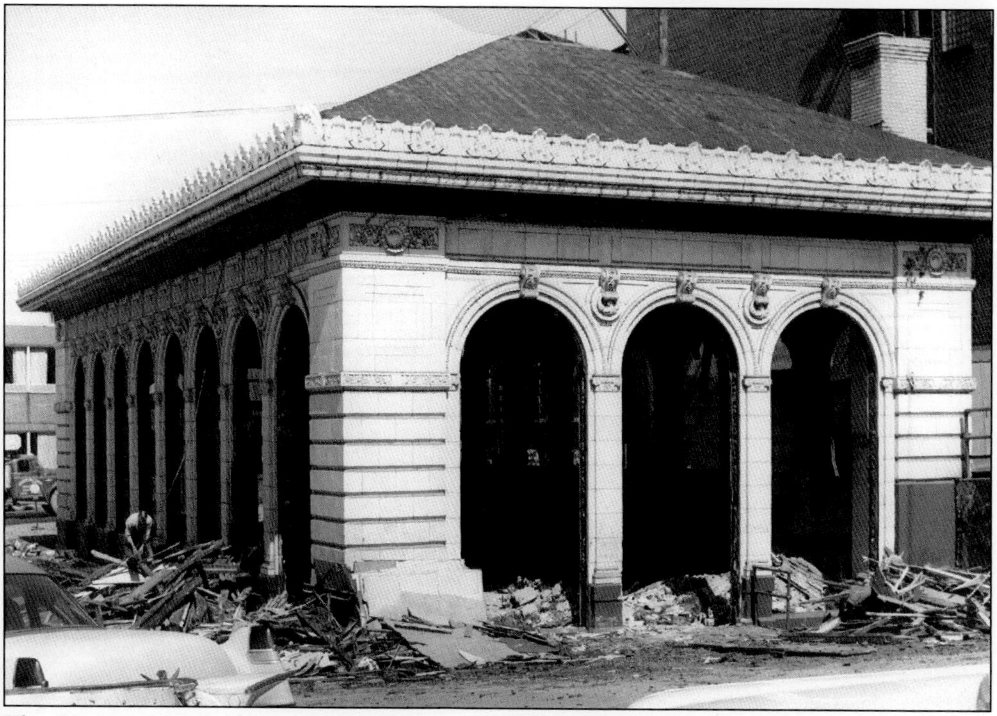

The Harmony and Short Line terminal on Cunningham Street in Butler fell victim to urban renewal in the 1960s. A tiered garage now provides parking for cars. (Courtesy of the Butler Eagle.)

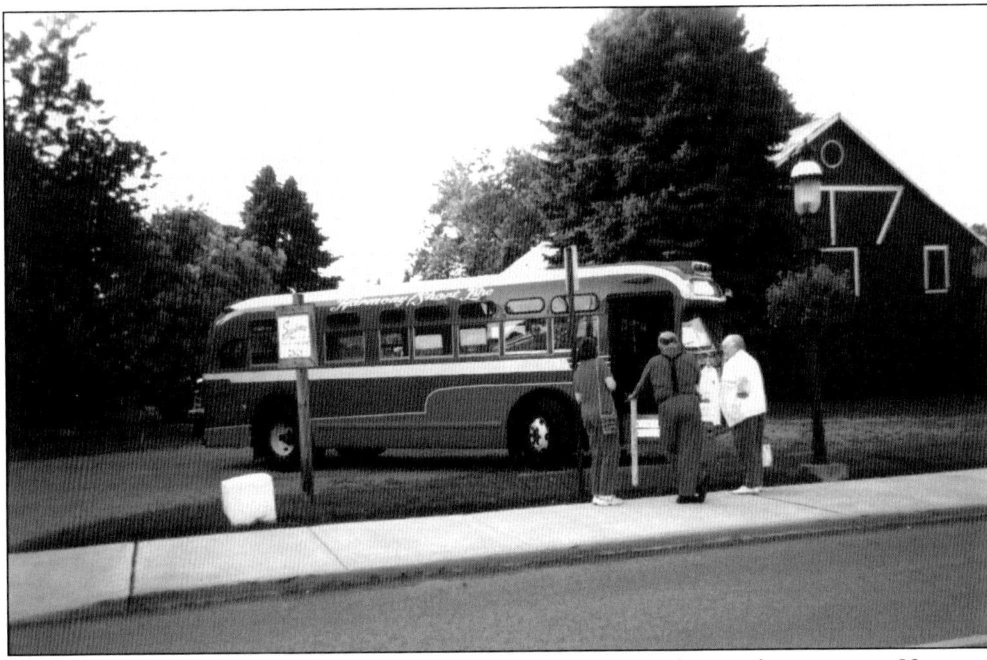

Coach 775, Harmony Short Line's 1947 General Motors transit bus, makes a stop in Harmony during the borough's bicentennial week. The bus was restored by the Antique Motor Coach Association of Pennsylvania, a nonprofit museum dedicated to the preservation of bus transportation systems. (Courtesy of Cathryn Rape.)

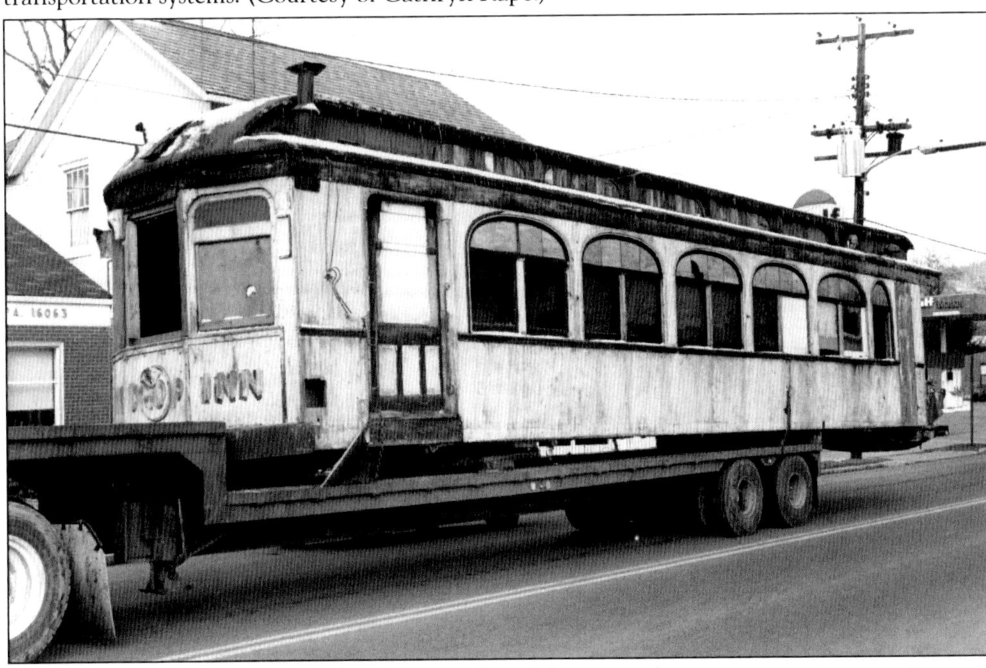

A well-worn Harmony route railway car, a relic of the interurban transportation era, is towed through Zelienople in 1989 headed for the Pennsylvania Trolley Museum in Washington County. The car last carried passengers in 1931 and had served as a diner in Butler County. (Courtesy of the Butler Eagle, photograph Ray Thompson.)

Six

Commerce

Three patriarchal figures stand out in Harmony history: Gen. George Washington, who became father of the country in the 18th century; George Rapp in the 19th century; and Dr. Arthur I. Stewart in the 20th century. Affectionately known to all as "Doc," Stewart was a father to the Harmony community and to local historical preservation.

While Washington passed through and Rapp stayed for a decade, Stewart served Harmony and the surrounding area for more than 60 years. He could rightly claim status as a father figure, having delivered an estimated 3,400 babies.

A native of Turtle Creek, Allegheny County, Stewart came to town in 1906, the year after the Harmony Society disbanded and a few years after the last service was held in the Harmony Mennonite meetinghouse.

He recalled when Harmony was the business hub of southwest Butler County with a foundry, two large flour mills, a lumber yard, two general stores, a stockyard, butchers, grocers, an oil well supply, carriage shops, three blacksmiths, livery stables, two hotels, and four restaurants.

He described a typical workday in the first few decades of the 20th century: "Farmers would arrive at the railroad station about 4 a.m. to meet the 'milkshake run' for delivery of their milk to Pittsburgh. Stores would open for business about 5 or 5:30 a.m. This included the doctor's office. Business was usually done by bartering. Four or five local freights would stop each day and require about a half hour to unload and load. At 7 p.m. the mail train would arrive and a large group of town folk would gather to see who was arriving and leaving. Then this group would follow the mail boy to the post office and while waiting for the mail to be sorted, they would gossip outside. At dusk the kids gathered on the diamond to play ball until 9 or 10 p.m. Stores would close about 10:30 or 11 p.m. At midnight the older boys coming home from dating would gather on the diamond for some barbershop quartet singing. Then all was quiet for a few hours until the farmers began arriving again."

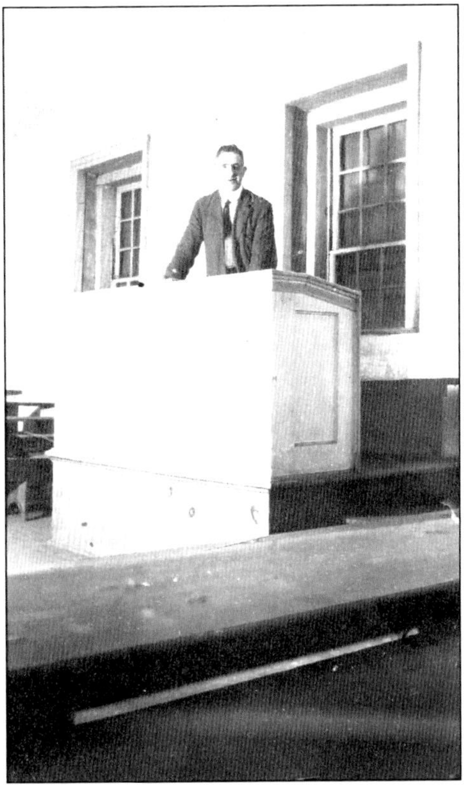

At left, Dr. Arthur Stewart stands in the Harmony Mennonite meetinghouse in the early 1900s. The young physician was a newcomer in 1906 but quickly became a community leader. He married Isabella Hardie, a descendant of Mennonite pioneer Abraham Ziegler, and delved deeply into the history of his adopted town. Below, he looks over his history scrapbooks in 1970 shortly before he was the guest of honor at Doc Stewart Day. (Courtesy of Ray Thompson.)

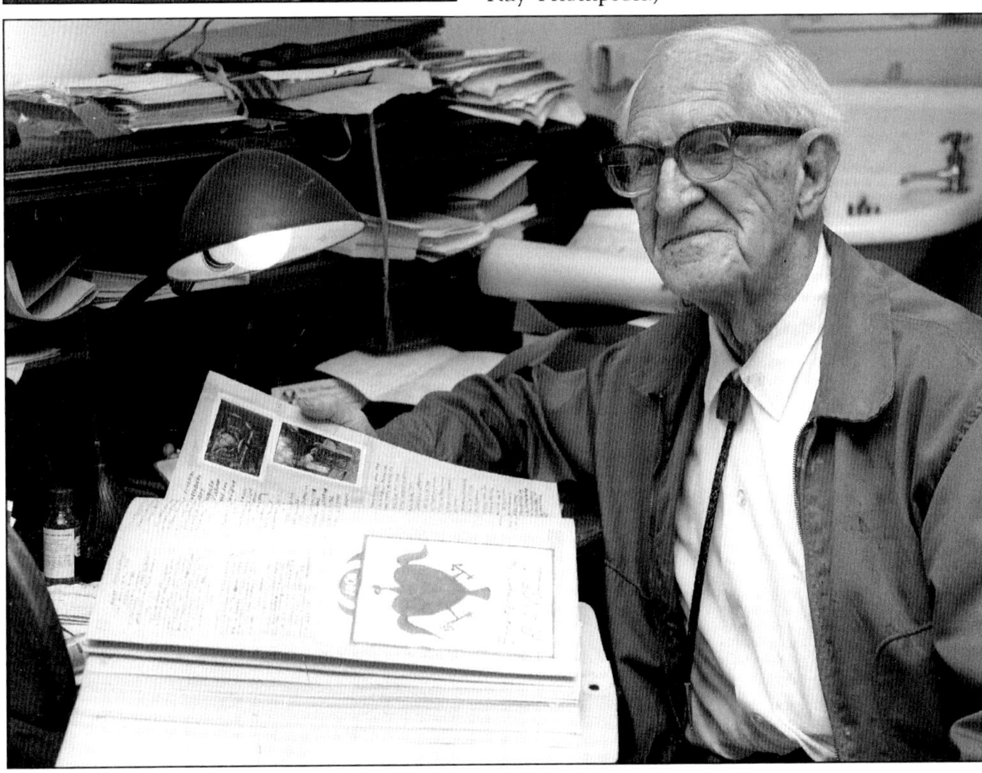

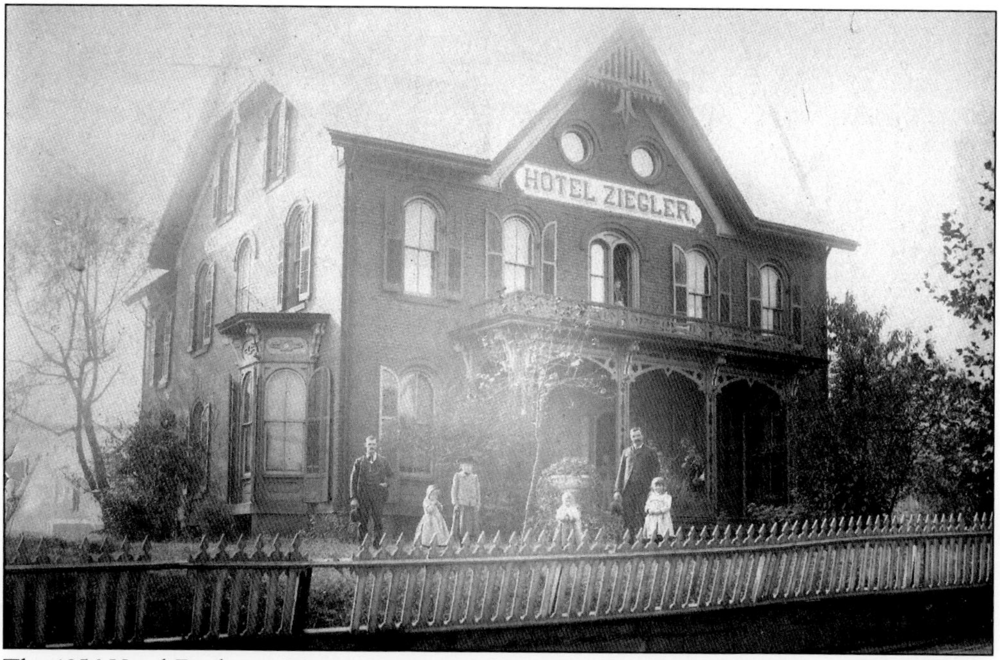

The 1856 Hotel Ziegler on Mercer Street was the home of bank president Austin Pearce. Louis Napoleon Ziegler bought the house from Pearce and opened a hotel in the late 1800s. Stewart boarded there when he first came to town. The well-preserved building is now the Harmony Inn restaurant. (Courtesy of Kathryn Ziegler Bauder.)

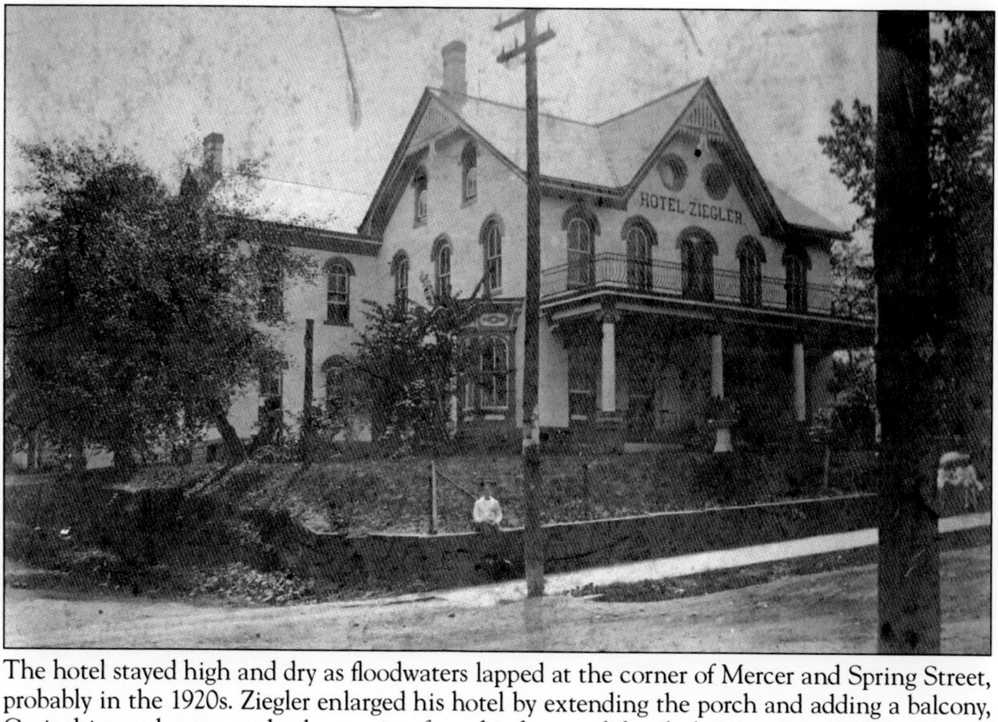

The hotel stayed high and dry as floodwaters lapped at the corner of Mercer and Spring Street, probably in the 1920s. Ziegler enlarged his hotel by extending the porch and adding a balcony, Corinthian columns, and a large wing for a kitchen and family living quarters. (Courtesy of Kathryn Ziegler Bauder.)

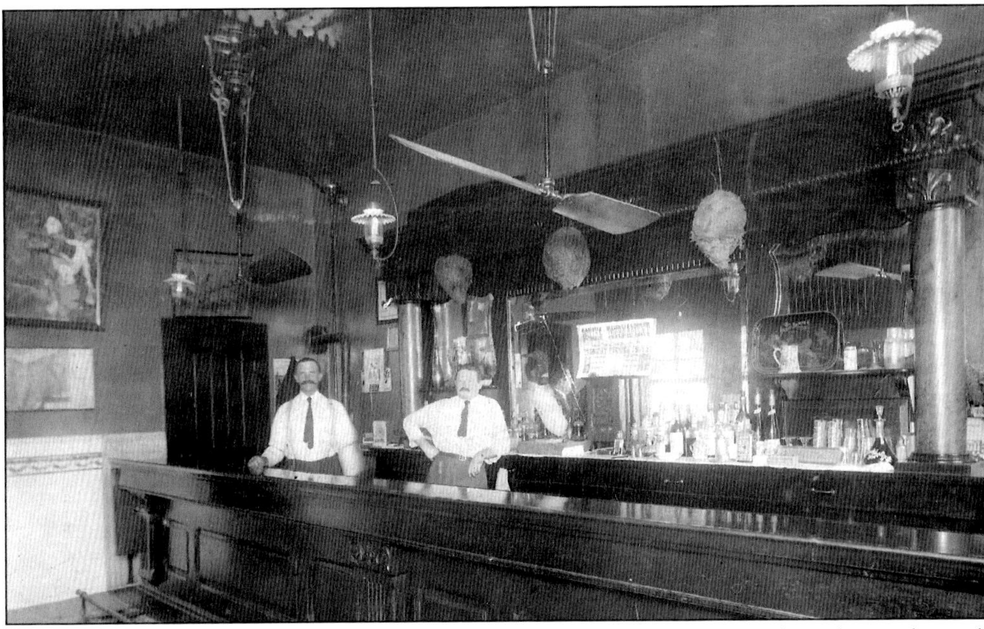

Owner Louis Napoleon Ziegler (right) stands in the barroom of his Hotel Ziegler in the early 1900s. Suspended hornet nests decorate the ornate bar. His daughter Kathryn, who was born in the hotel, remembers another decoration, a lion in a cage, seen in the mirror at right. Current owners, Gary Barnes and Carl Beers, have retained original features, including the bar, stairway, woodwork, and pocket doors. (Courtesy of Kathryn Ziegler Bauder.)

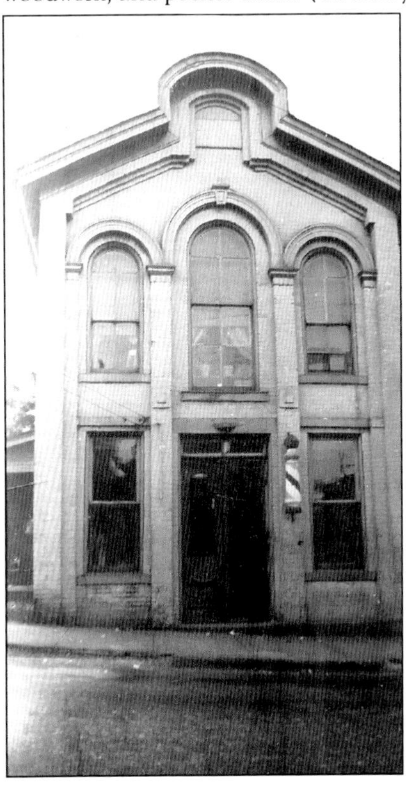

Harmony Savings, the Pearce family bank, stands across the street from the Hotel Ziegler. A barbershop was doing business there when this picture was taken in the 1930s. The current owner, Thomas Murray of the Murray Agency Realtors, restored the exterior. Murray also donated a lot nearby on Mercer Street to Historic Harmony. A log house given to Historic Harmony by Robinson Industries was moved from West German Street to that lot and now functions as a museum annex and weavers' center.

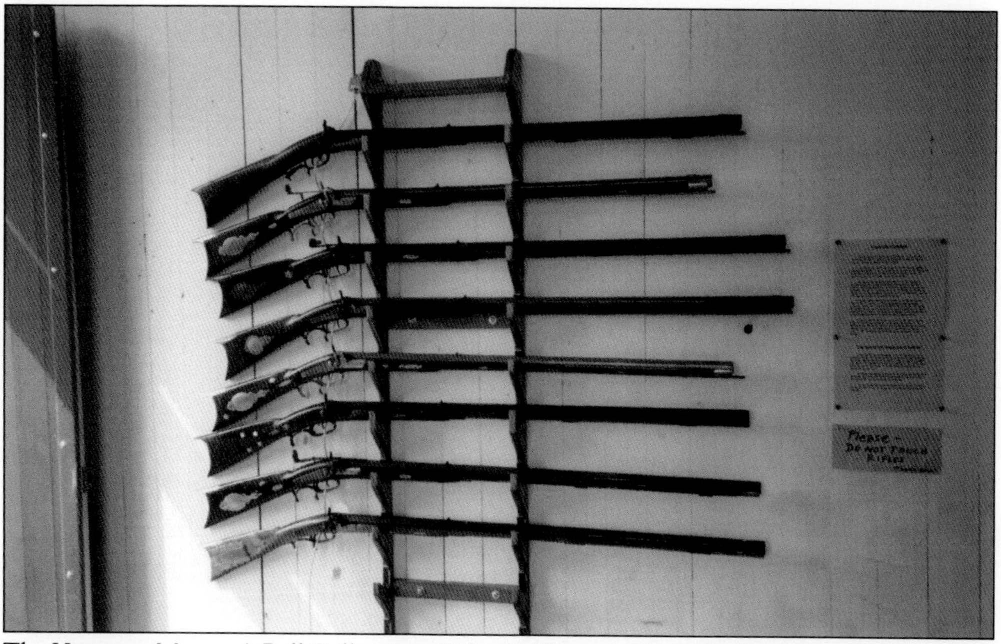

The Harmony Museum's Ball Collection of Charles Flowers rifles is displayed at a museum event. Working in a shop on Wood Street, Flowers crafted fine Pennsylvania long rifles between 1850 and 1897. His rifles, highly respected at shooting matches of his time, are viewed today as works of art as well as collectible firearms. Most Flowers rifles have a handsome, functional brass plate protecting the stock from percussion cap flash. Other common elements distinguishing his work are incised stock carvings, a decorative patch box, and German silver or brass mountings. Decoration usually includes asterisks that look like a blooming flower. The rifle collection was made possible by Hiram P. Ball, his wife Florence, and the estate of Henry A. Ball Sr. (Photographs by John Ruch.)

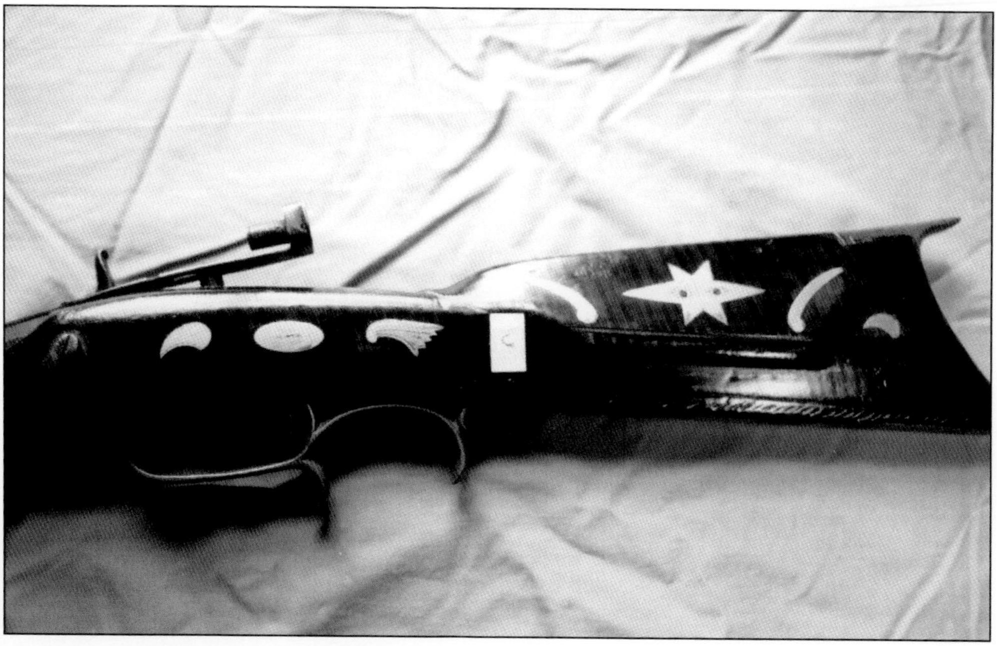

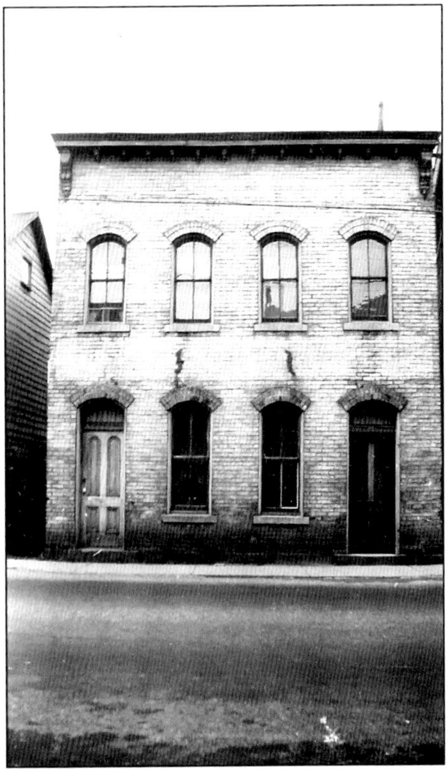

Several banks were established in Harmony in the 1800s when business was booming. Harmony National Bank was organized in 1876, and the owners constructed a brick building on Main Street two doors south of the diamond where the Ziegler Log House now stands. Below, the Swain and Moyer store owners paid a bill with a Harmony Savings Bank check. (Courtesy of Delsa White.)

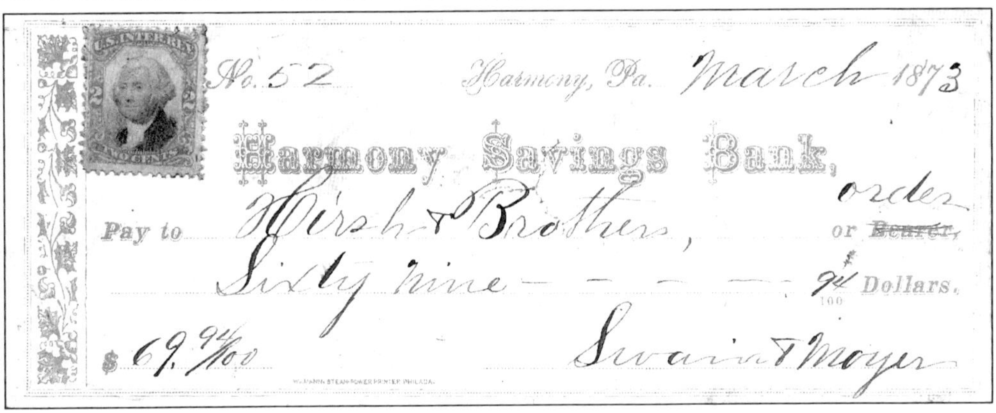

U.S. INTER. REV. 2 TWO CENTS

No. 52 Harmony, Pa. March 1873

Harmony Savings Bank,

Pay to Hirsh & Brothers, or ~~Bearer,~~ order

Sixty nine — — — — — 94/100 Dollars.

$ 69.94/100 Swain & Moyer

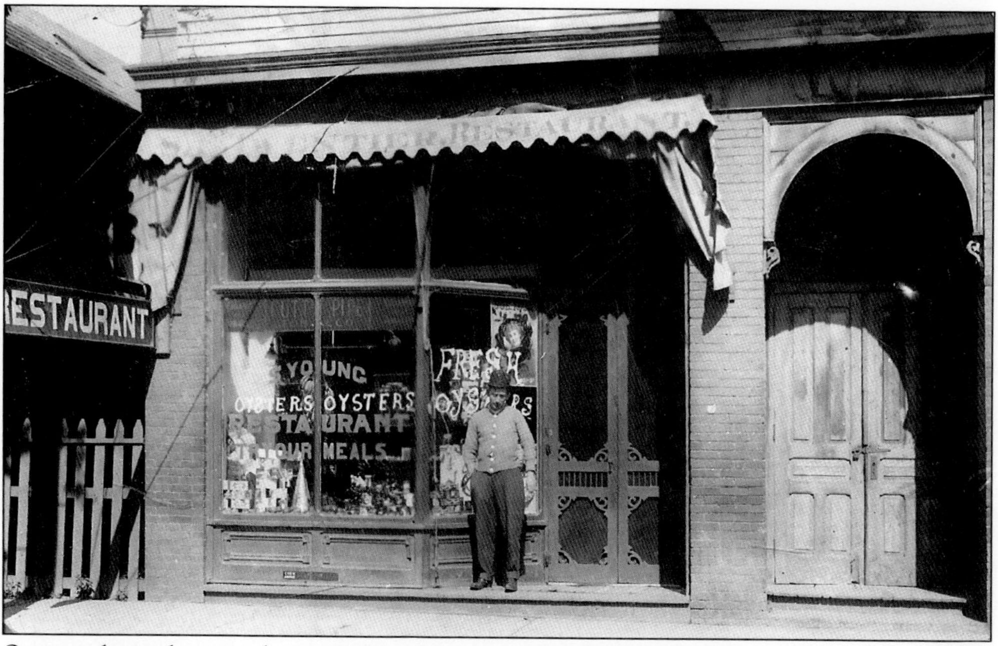

Oysters obviously were the specialty when this photograph was taken at Young's Restaurant in the Odd Fellows hall, also called the opera house, on Mercer Street. According to the 1909 *International Magazine of Industry*, the restaurant was opened in the 1880s by Mr. Young, a native of Evans City. It offered a cozy dining room where ladies were served. Otto and Gert's ice cream parlor and lunch room is located here now.

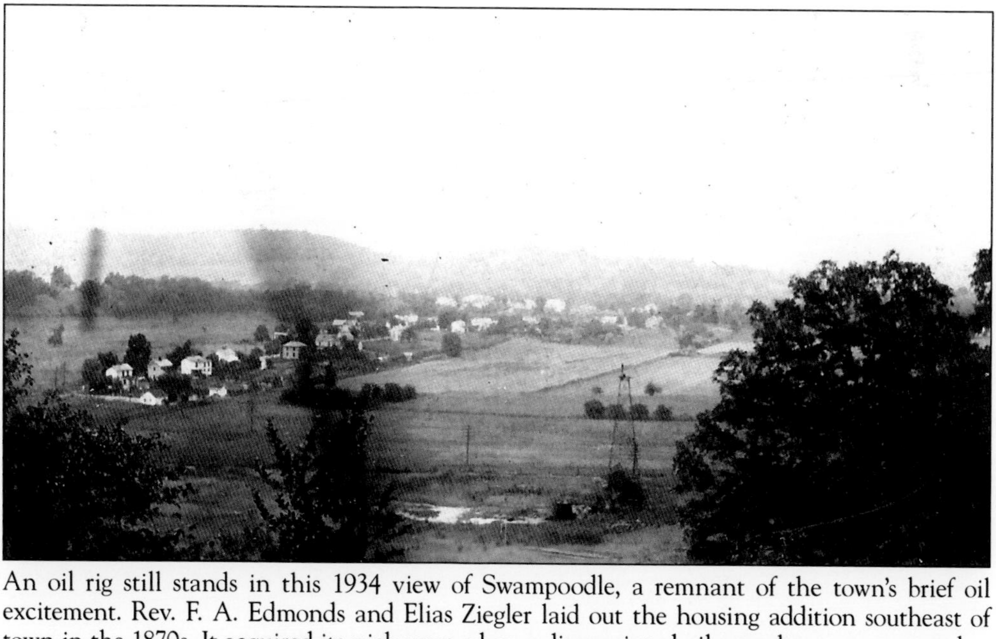

An oil rig still stands in this 1934 view of Swampoodle, a remnant of the town's brief oil excitement. Rev. F. A. Edmonds and Elias Ziegler laid out the housing addition southeast of town in the 1870s. It acquired its nickname when a disappointed oil speculator was reported to have commented, "I swamped my boodle there." Several wells were drilled in this part of town, but that activity was soon eclipsed by the discovery of a flowing oil well north of Harmony.

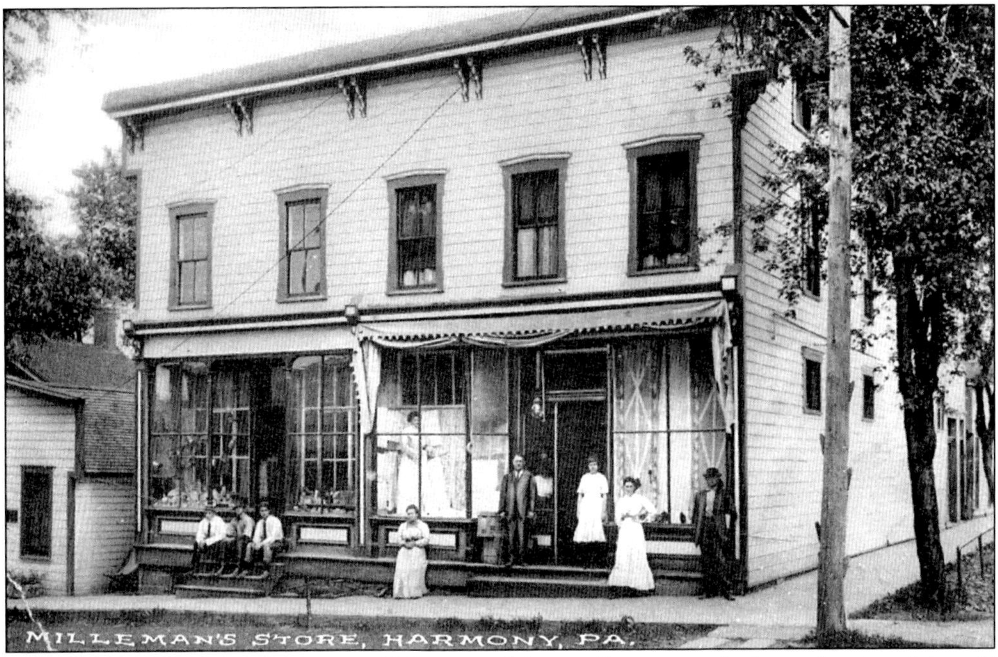

The Milleman Store at the corner of Mercer and Spring Streets was built on the site of the old Harmony distillery. Owners H. C. Milleman and his son sold clothing, groceries, and general merchandise. Later Charles and Ralph Druschel operated a Clover Farm Store here. Several members of the Druschel family worked in the store from the 1930s to 1950s. The photograph below offers a look inside the old Milleman Store where two clerks are at work, a customer sits at the counter, and a boy uses the wall telephone with a hand crank.

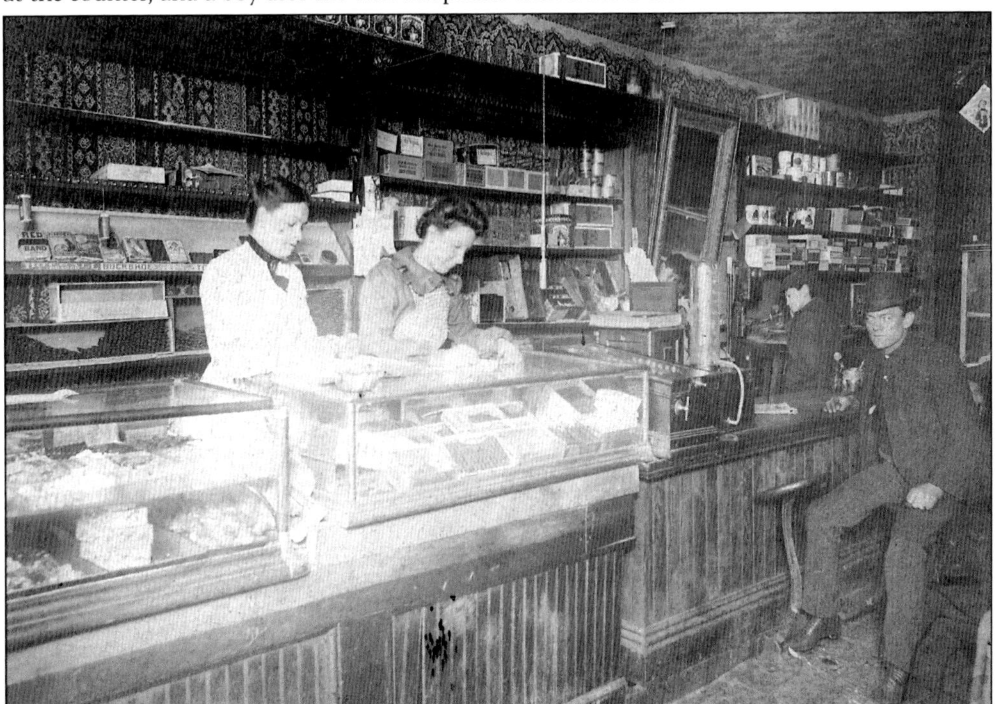

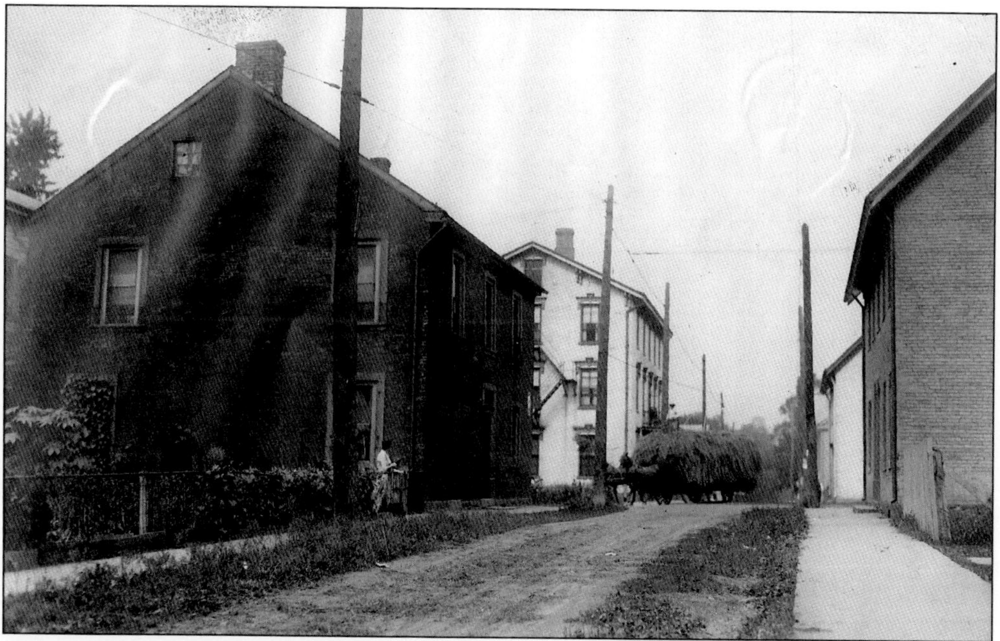

A hay wagon crosses the diamond in this 1915 view of Mercer Street. The Harmony Society's store (near left) and the Beam Hotel (far left) look much as they do today. The building on the right was removed to make way for a new sanctuary on Grace Reformed Church. On East Mercer Street, below, the Harmonist Muller house stands at left. Across the street, a Harmonist house with an 1811 lintel stone is no longer standing.

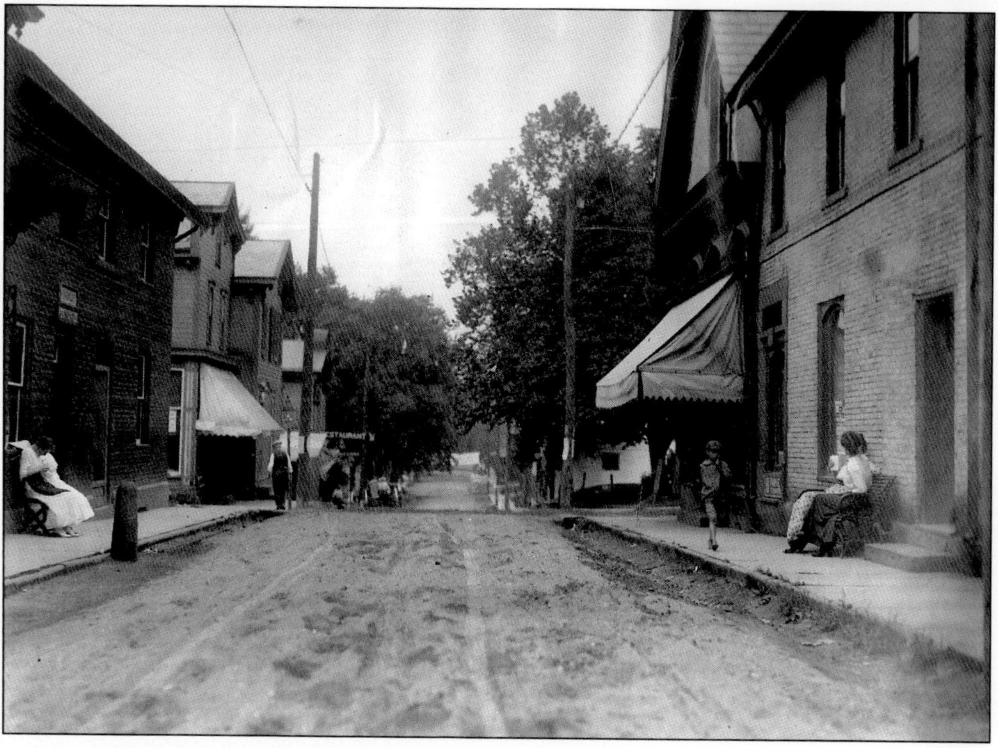

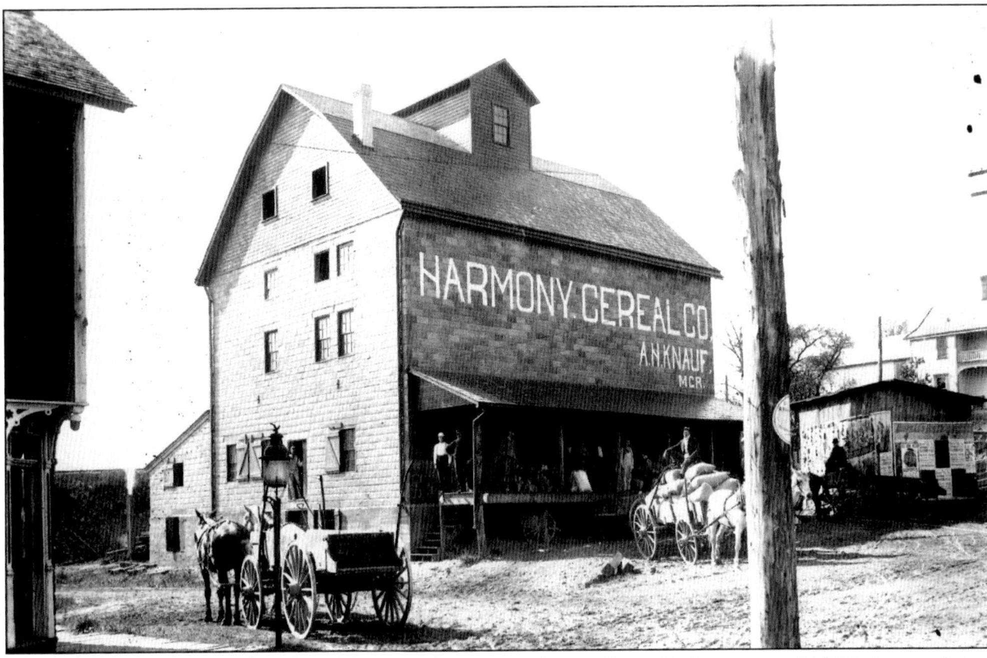

The mill at German and Spring Streets is known today as Knauf's, but around 1900, it was doing business as Harmony Cereal Company. A. H. Knauf of Evans City built the mill about 1900 on the foundation of his earlier mill that burned. A corner of the Dambach Lumber building can be seen at left.

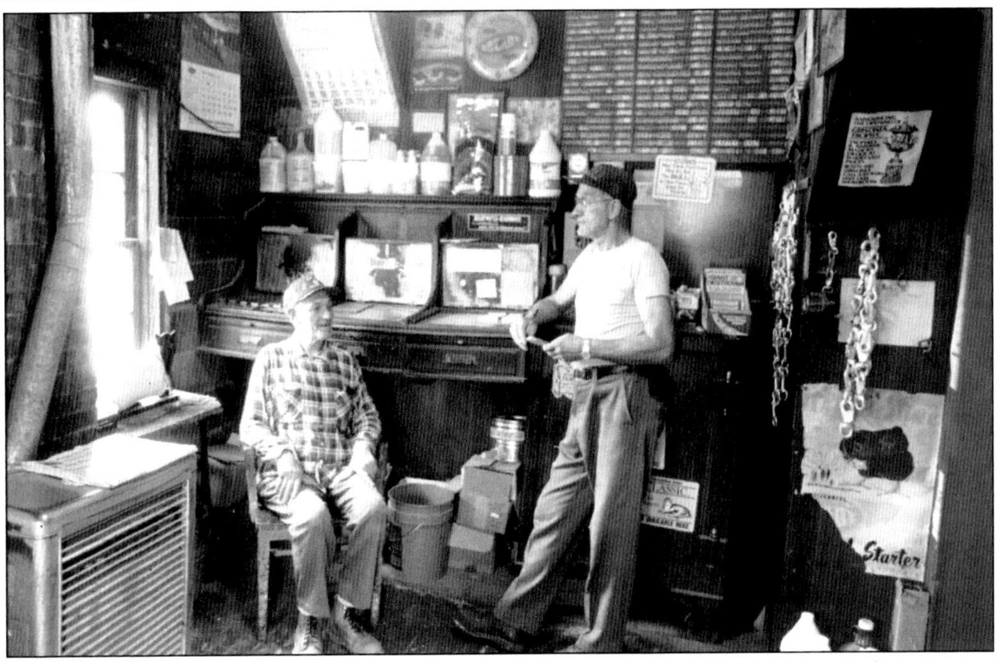

Brothers Franklin (left) and Clyde Knauf, shown in their office in 1993, were the third generation to operate the mill started by their grandfather. Locals liked to gather around the stove in the office or on the long loading dock in good weather to pass the time. (Courtesy of the Butler Eagle, photograph by Ray Thompson.)

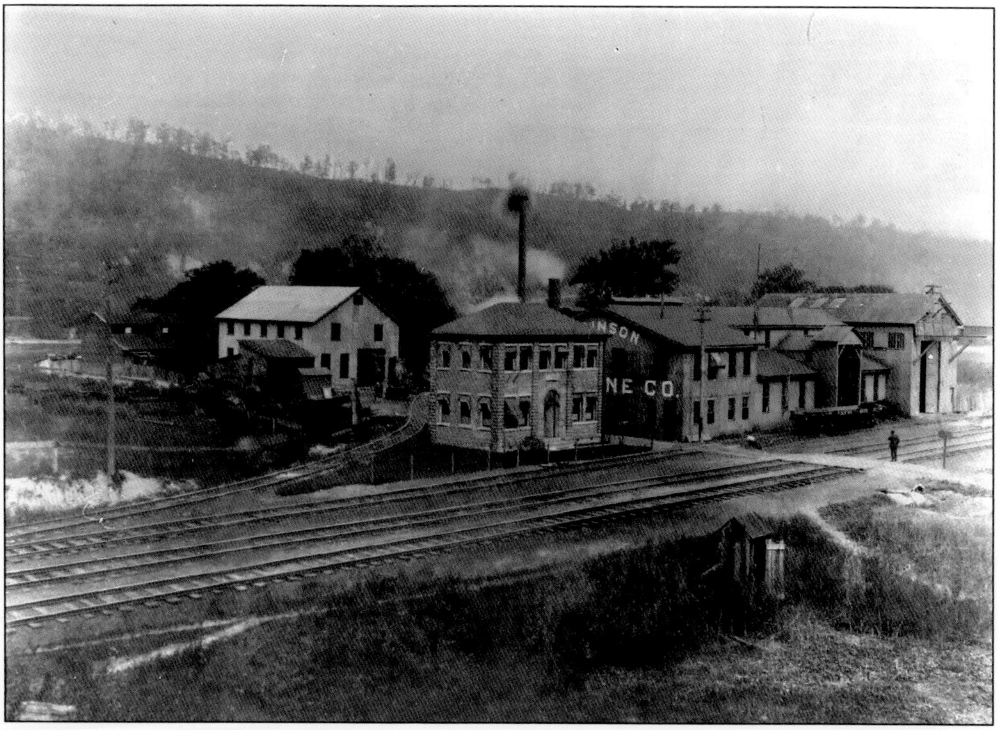

The Robinson Ventilating Company complex shown in this vintage photograph was the forerunner of Robinson Industries, which has been headquartered in Harmony since 1921. J. R. Robinson formed the company in Pittsburgh in 1908 to sell fans. Today Robinson Industries is an air-moving specialist company and manufacturer of industrial fans. (Courtesy of Robinson Industries.)

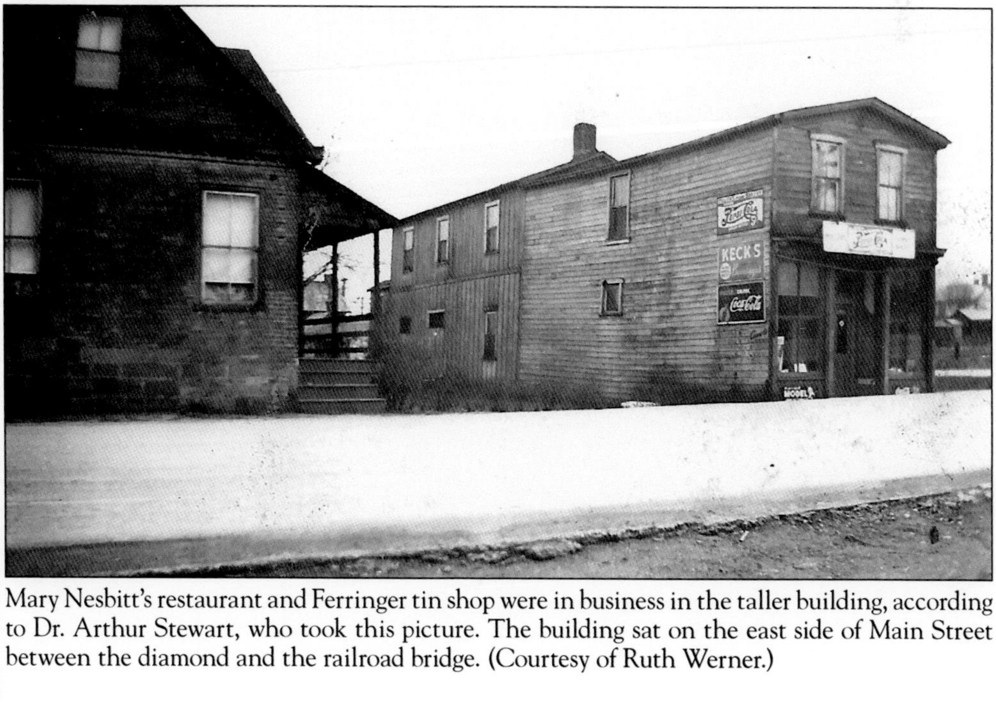

Mary Nesbitt's restaurant and Ferringer tin shop were in business in the taller building, according to Dr. Arthur Stewart, who took this picture. The building sat on the east side of Main Street between the diamond and the railroad bridge. (Courtesy of Ruth Werner.)

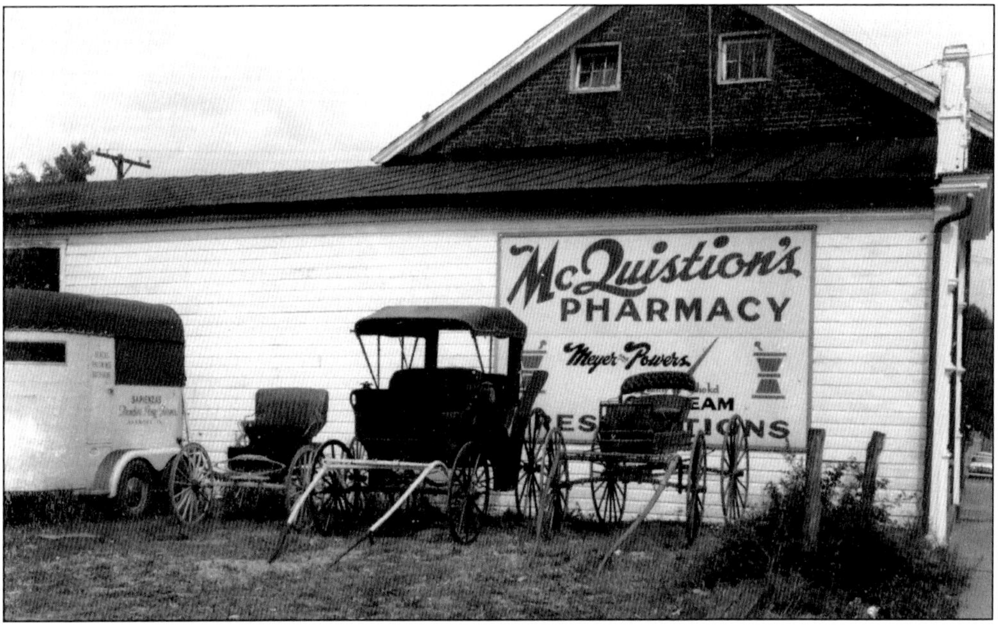

This shot of Joseph Sapienza's antique vehicle collection also offers a good look at Ralph McQuistion's pharmacy next door. Judge John H. Wilson and others who grew up in town remembered the chocolate sodas they enjoyed at McQuistion's soda fountain. The former pharmacy is attached to the Harmonist Muller house at Mercer and Wood Streets and now houses the Exchange at Harmony antiques and gift shop. (Courtesy of Tim Sapienza.)

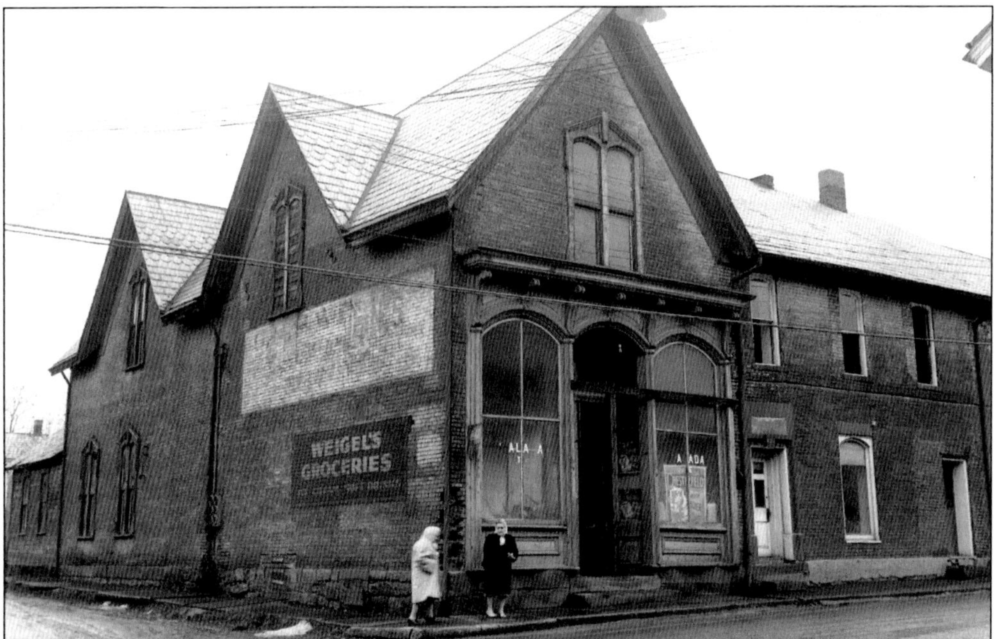

Harmony had a number of grocery stores, including this one at the corner of Mercer and Wood Streets in a former Harmony Society factory. Beginning about 1870, it was the Swain store, and later it was known as Sitler, Swain and Moyer. In its last years, it was Weigel's. The building is no longer standing.

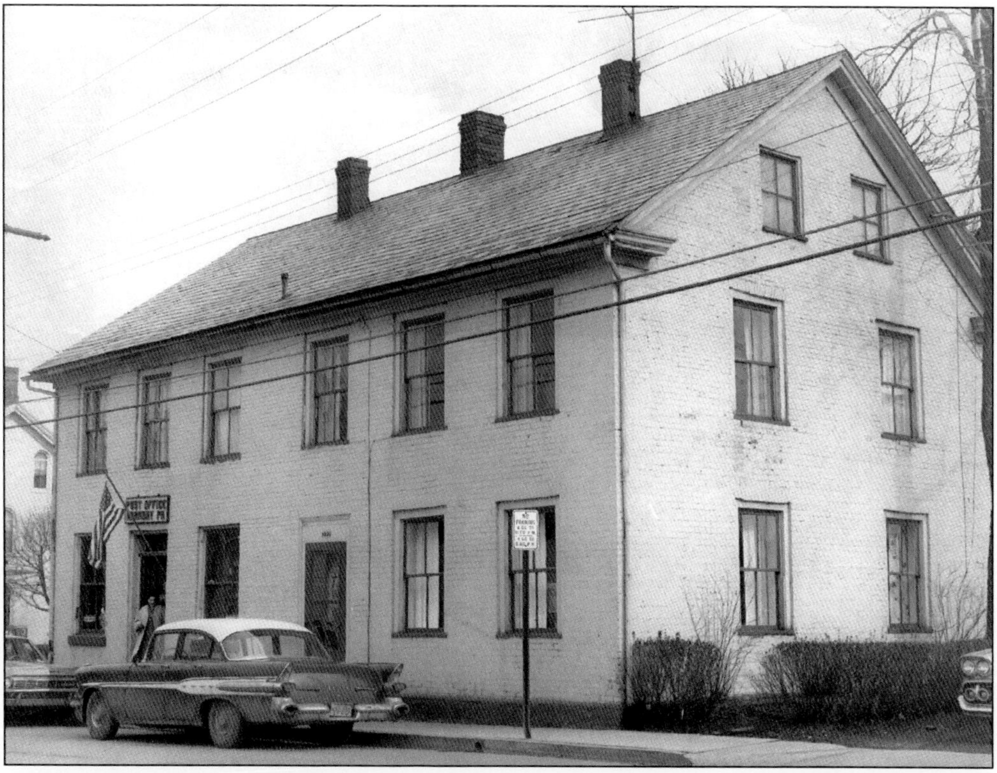

A customer leaves the Harmony Post Office in the 1960s. The post office was in the Wagner-Bentle house on Mercer Street, a residence for two Harmony Society families. Later it was the Fiedler family home and office of Dr. Daniel Fiedler. Now owned by Historic Harmony, it contains museum exhibits and the museum shop. (Courtesy of the Butler Eagle.)

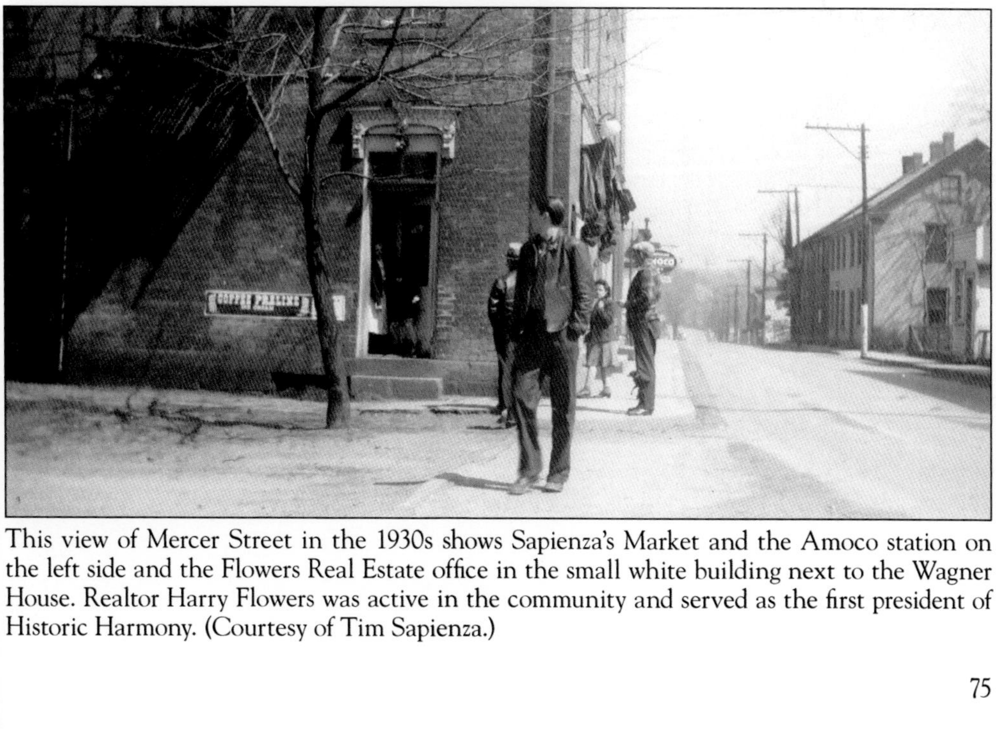

This view of Mercer Street in the 1930s shows Sapienza's Market and the Amoco station on the left side and the Flowers Real Estate office in the small white building next to the Wagner House. Realtor Harry Flowers was active in the community and served as the first president of Historic Harmony. (Courtesy of Tim Sapienza.)

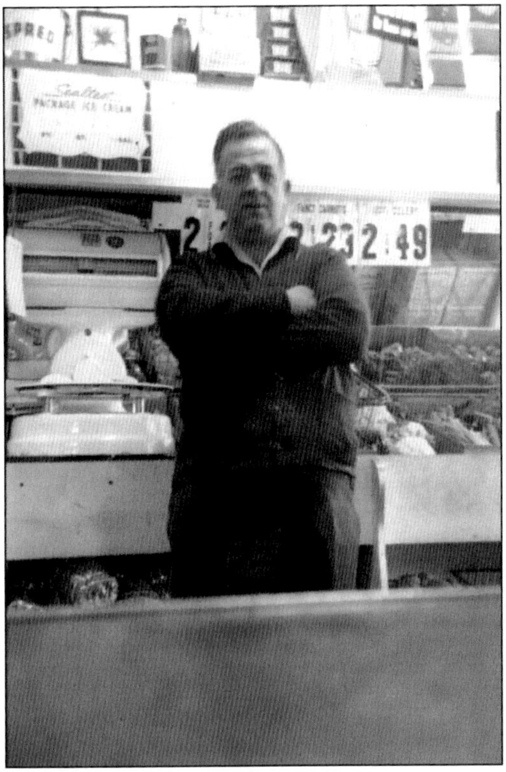

Joseph Sapienza Jr. works in his market at Main and Mercer Streets in 1951. He opened the business in the old Harmony Society warehouse in the 1920s and moved across the street a decade later. Sapienza's Market on the diamond quickly became a cornerstone of the neighborhood. Below is a view of the market in the 1950s. (Courtesy of Tim Sapienza.)

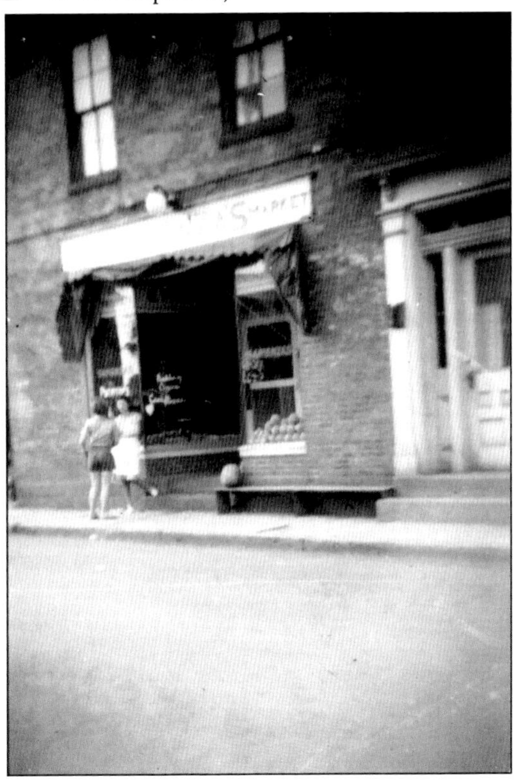

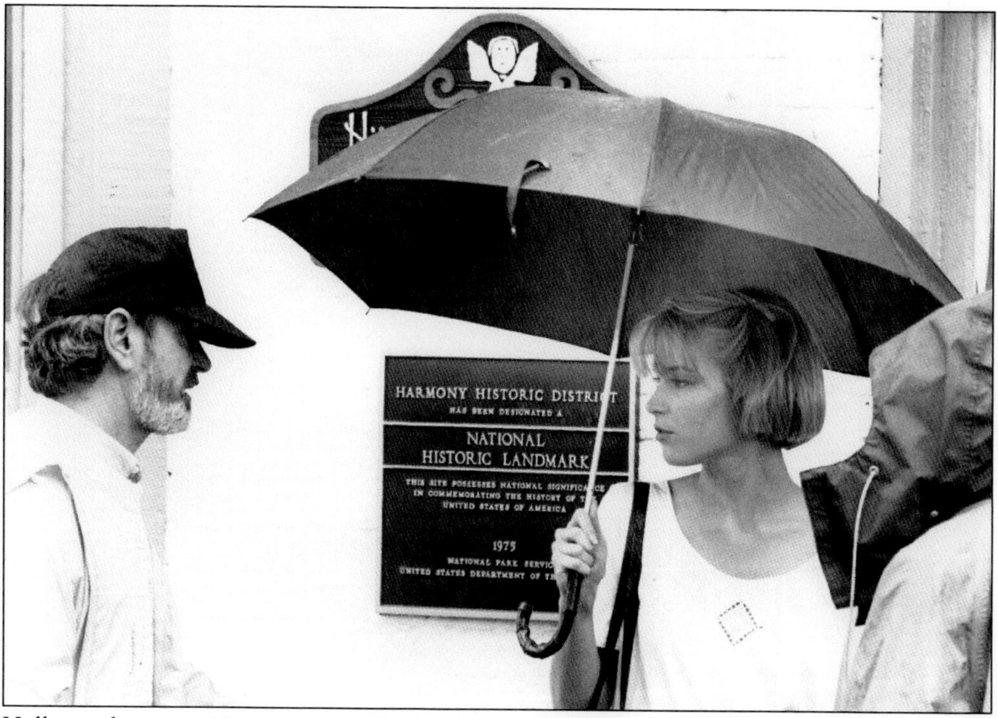

Hollywood came to Harmony in 1990 when the cast and crew of the film *Iron Maze* shot several scenes on Main and Mercer Streets. The old McQuistion Pharmacy space was transformed into a saloon for the occasion. Here actress Bridget Fonda confers with the director in front of the Harmony Museum. (Courtesy of the Butler Eagle, photograph Ray Thompson.)

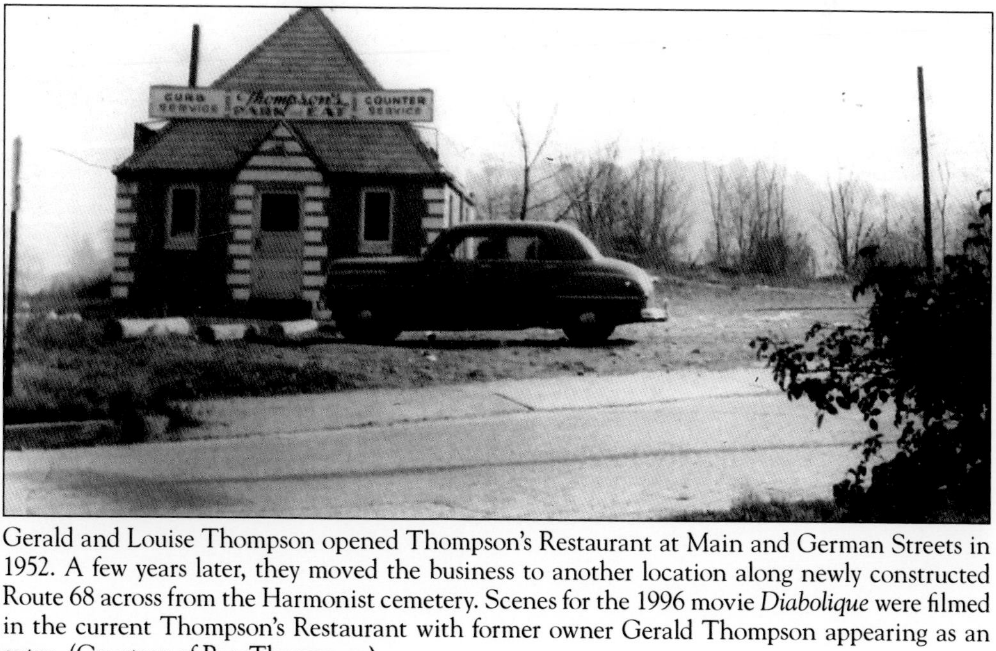

Gerald and Louise Thompson opened Thompson's Restaurant at Main and German Streets in 1952. A few years later, they moved the business to another location along newly constructed Route 68 across from the Harmonist cemetery. Scenes for the 1996 movie *Diabolique* were filmed in the current Thompson's Restaurant with former owner Gerald Thompson appearing as an extra. (Courtesy of Ray Thompson.)

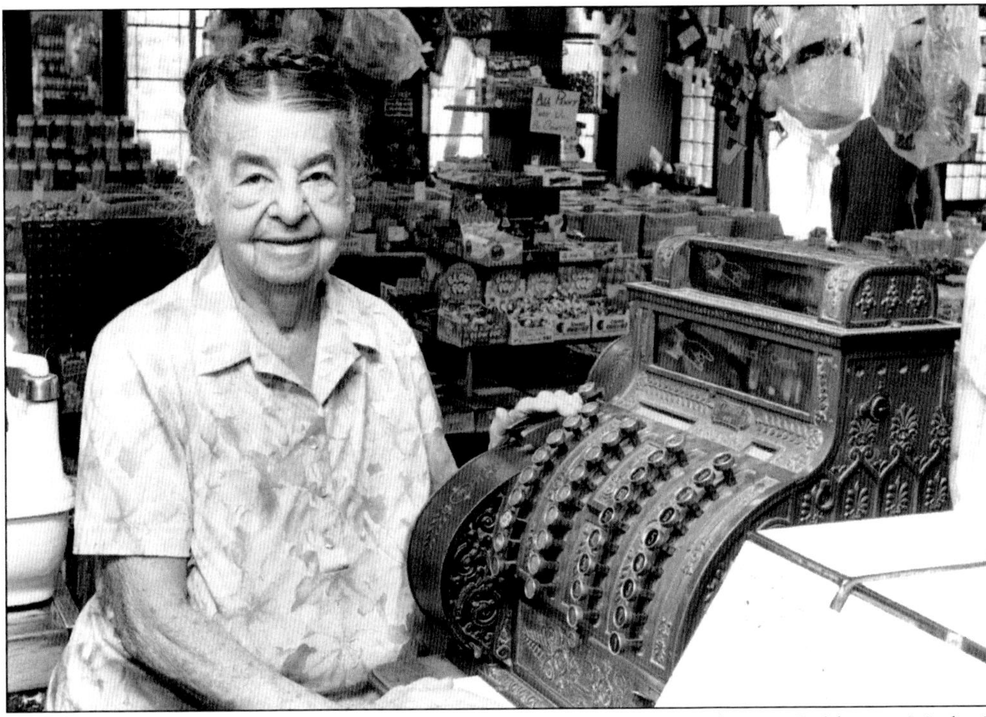

Dorothy Baldinger works at the antique cash register in 1988 during Baldinger Market's 55th year. The farm market she and her husband, Allan M. Baldinger, established on U.S. Route 19 in Jackson Township became famous for its old-fashioned atmosphere and bins of penny candy. Generations of children have enjoyed selecting candy there. When it looked as if the market would close, neighbors and patrons circulated petitions asking for help in retaining the business. Zelienople businessman Patrick Boylan came to the rescue by buying a building on U.S. Route 19 in Zelienople and remodeling it to replicate the original market. Baldinger's opened at its new location in November 2008. (Courtesy of the Butler Eagle, photograph by Ray Thompson.)

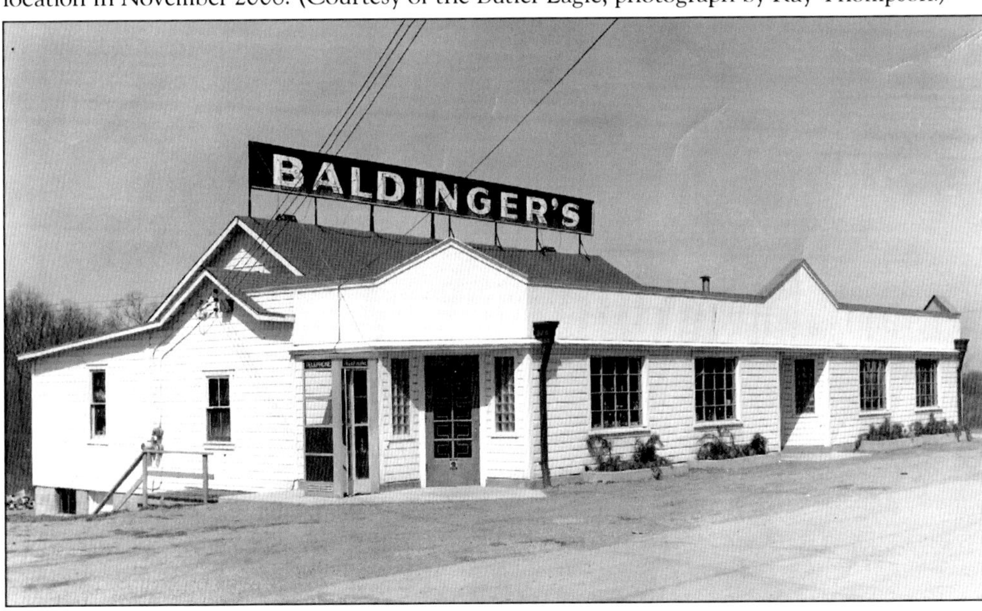

Seven

Civic and Social Life

Life in Harmony has always revolved around the Connoquenessing Creek for commercial use and recreation. The stream has attracted summer visitors to board at local hotels and rooming houses and to build vacation cottages along its banks.

Service groups have long supplemented town governmental services. The Harmony Volunteer Fire Company, established 1874, has taken the lead in many activities, including organizing an ambulance service, sponsoring a young people's drum and bugle corps, spearheading the drive to finance war memorials, and founding the Harmony Museum. For many years, the firemen held carnivals at Rapp Park to fund equipment purchases.

Circuses were also popular attractions. Butler County president Judge John Wilson, a Harmony native, recalled circuses on the commons, noting, "When Dan Rice came with his show there was an extra big turnout as he was related to many of the residents." Rice (1823–1900), an internationally famed political humorist, clown, and animal trainer, headquartered his traveling circus in Girard, Pennsylvania, in 1853. Some believe Rice's trademark top hat, star-spangled suit, and chin whiskers provided inspiration for the caricature of Uncle Sam.

Music is a recurring theme throughout town history. Harmony Society members played instruments and sang on the way to their fields. After founding Economy in Beaver County in 1824, they organized one of the first orchestras in America. Harmony residents have continued the musical tradition with the firemen's band, the Harmonettes Drum and Bugle Corps, school bands, and public concerts.

In the 1800s, fraternal groups flourished, including Kinnear Lodge No. 648, International Order of Odd Fellows, Harmony Lodge No. 429, Free and Accepted Masons, and Knights of Pythias Eden Lodge No. 311. During this period, The Odd Fellows hall, also called the opera house, was constructed. In addition to being a meeting hall, it was an entertainment center for shows, band concerts, lyceums, and amateur plays. The Economy Band, directed by John Duss, one of the last Harmony Society trustees, performed at the opera house. It also has held a dance hall, restaurant, bowling alley, bingo parlor, basketball court, garage, fan factory, bottling works, and antiques shop. Today it is Otto and Gert's ice cream parlor and lunch room.

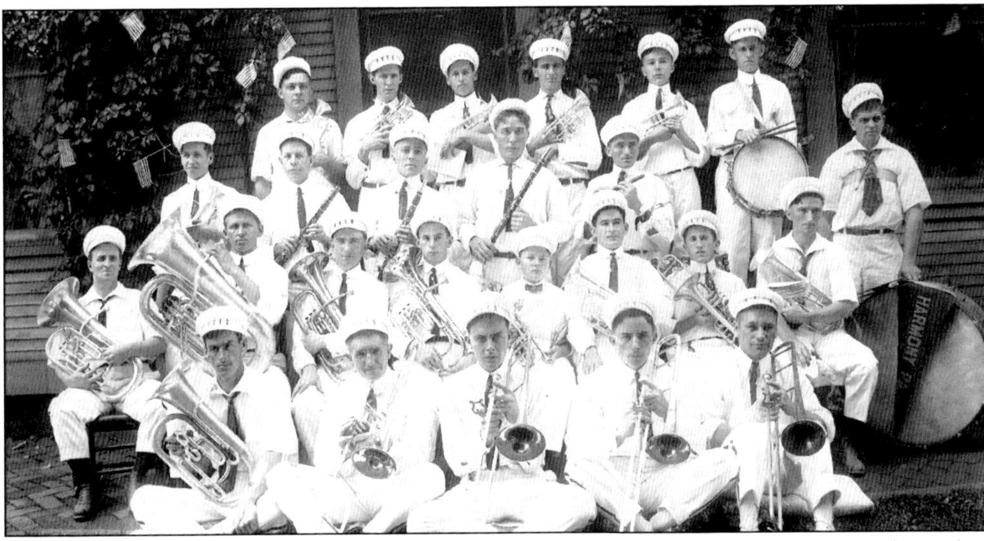

The Harmony Volunteer Fire Company, celebrating its 135th anniversary in 2009, has taken the lead in community life, including founding the Harmony Museum. Dr. Arthur Stewart, second from left in front, was instrumental in organizing Historic Harmony. Band members from left to right are (first row) Russell Sitler, Stewart, Ferd Shaffer, Elmer Allen, and Charles Milleman; (second row) Charles Teets, Fred Westerbeck, Jacob Rape, Clarence Dambaugh, Ralph McQuistion, Edward Casserly, Art Dambach, and Edward Rape; (third row) Fred Weigel, Frank Simon, Ezra Flowers, Curt Lewis, Thayer Peters, and Lee Stauffer; (fourth row) Edward Stauffer, Elmer McCormick, Frank Weigel, Stewart Flick, Bill Flowers, and Cliff Bloom.

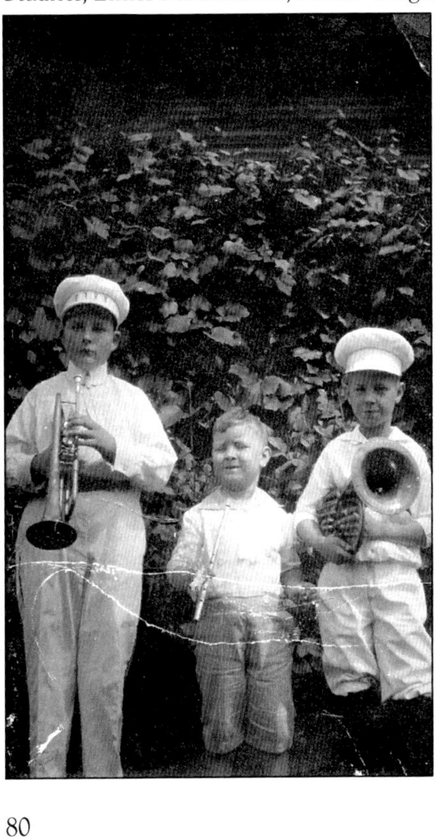

Harmony Firemen's Band trumpeter Ralph McQuistion (left) prepares to practice with an unidentified horn player at right and an aspiring musician at center. Stewart, a band member, wryly commented that the group consisted of 50 pieces, "all forming a unit to render the citizens miserable during their period of learning to play." (Courtesy of Nancy Wiser.)

Ralph McQuistion continued making music for years as director of the Grace Reformed Church Orchestra that began performing concerts in 1927, and as director of the Harmony Junior Band. He also served as a Historic Harmony board member, worked as Harmony postmaster, and owned McQuistion's Pharmacy. (Courtesy of Nancy Wiser.)

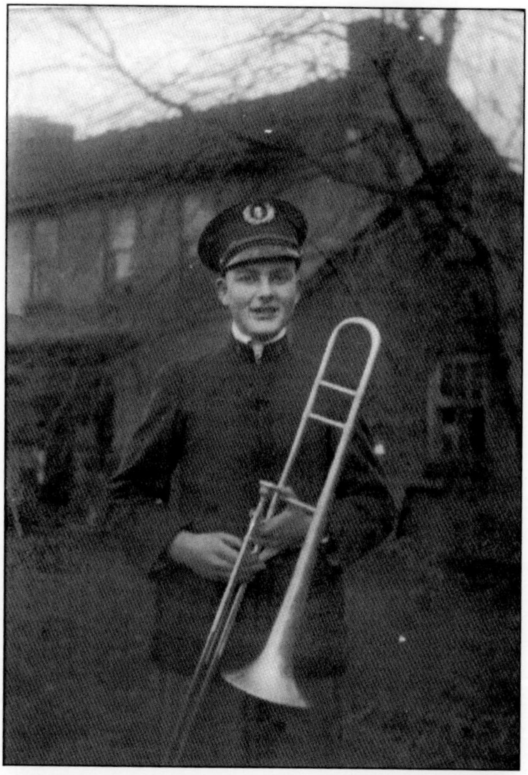

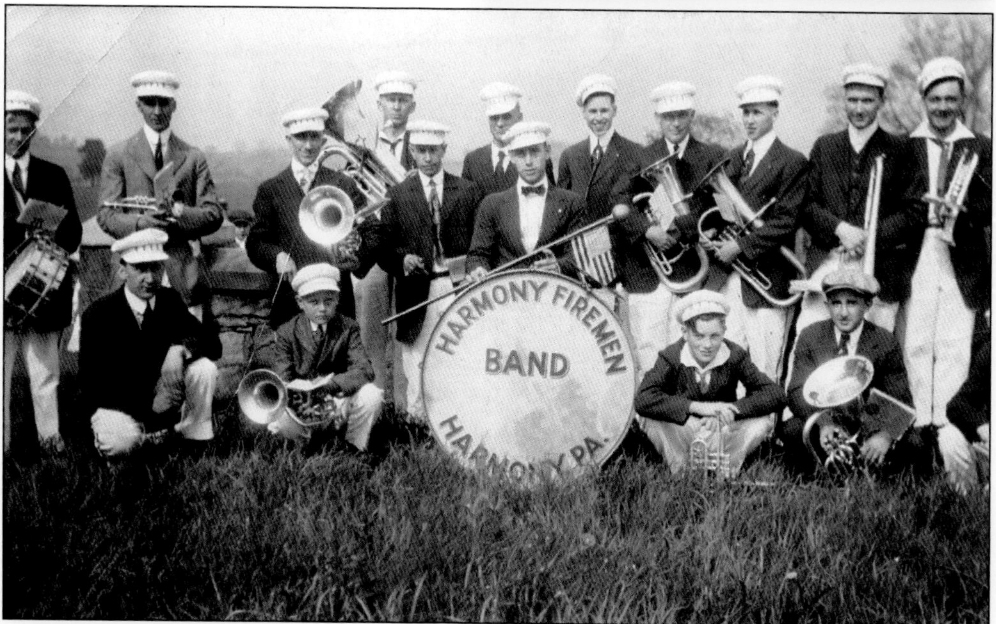

Harmony firemen's band members gather to play taps during a Memorial Day service at the Mennonite cemetery. From left to right are (first row) ? Bloom, Clarence Nesbitt, Russ Nesbitt, and Curly Stover; (second row) Cliff Bloom, Stewart Flick, Jake Rape, Frank Simon, and Joe Shaffer; (third row) Fred Westerbeck, unidentified, Fred Weigel, Lee Blackburn, Frank Weigel, George Suplee, and Edward Stauffer. (Courtesy of Nancy Wiser.)

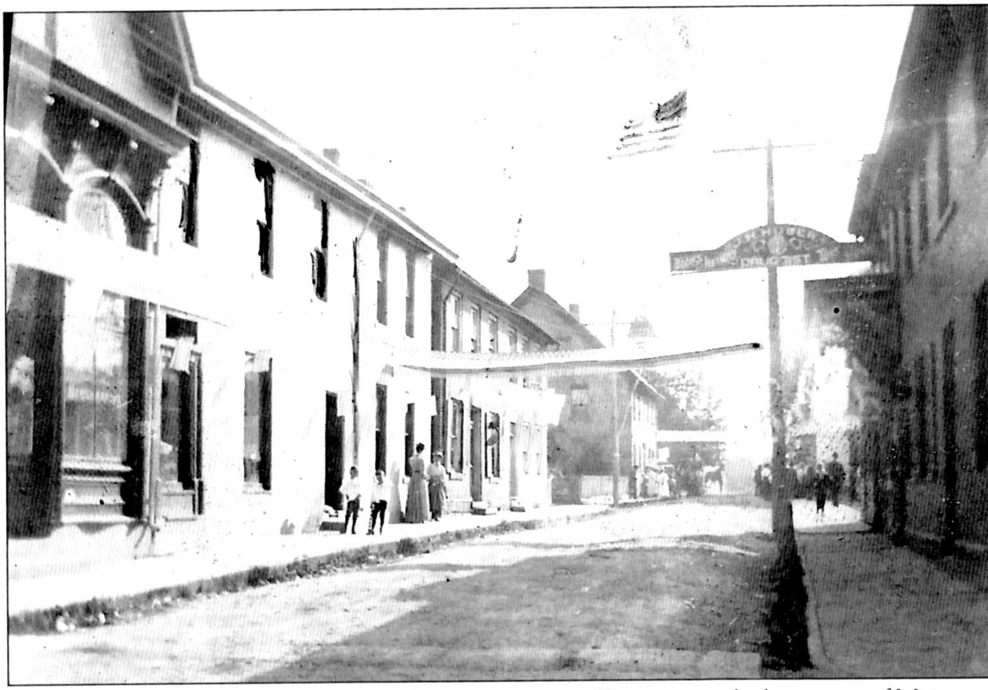

Flags and banners flutter along Mercer Street as a team of horses rounds the corner of Main and Mercer Streets in this scene from the early 1900s. The Harmonist church clock tower and huge American flag can be seen in the distance. The flag was first raised in the diamond in 1899.

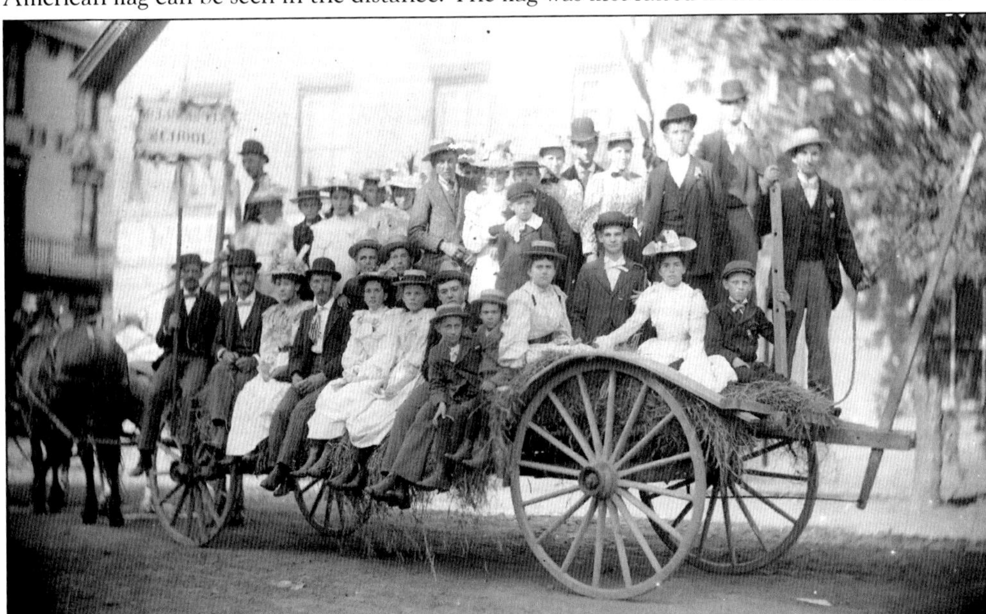

Sunday school members from the Reformed Church in Middle Lancaster pause in the Harmony diamond on this sunny day. Those identified include (first row) Rhinart Bintrim holding a sign, Franklin Brenner, Clara Barkley, Al Scheidemantle, Carrie Eicholtz, Bessie Musselman (later the wife of Albert Brenner), Sadie Scheidemantle, Homer Metz, and Lizzie Eicholtz; (second row) Lettie Metz, Albert Brenner, and Anna Brenner Boots.

A Harmony girl in patriotic costume waves the flag, perhaps in preparation for the traditional Fourth of July parade through Zelienople and Harmony. Her dress may indicate she was a member of the Maccabees order. (Courtesy of Nancy Wiser.)

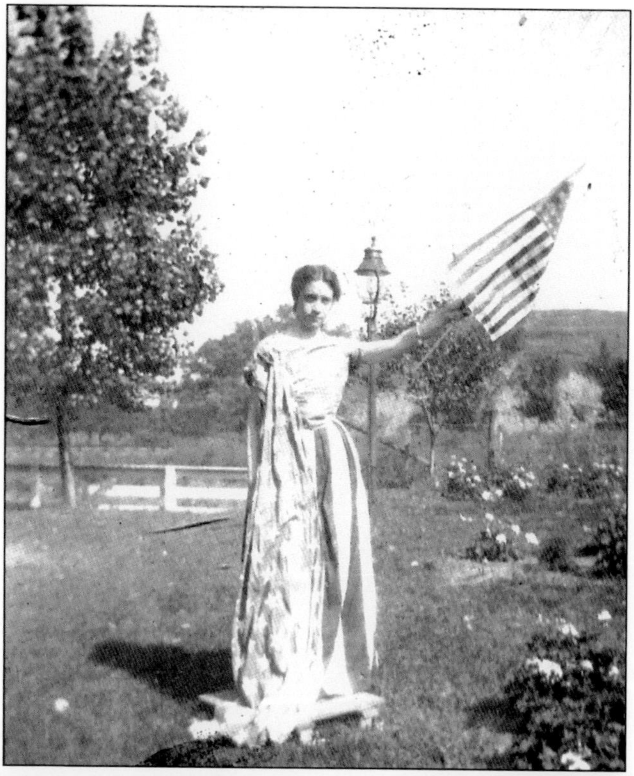

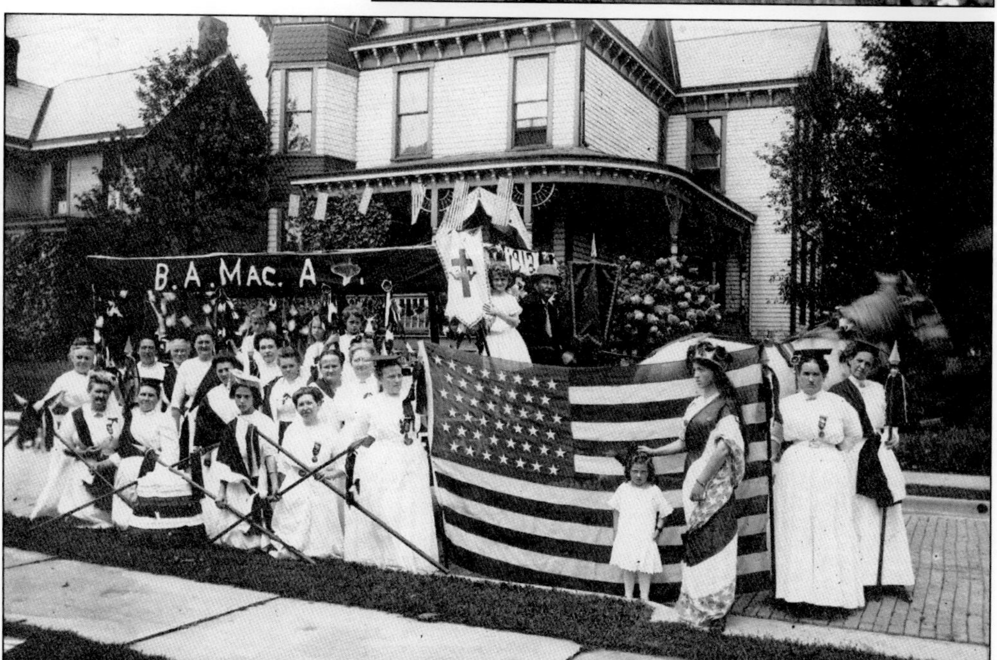

Costumed members of the local Maccabees chapter pause during a parade on New Castle Street in Zelienople in 1912. Identified include Margaret Bame Stamm, fourth from left in the second row, and Mrs. Elmer Shantz, standing second from right. (Courtesy of Bernice Stamm Lewis.)

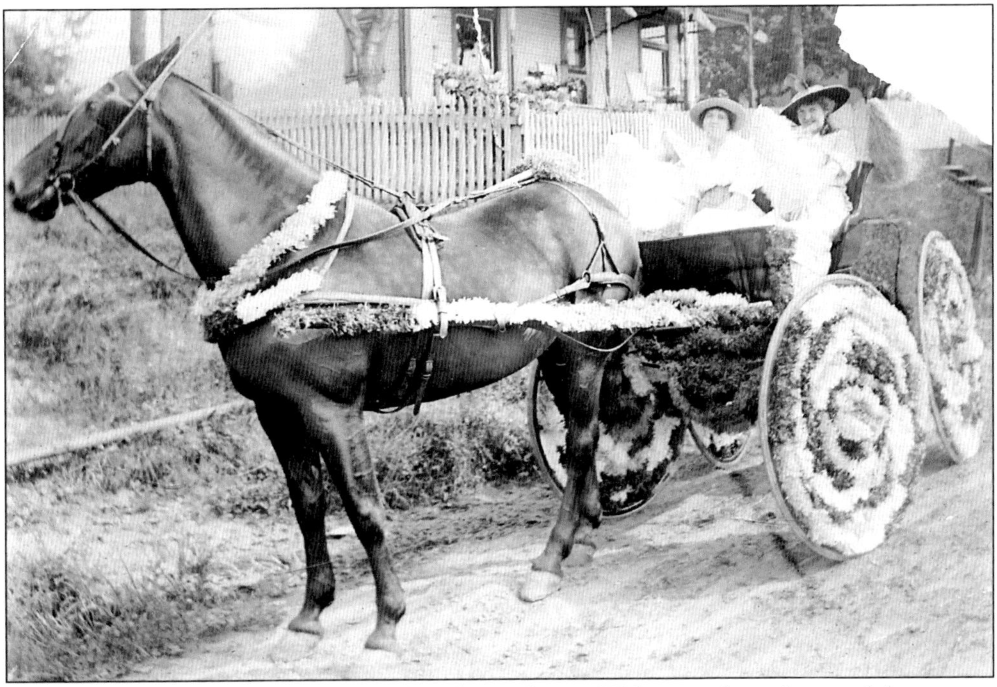

Sisters Nancy Sharrer Ziegler (left) and Kathryn Sharrer Walters, in fancy hats and dresses, are on their way to join a Fourth of July parade in Harmony or Zelienople. Their wagon and horse are also decked out for the holiday. (Courtesy of Kathryn Ziegler Bauder.)

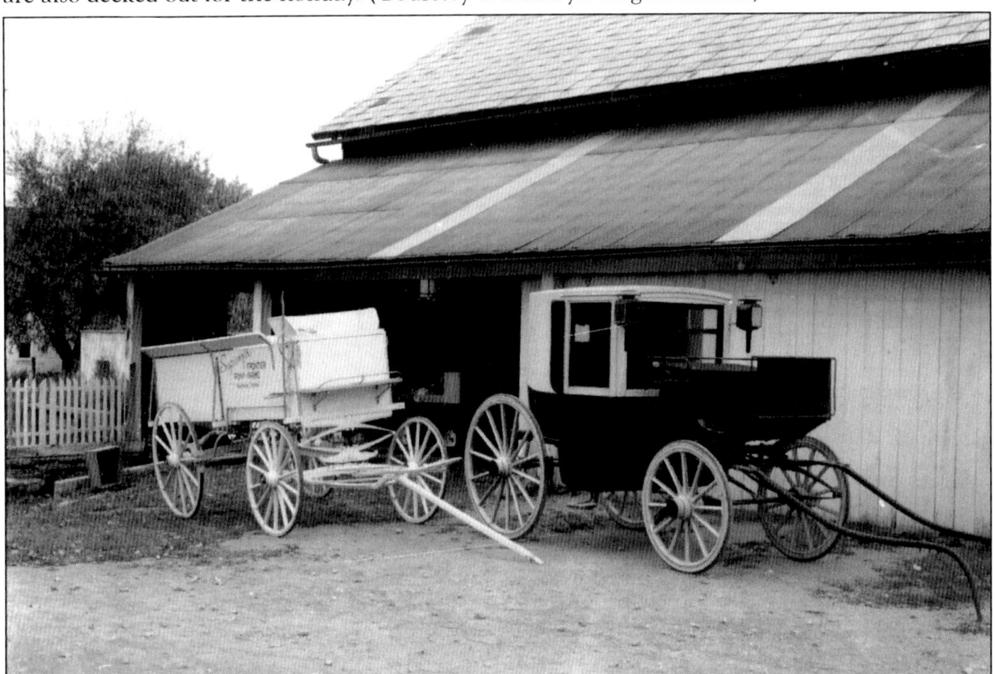

Joseph Sapienza Jr. usually had a vehicle ready to hitch to a horse. This carriage and wagon advertising his Frontier Pony Farm is part of the collection he stored in his barn on Mercer Street. (Courtesy of Tim Sapienza.)

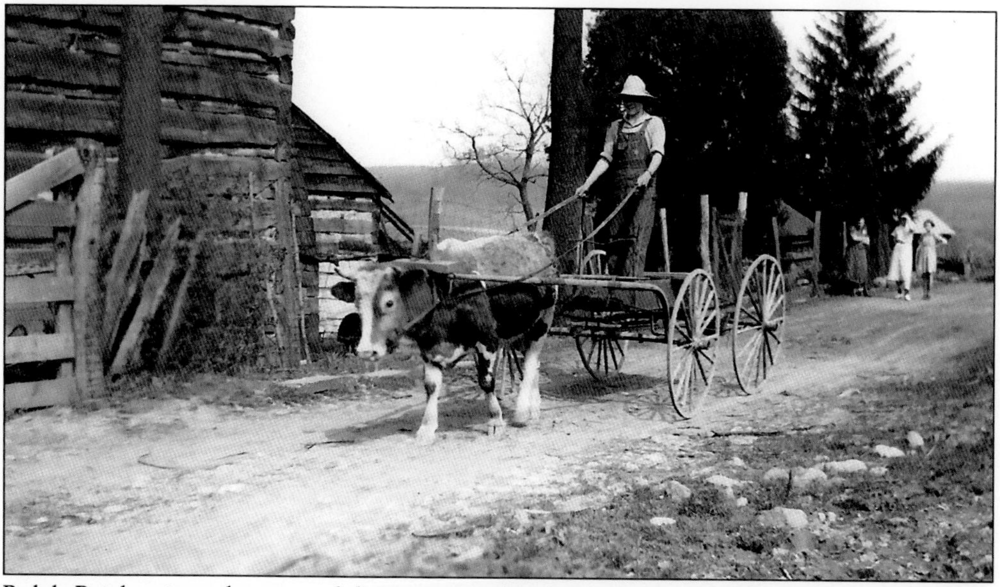

Ralph Beighey is at the reins of the wagon, as his favorite bull pulls him along a path on the Beighey farm in Middle Lancaster. Beighey and the bull were often seen in parades. Santa Claus used to ride through Zelienople aboard the Beighey wagon in the annual Christmas parade. (Courtesy of Ruth Werner, photograph by Dr. Arthur Stewart.)

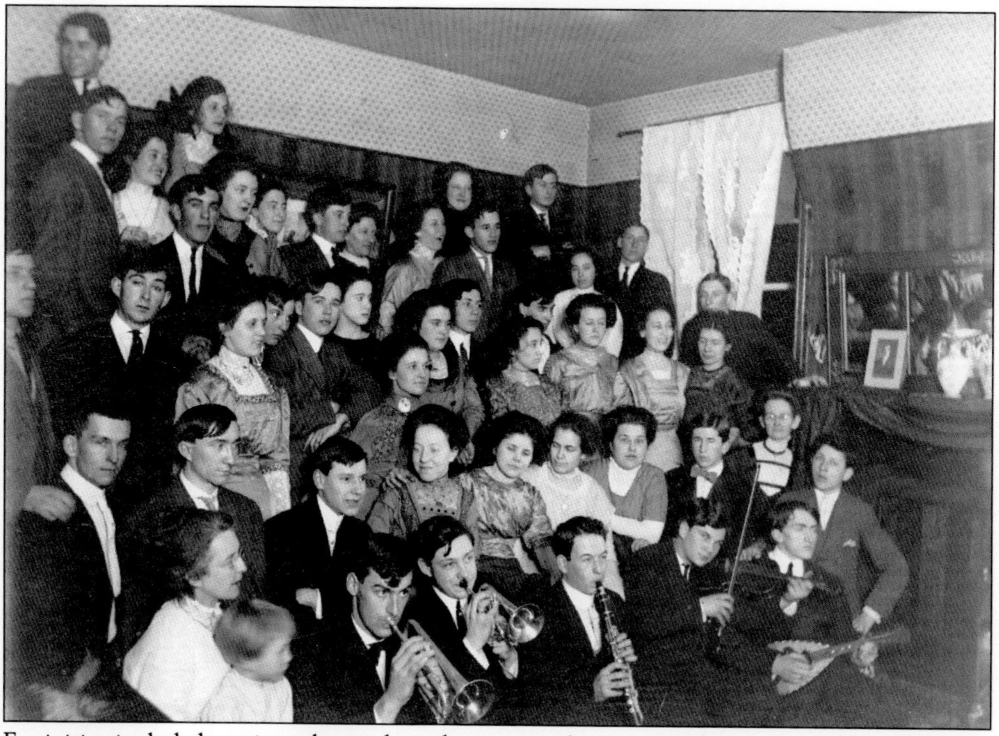

Festivities included music making when this group of young people got together in Harmony during World War I. According to a notation on the picture, the occasion was a farewell party for Bill Flowers who was leaving for military duty. The party was held at the home of Vesta Ziegler. (Courtesy of Nancy Wiser.)

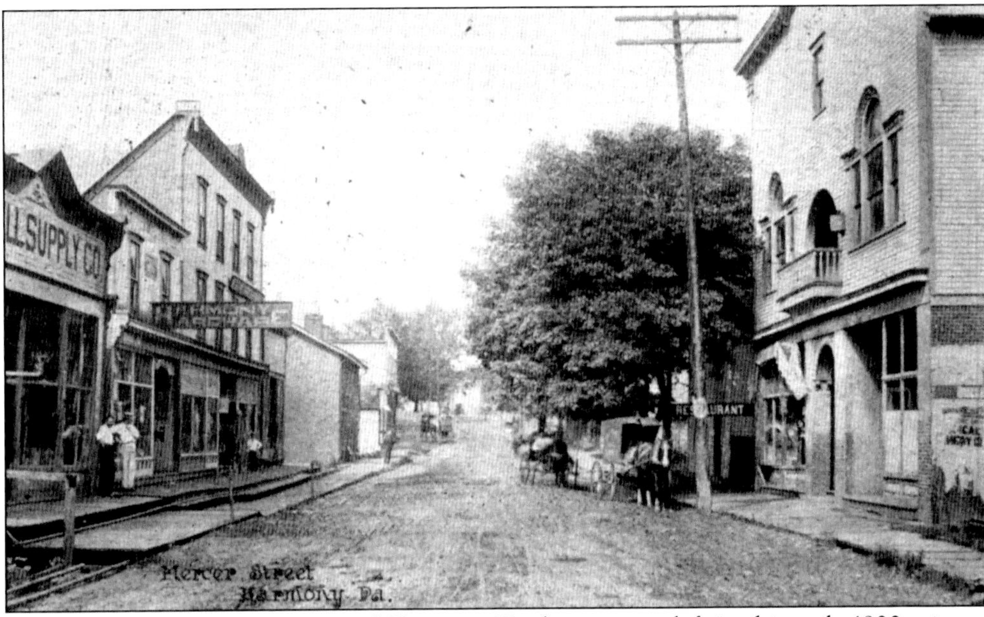

The Oil Well Supply Company and Harmony Hardware are at left in this early 1900s view of Mercer Street. Ed Shever operated the hardware for many years. Today's tenants in the hardware building are Lazier's Harmony Music Studios, Siri's School of the Performing Arts, and the Salon by Marian Davis. The Odd Fellows hall, also called the opera house, at right, is now occupied by Otto and Gert's. Its second-floor stage was the scene of lyceum lectures, plays by stock companies, socials, and dances. John S. Duss brought the Harmony Society's Economy Band here to perform. In addition to the Odd Fellows, other groups met in the hall, including the Knights of Pythias and the Pythian Sisters, who issued the card below. (Courtesy of Delsa White.)

Pythian Sisters Benefit

I. O. O. F. HALL, HARMONY

Tuesday Evening, May 10, 1927

8:30 p. m.

Admission Fifty Cents

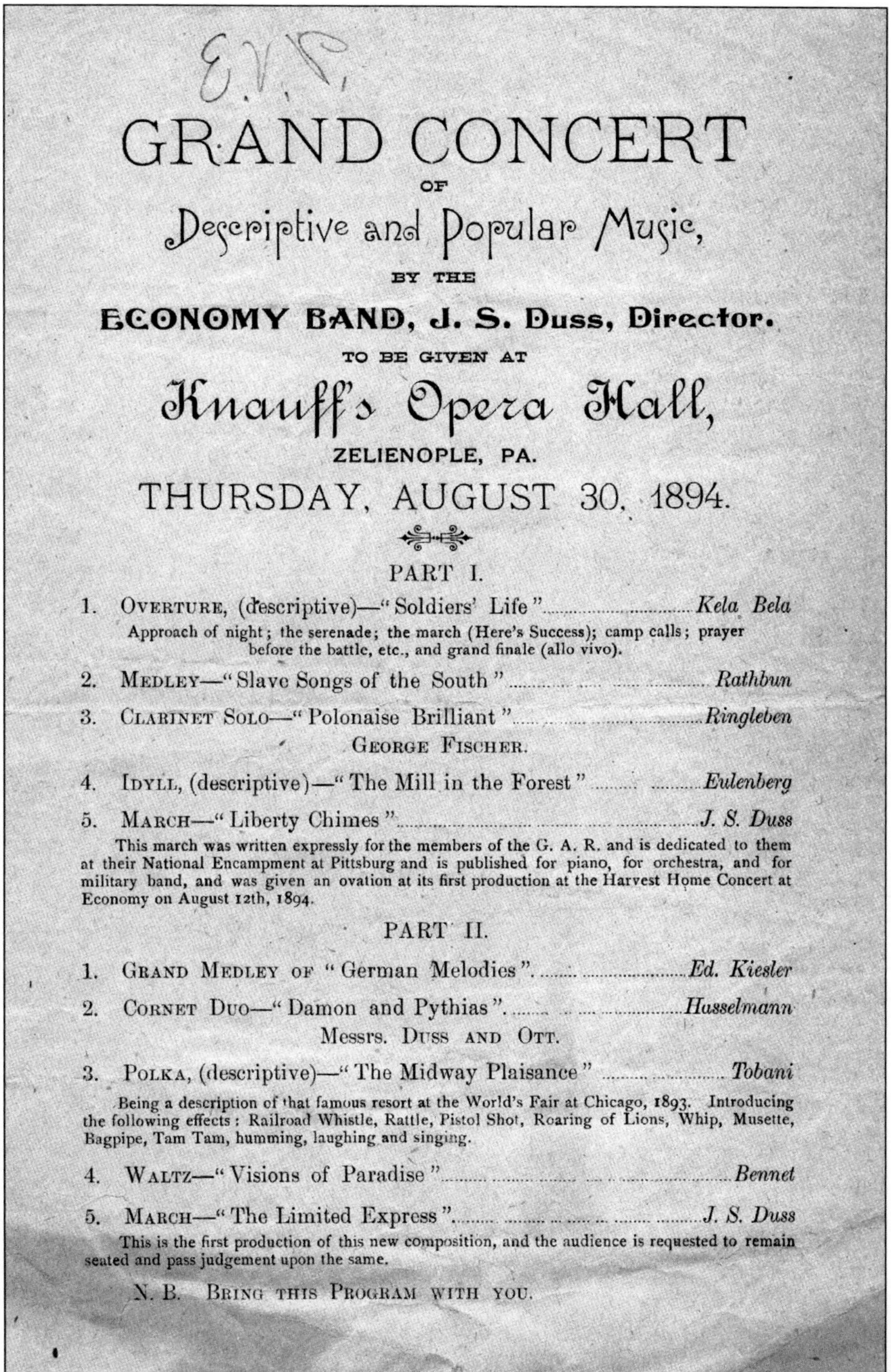

GRAND CONCERT

OF

Descriptive and Popular Music,

BY THE

ECONOMY BAND, J. S. Duss, Director.

TO BE GIVEN AT

Knauff's Opera Hall,

ZELIENOPLE, PA.

THURSDAY, AUGUST 30, 1894.

PART I.

1. OVERTURE, (descriptive)—"Soldiers' Life" .... *Kela Bela*
   Approach of night; the serenade; the march (Here's Success); camp calls; prayer before the battle, etc., and grand finale (allo vivo).
2. MEDLEY—"Slave Songs of the South" .... *Rathbun*
3. CLARINET SOLO—"Polonaise Brilliant" .... *Ringleben*
   GEORGE FISCHER.
4. IDYLL, (descriptive)—"The Mill in the Forest" .... *Eulenberg*
5. MARCH—"Liberty Chimes" .... *J. S. Duss*
   This march was written expressly for the members of the G. A. R. and is dedicated to them at their National Encampment at Pittsburg and is published for piano, for orchestra, and for military band, and was given an ovation at its first production at the Harvest Home Concert at Economy on August 12th, 1894.

PART II.

1. GRAND MEDLEY OF "German Melodies" .... *Ed. Kiesler*
2. CORNET DUO—"Damon and Pythias" .... *Husselmann*
   Messrs. DUSS AND OTT.
3. POLKA, (descriptive)—"The Midway Plaisance" .... *Tobani*
   Being a description of that famous resort at the World's Fair at Chicago, 1893. Introducing the following effects: Railroad Whistle, Rattle, Pistol Shot, Roaring of Lions, Whip, Musette, Bagpipe, Tam Tam, humming, laughing and singing.
4. WALTZ—"Visions of Paradise" .... *Bennet*
5. MARCH—"The Limited Express" .... *J. S. Duss*
   This is the first production of this new composition, and the audience is requested to remain seated and pass judgement upon the same.

N. B. BRING THIS PROGRAM WITH YOU.

This program was distributed before a concert by the Economy Band, directed by John S. Duss, a Harmony Society member at Economy (now Ambridge). Duss also brought his musicians to the Harmony opera house. When the society disbanded in 1905, Duss and his wife were the last remaining trustees.

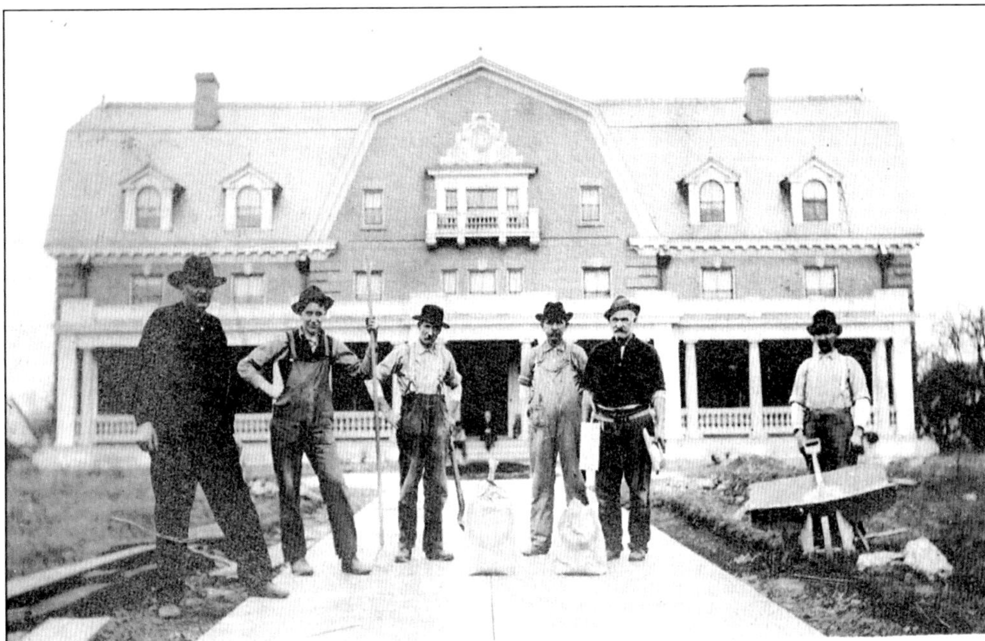

J. A. Young & Son's Gang, Pythian Home, Harmony, Pa

The Knights of Pythias Home for the Aged opened on January 3, 1907, a few years after Knights of Pythias Eden Lodge No. 311 was instituted in Harmony. The home and farm occupied the former Fiedler farm on Mill Road, known today as Evergreen Mill Road, in Jackson Township a mile east of Harmony. The renovated and expanded home is now the Evergreen Nursing Center. Below is the stone barn on the Pythian grounds. (Courtesy of Delsa White.)

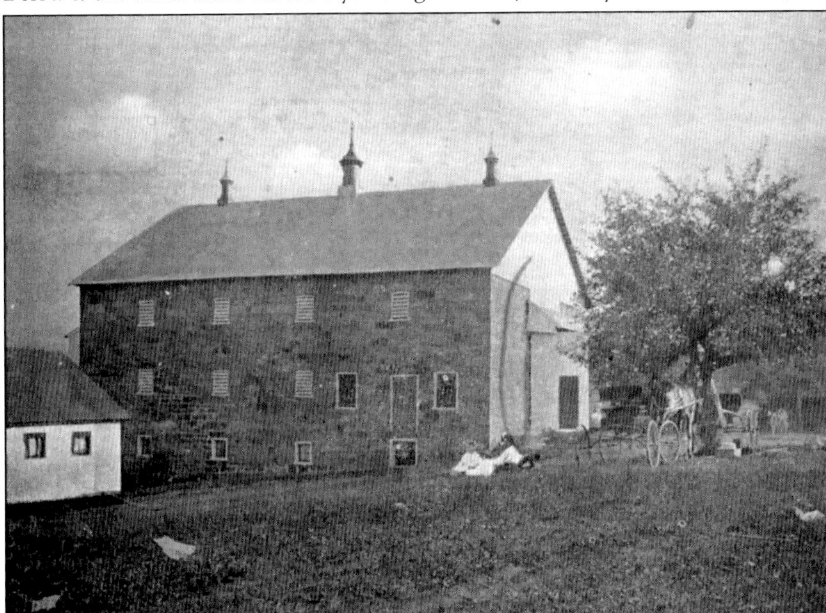

KNIGHTS OF PYTHIAS BARN, HARMONY, PA.

Dr. Daniel Fiedler served as physician at the Knights of Pythias Home for the Aged that was built on his family's farm. The home of his parents, Butler County associate judge Daniel Fiedler and Magdalena Shontz Ziegler, burned in 1901. Dr. Daniel Fiedler was the home's physician from its opening until his death in 1920.

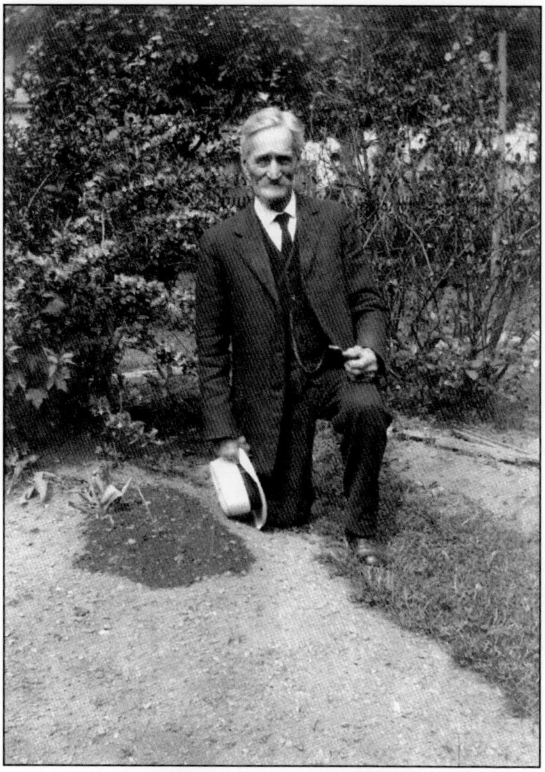

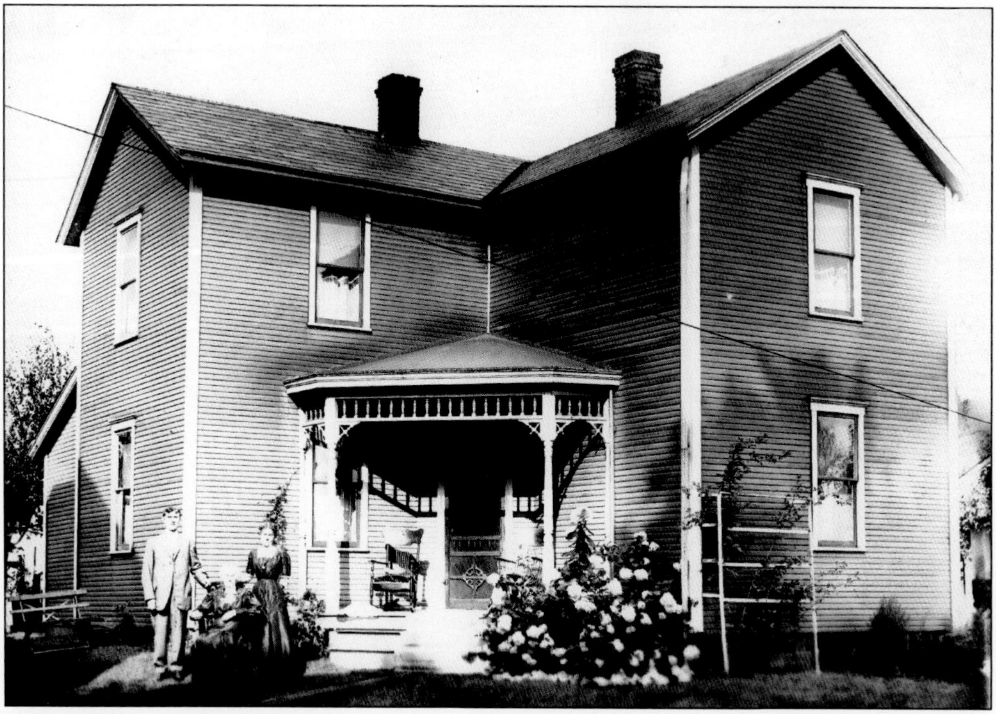

John and Etta Kloffenstein and her mother, Mrs. Grant, stand in front of their house on North Main Street about 1912. The house looks much the same today.

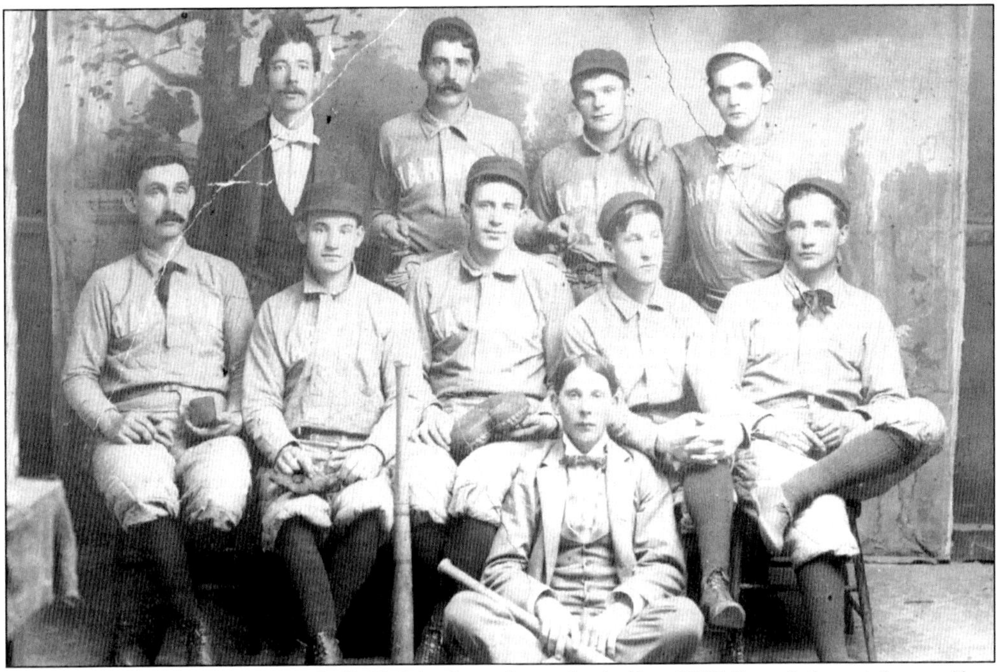

Members of the Harmony Baseball Club look ready to play ball in 1897. From left to right are (first row) Fred Strutt; (second row) John "Honey" Allen, ? Brown, Fred Jaxon, Steele Kent, and Frank Kent; (third row) Bill Gibson, Wes Hoover, Charles Kelly, and Newt Eppinger. George "Rube" Waddell lived in Harmony before his career as a professional pitcher. Waddell was posthumously inducted into the Baseball Hall of Fame in 1946.

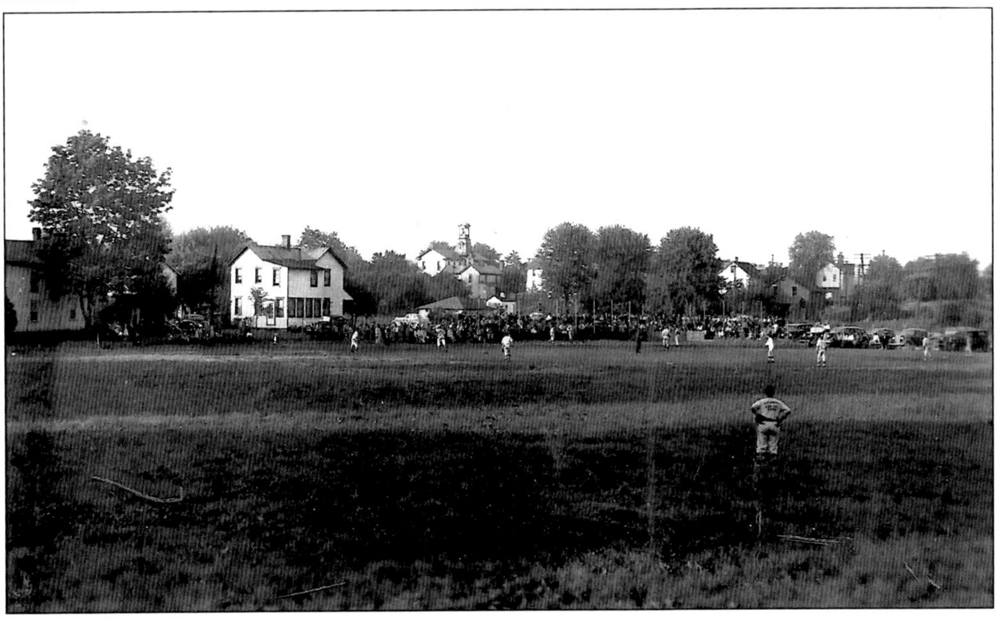

Ball teams compete in Rapp Park on the west end of Mercer Street, probably in the 1930s. The school tower holds a bell that was replaced with the Harmony Society clock in 1938. Rapp Park was the community's playground and site of the annual firemen's carnivals before being commercially developed. (Courtesy of Ruth Werner.)

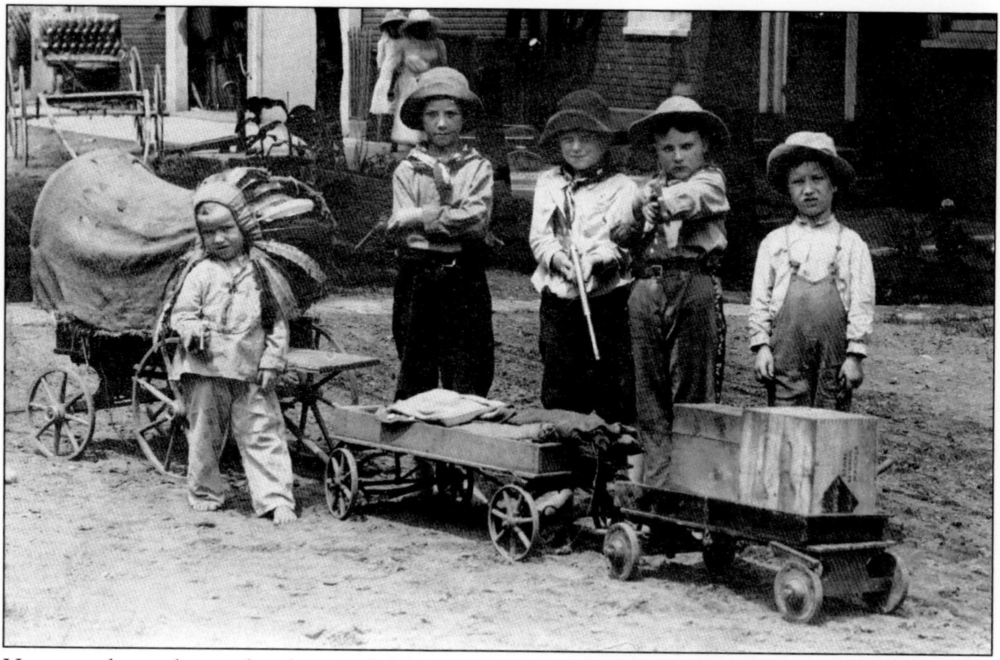

Harmony boys play under the watchful eyes of two nicely dressed girls in the early 1900s. The scene is outside Weigel's Blacksmith Shop on North Main Street. From left to right are Chip Shaffer, Orrie Shaffer, Russell Nesbitt, Ralph McQuistion, and Paul Shaffer.

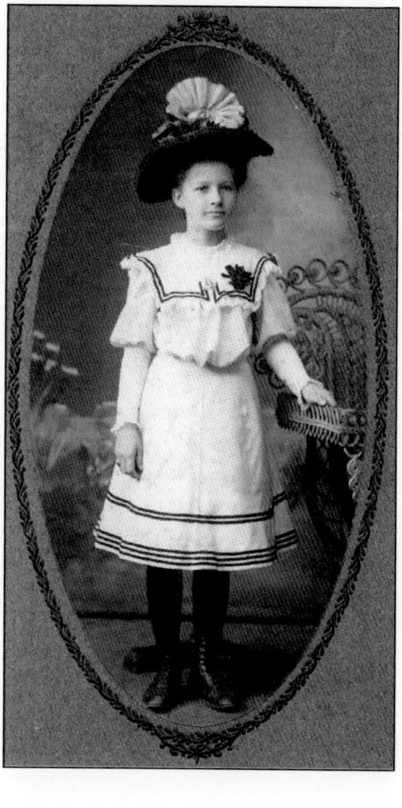

Alice Hodil Flinner wears a fine hat in this portrait photograph taken around 1905. She was one of six daughters of Jacob and Martha Hodil of Harmony. (Courtesy of Nancy Wiser.)

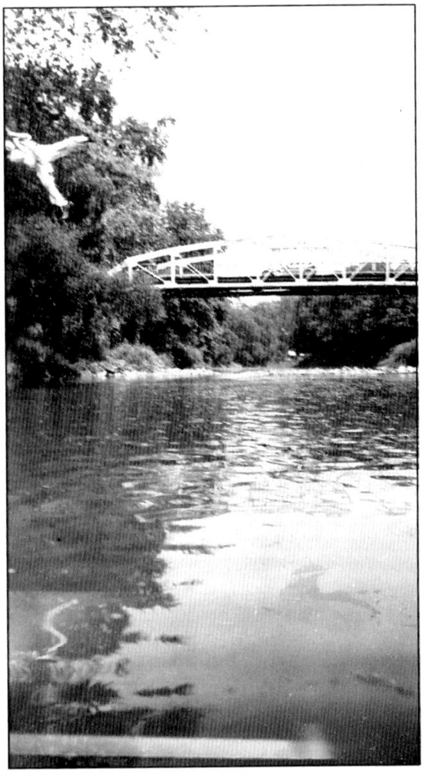

The Connoquenessing Creek was the center of summer fun in old Harmony. The coolie, the salty, the rock, and the deep hole were favorite swimming spots. The dam at Zelienople raised the creek level by six feet, providing three miles of deep water for boating, swimming, and fishing between Zelienople and Edenau. When the dam deteriorated, the water level fell.

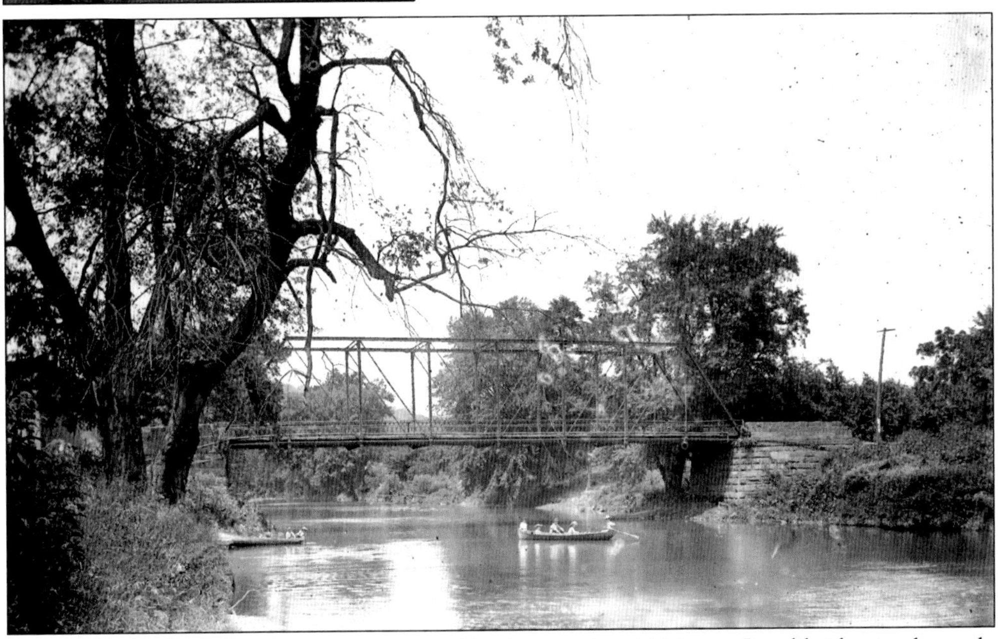

Canoeists paddle on the Connoquenessing Creek near the old Mercer Road bridge in the early 1900s. The interurban train company publicized its Harmony route by describing the delights of a trolley trip from Pittsburgh "through a land of the rarest natural beauty to four prosperous growing cities and many smaller communities." A chief draw, it was touted as "Connoquenessing Creek, the Sportsman's Elysium."

Brothers Robert (left) and Thomas Wiser have fun with an old keg in the huge basement fireplace of their home, the former William Latchaw house, on North Main Street in 1937. (Courtesy of Nancy Wiser.)

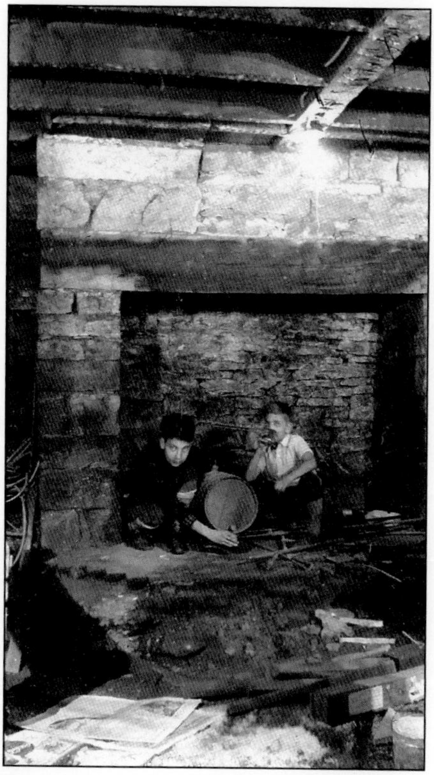

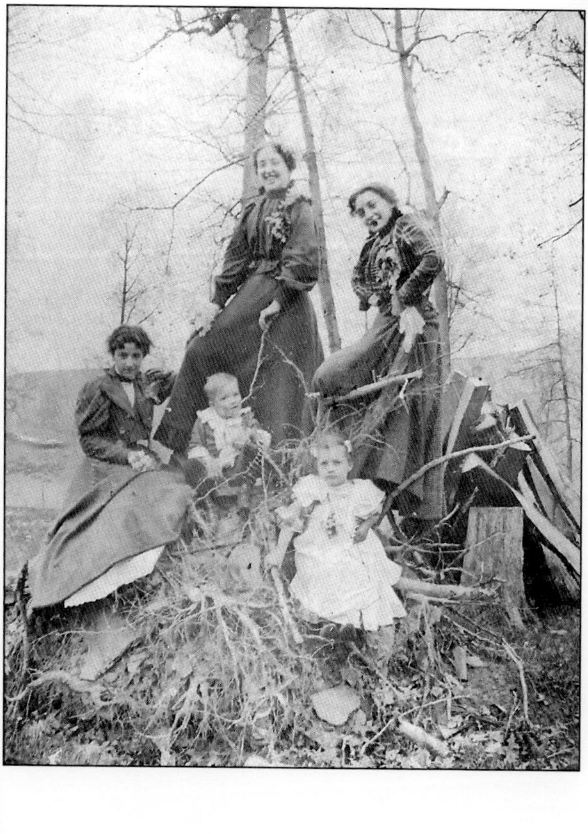

This group takes a break from gathering wood or building a bonfire in the 1890s to strike a pose for the camera. From left to right are (first row) Carrie (Hodil) Woodruff, Jane Webster, and Alice (Hodil) Flinner; (second row) Anna Harvey and Retta (Hodil) Kristophel. (Courtesy of Nancy Wiser.)

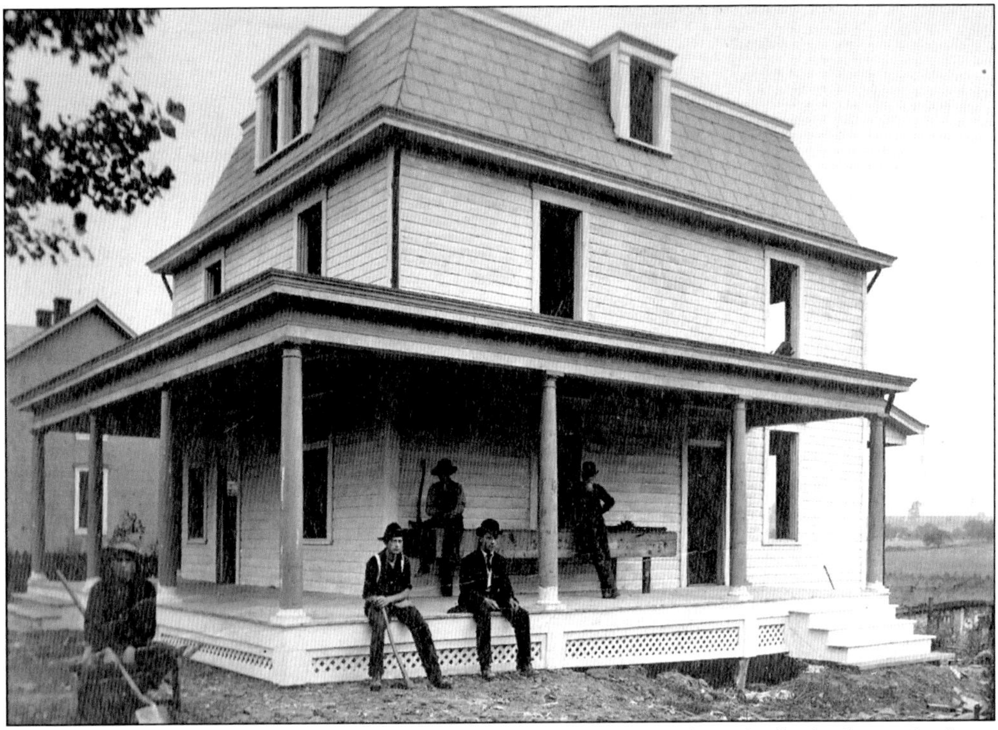

Louisa Seber Schaeffer Fiedler was a twice-widowed seamstress when she had a house built on Spring Street in Harmony's Swampoodle section. Workmen taking a break on the porch during construction are, from left to right, (seated) Al Klinefelter and O. I. Burkett, (standing) Ed Leisie and contractor George Klinefelter. At left in the yard is Louisa's son, Hal Fiedler. The cost of construction was $1,600. Louisa moved into the home on November 7, 1907. Below, Louisa stands on the porch with her daughter Esther Fiedler Stamm and daughter-in-law Elsie Rape Fiedler. (Courtesy of Bernice Stamm Lewis.)

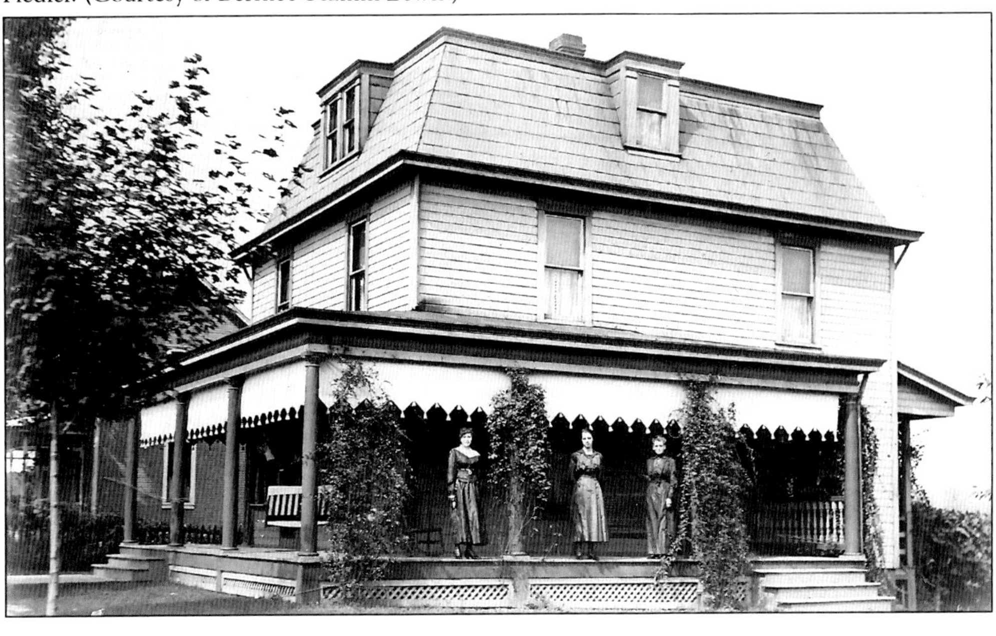

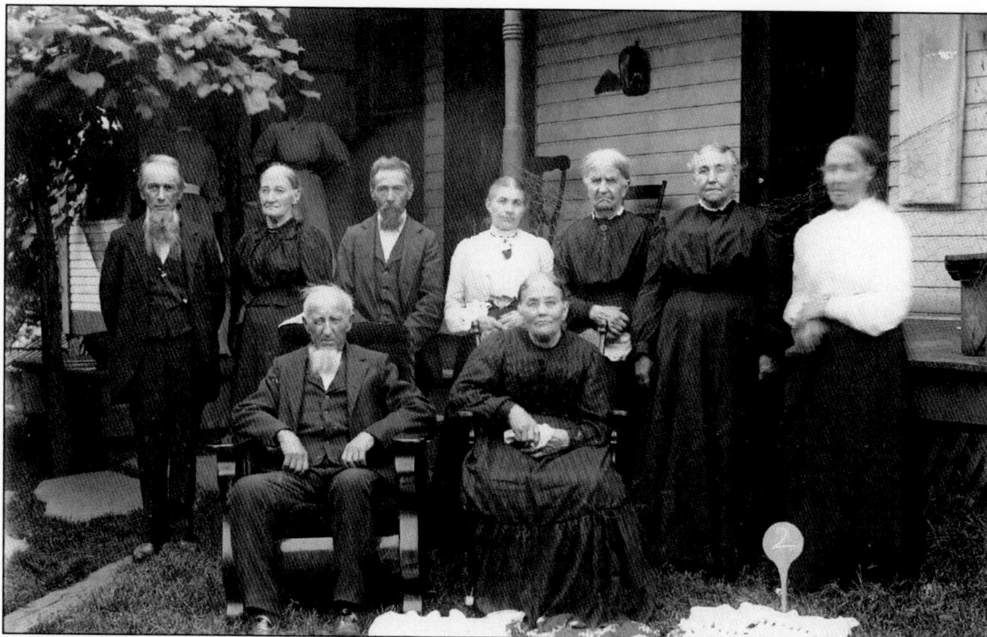

Jacob and Elizabeth Goehring Brenner of Lancaster Township celebrate their golden wedding anniversary on August 30, 1906. From left to right are (first row) Jacob and Elizabeth Brenner; (second row) George Dindinger, Maria Dindinger, Charlie Goehring, Caroline Goehring, Charlotte Brenner, Sophia Young, and Mary Nagle; (on porch) Mary Brenner and Catharine Brenner. Below, the Brenner family gathers for a reunion in 1932.

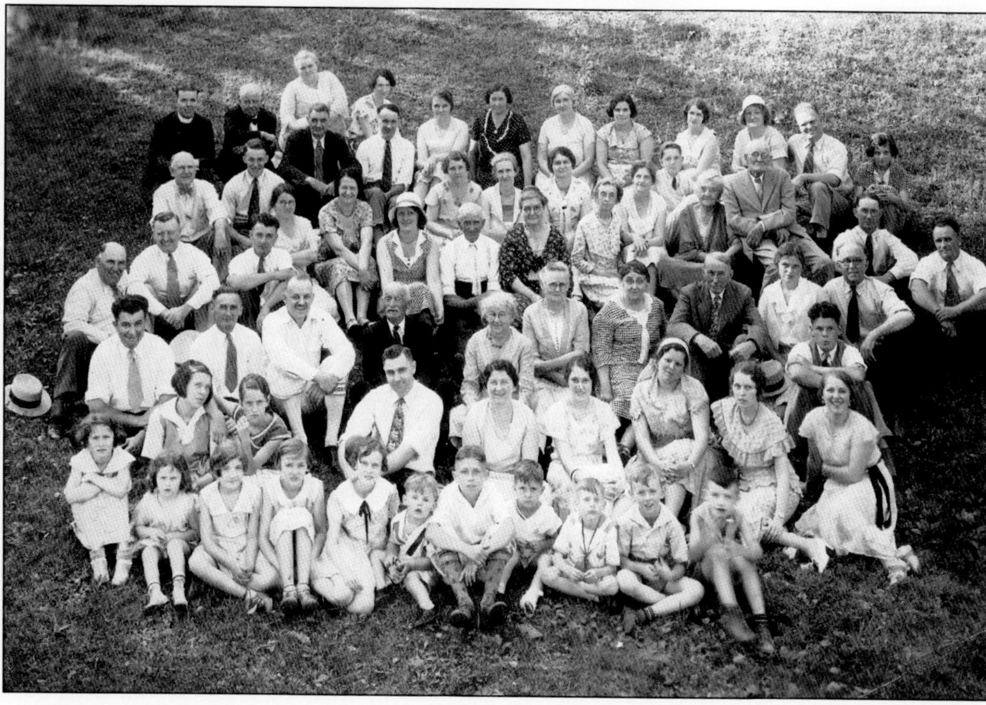

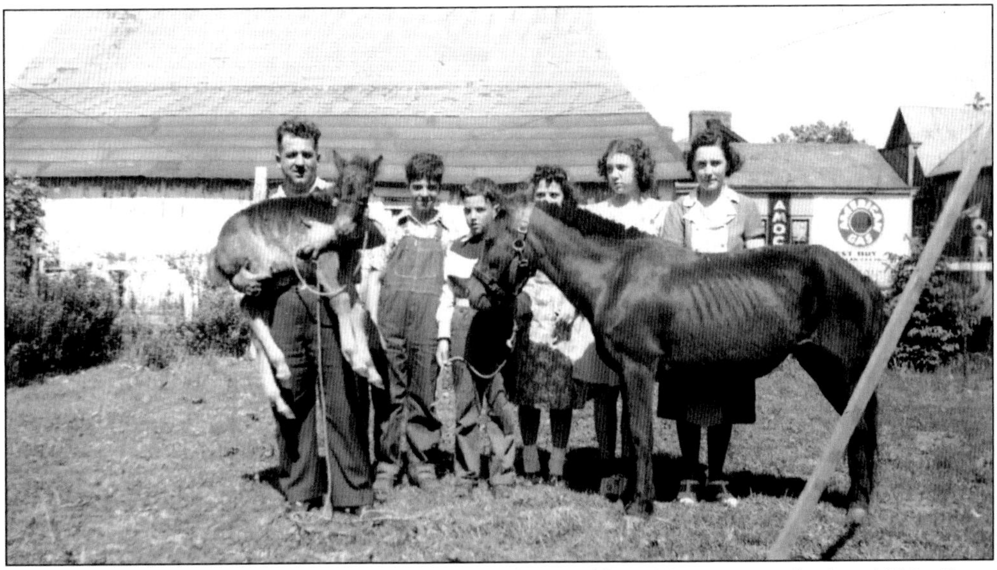

The Sapienza family welcomes a new addition to their stable in Harmony in the late 1930s. From left to right are Joseph Sapienza Jr., sons Joseph III and Louis, and daughter Rosalie. The other girls are unidentified. (Courtesy of Tim Sapienza.)

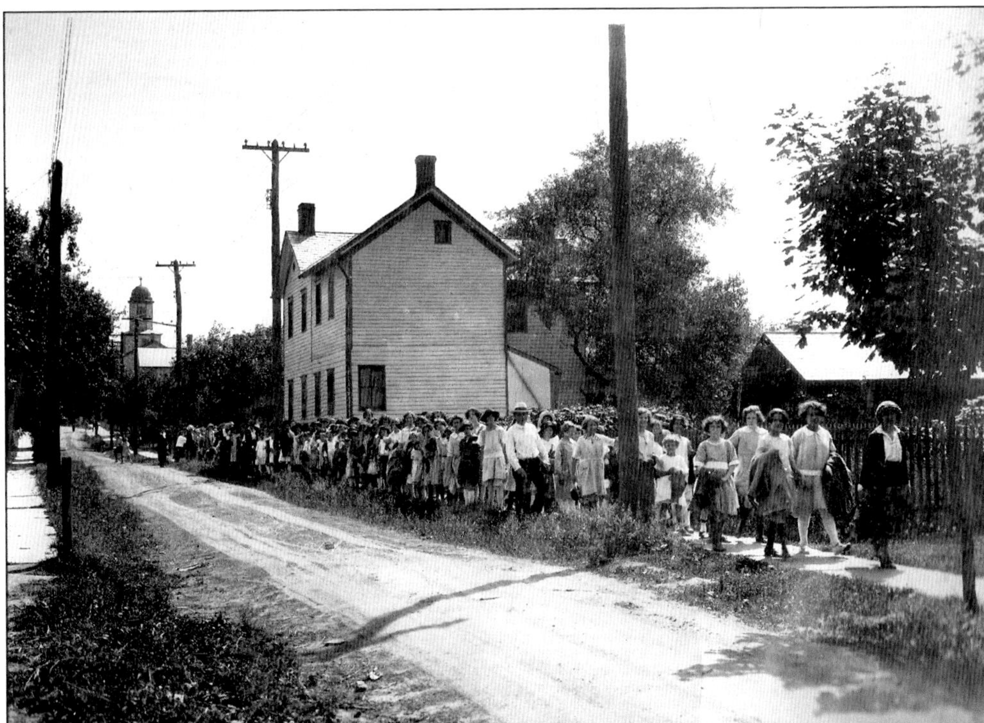

City children walk along Mercer Street in July 1922 on their way to the newly-opened Emma Farm Camp. Providing summer recreation for city mothers and children, the camp was established by the Isaac and Morris Kaufmann families and supported by the Pittsburgh Community Fund and Federation of Jewish Philanthropies of Pittsburgh.

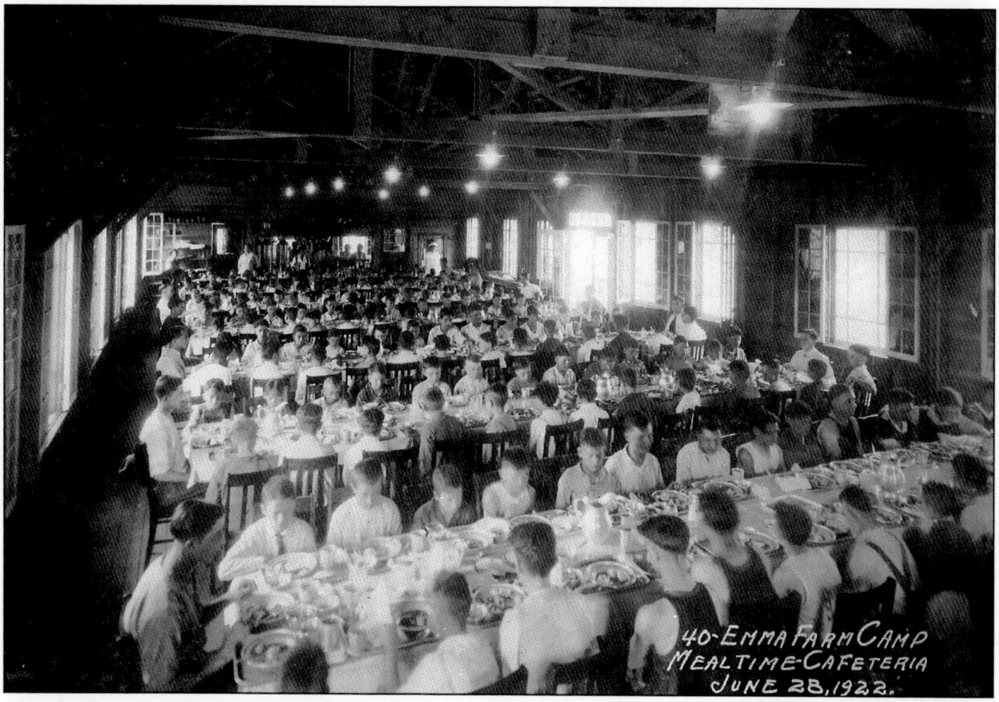

Hundreds of children were ready for dinner in the new dining hall at the Emma Farm Camp in June 1922. Below are staff workers during the 1966 summer season. Many local residents worked at the farm during its 50 years in Harmony. The camp was moved to West Virginia in 1972. Indian Brave Campground now occupies the site.

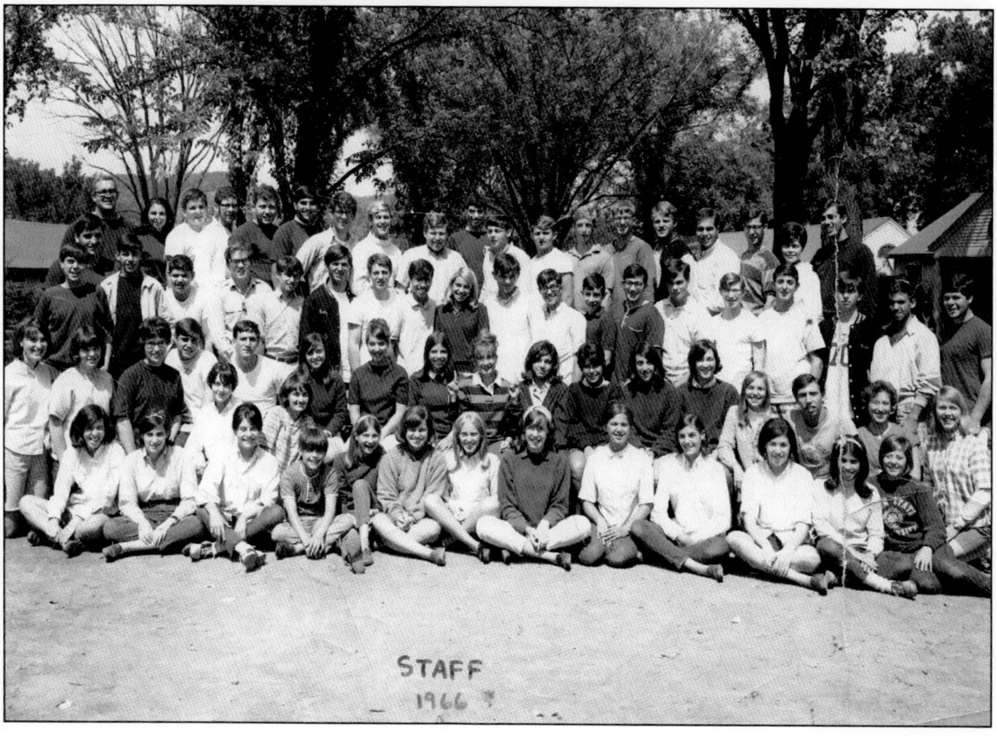

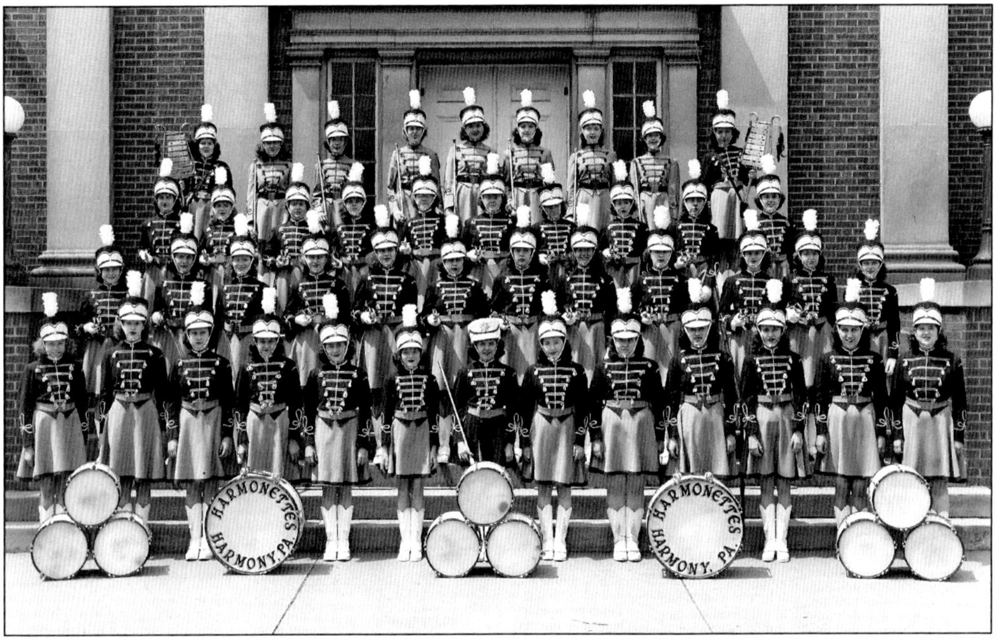

The Harmonettes Drum and Bugle Corps assembled in 1948 on the Grace Reformed Church steps. The Harmony Volunteer Fire Company organized the all-girl marching unit in 1946, and members soon began winning competitions throughout the tri-state region. Below, the Harmonettes, wearing maroon and grey uniforms, march in a parade in Zelienople. (Above, courtesy of Janet Shaffer Miesel; below, courtesy of Nancy Wiser.)

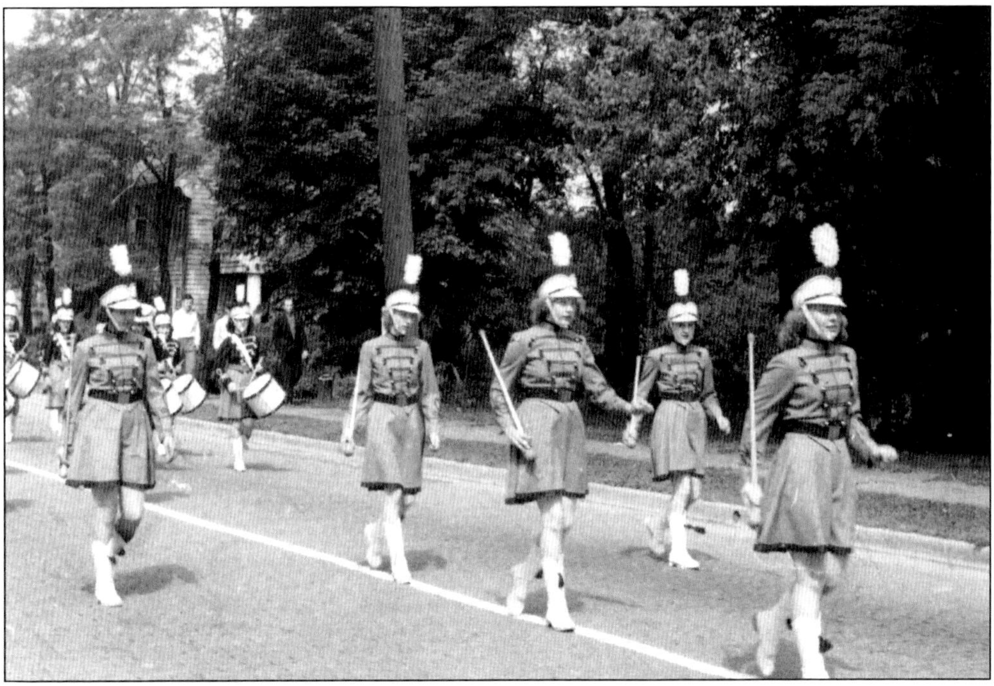

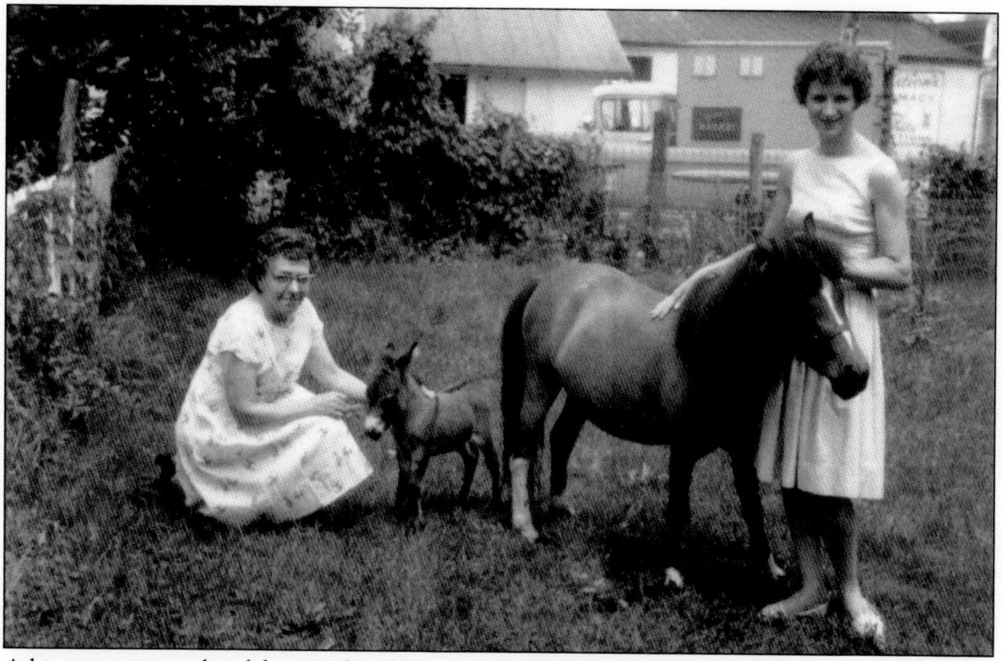

A big attraction at local fairs in the 1950s was "the Smallest Mule in the World," seen here with Lucy Sapienza and her daughter-in-law Betty Sapienza. The family, including their husbands Joseph Sapienza Jr. and his son Joseph Sapienza III, exhibited the tiny pet whose mother is the pony at right. (Courtesy of Tim Sapienza.)

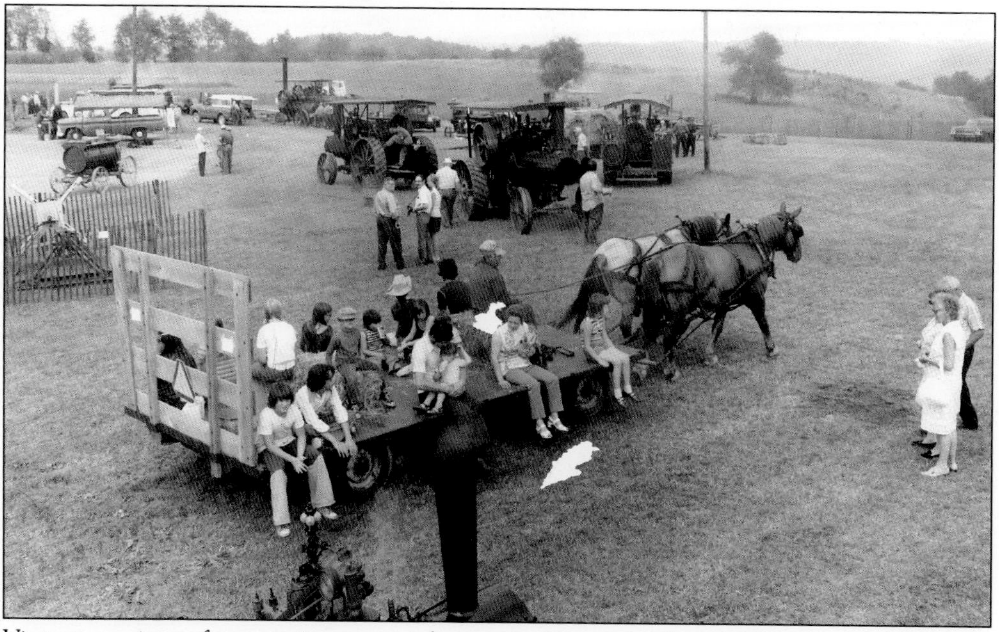

Vintage engines, farm equipment, and wagon rides were featured at the Northwestern Pennsylvania Steam Engine and Old Equipment Association's Steam Show in 1973. The show was held in Middle Lancaster at the time. A few years later, the group moved its events to new grounds in Portersville where it continues to attract crowds each year. (Courtesy of Ray Thompson.)

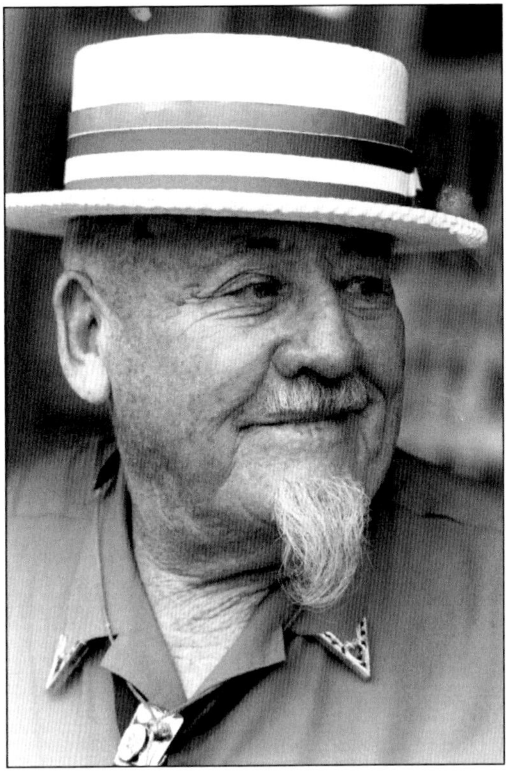

Middle Lancaster businessman Charlie Burgh was a musical icon in the region. He and his Burgh Gang band, often making music atop an antique fire truck, were regulars at festivals and parades. Burgh played banjo with the Hap Clark Orchestra and owned Burgh's Pleasure Palace dance hall. (Courtesy of the Butler Eagle, photograph by Ray Thompson.)

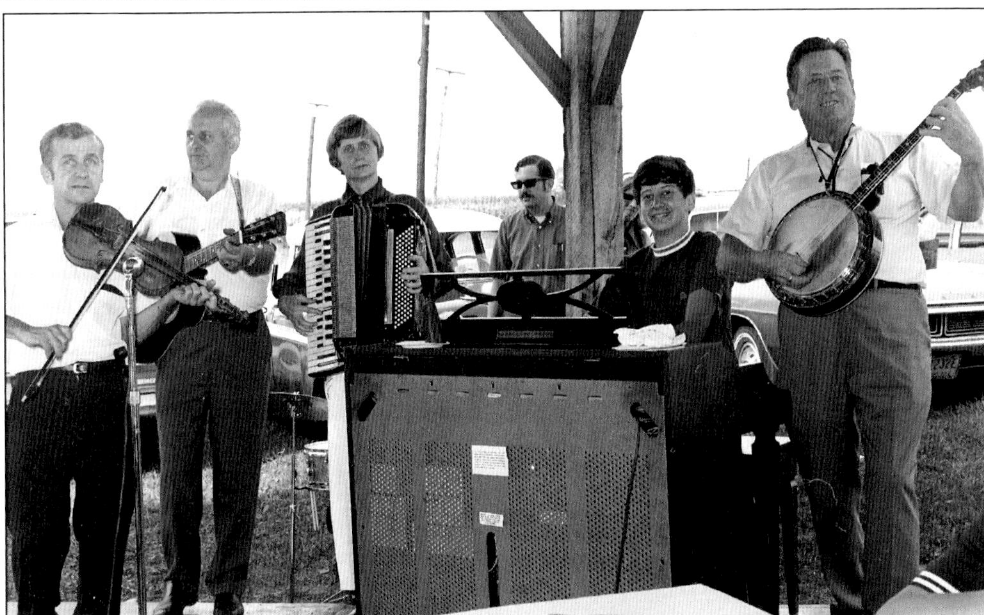

The Burgh Gang plays in Middle Lancaster in the 1970s. From left to right are an unidentified fiddler; guitarist Emmitt Mateer; his wife, Dawn Mateer, of New Brighton; John Burgh on piano; and Charlie Burgh on banjo. John Burgh, a trained musician, carries on his father's tradition by performing with his band at local events. (Courtesy of the Butler Eagle, photograph by Ray Thompson.)

Eight

Disasters and War

The pacifist Harmonists ran afoul of the law during the War of 1812 when they refused to be drafted. Although they paid fees in lieu of military service, they were taken to court and fined. Soldiers of the Black Rock Company camped on the Harmony commons before marching through the Harmony Society's town and across their bridge on their way to join Oliver Hazard Perry on Lake Erie.

Militia organizations customarily appointed muster days when soldiers of each district were required to meet for drills. The local meeting place was the Harmony commons. Observers noted that much of the muster agenda involved wrestling, bare-fisted fighting, and throwing the shoulder stone. Often fights broke out. The musters usually lasted two days and ended with a banquet. The Harmony Blues unit had a feast at Beam's Tavern in 1825. The Jackson Volunteer Guards drilled on the commons in 1845.

After the Civil War, G. D. Swain of Harmony chaired the Butler County Monument Association, which commissioned and raised funds for a statue honoring Butler County soldiers who served in the conflict. The monument was erected in Butler's Diamond Park in 1894.

For more than a century, both German and English were frequently spoken in Harmony, and pastors conducted church services in both languages. The use of German in the community quickly diminished after the start of World War I.

Natural disasters also changed Harmony. A fire destroyed much of the northwest quarter of town in 1852. Four years later, a tornado ripped off roofs. The replacement roofs were not as steeply pitched as those on old Harmonist structures, altering the look of the town. A 1985 tornado caused extensive damage in Jackson Township and killed six people in southern Butler County. The Connoquenessing Creek has periodically flooded the town, most notably in 1955 and 2004. Historians recorded that the "pumpkin flood" of 1832 washed pumpkins and whiskey barrels through the town.

Harmony residents have typically met wars and disasters by volunteering for service, helping neighbors rebuild damaged homes and lives, and revering their military veterans.

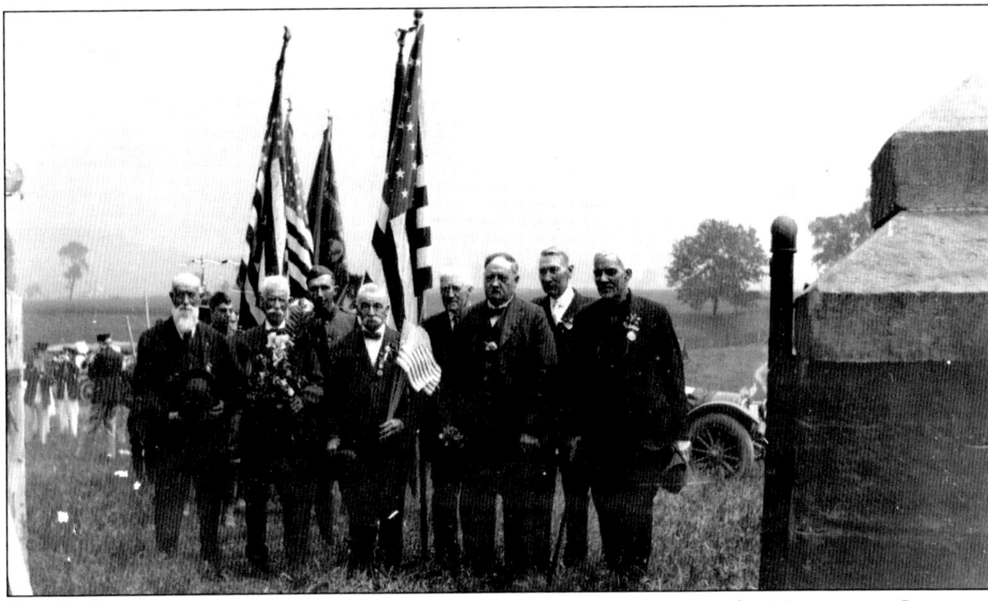

Civil War veterans carry flags during a Memorial Day ceremony in the Mennonite Cemetery north of Harmony. From left to right are Nelson Keefer, ? Wheller, ? McCormick, Jacob Hodil holding a small flag, Albert Bintrim in a soldier suit, ? Stiver, unidentified, and ? McMillen. Harmony firemen's band members play in the background. (Courtesy of Nancy Wiser.)

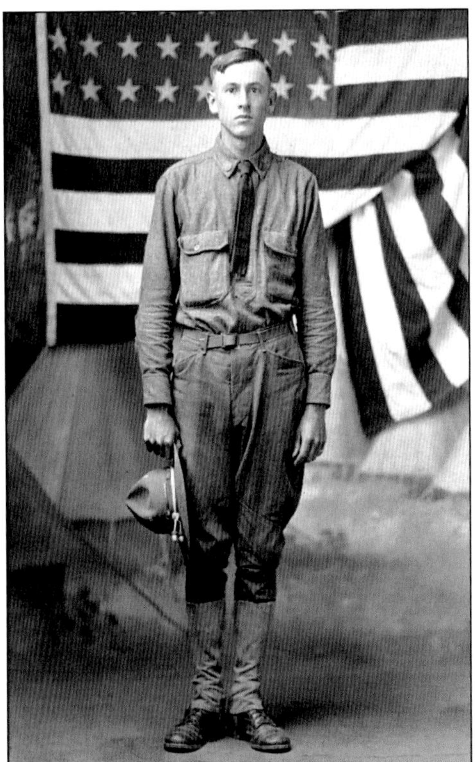

Paul Weigel, shown in uniform in 1918, was one of the local youths who served during World War I. The conflict marked the end of German language usage in Harmony where it had been heard for more than a century. (Courtesy of Nancy Wiser.)

The Harmony War Savings Committee issued this letter in June 1918 urging citizens to buy war savings stamps.

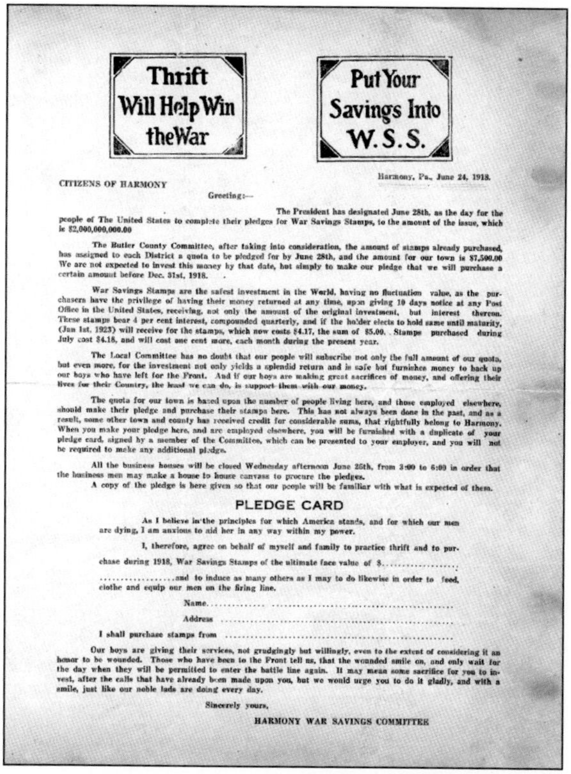

Thrift Will Help Win the War

Put Your Savings Into W. S. S.

Harmony, Pa., June 24, 1918.

CITIZENS OF HARMONY

Greeting:—

The President has designated June 28th, as the day for the people of The United States to complete their pledges for War Savings Stamps, to the amount of the issue, which is $2,000,000,000.00

The Butler County Committee, after taking into consideration, the amount of stamps already purchased, has assigned to each District a quota to be pledged for by June 28th, and the amount for our town is $7,500.00 We are not expected to invest this money by that date, but simply to make our pledge that we will purchase a certain amount before Dec. 31st, 1918.

War Savings Stamps are the safest investment in the World, having no fluctuation value, as the purchasers have the privilege of having their money returned at any time, upon giving 10 days notice at any Post Office in the United States, receiving, not only the amount of the original investment, but interest thereon. These stamps bear 4 per cent interest, compounded quarterly, and if the holder elects to hold same until maturity, (Jan 1st, 1923) will receive for the stamps, which now costs $4.17, the sum of $5.00. Stamps purchased during July cost $4.18, and will cost one cent more, each month during the present year.

The Local Committee has no doubt that our people will subscribe not only the full amount of our quota, but even more, for the investment not only yields a splendid return and is safe but furnishes money to back up our boys who have left for the Front. And if our boys are making great sacrifices of money, and offering their lives for their Country, the least we can do, is support them with our money.

The quota for our town is based upon the number of people living here, and those employed elsewhere, should make their pledge and purchase their stamps here. This has not always been done in the past, and as a result, some other town and county has received credit for considerable sums, that rightfully belong to Harmony. When you make your pledge here, and are employed elsewhere, you will be furnished with a duplicate of your pledge card, signed by a member of the Committee, which can be presented to your employer, and you will not be required to make any additional pledge.

All the business houses will be closed Wednesday afternoon June 26th, from 3:00 to 6:00 in order that the business men may make a house to house canvass to procure the pledges.

A copy of the pledge is here given so that our people will be familiar with what is expected of them.

PLEDGE CARD

As I believe in the principles for which America stands, and for which our men are dying, I am anxious to aid her in any way within my power.

I, therefore, agree on behalf of myself and family to practice thrift and to purchase during 1918, War Savings Stamps of the ultimate face value of $.................. ....and to induce as many others as I may to do likewise in order to feed, clothe and equip our men on the firing line.

Name..

Address ....

I shall purchase stamps from ....

Our boys are giving their services, not grudgingly but willingly, even to the extent of considering it an honor to be wounded. Those who have been to the Front tell us, that the wounded smile on, and only wait for the day when they will be permitted to enter the battle line again. It may mean some sacrifice for you to invest, after the calls that have already been made upon you, but we would urge you to do it gladly, and with a smile, just like our noble lads are doing every day.

Sincerely yours,

HARMONY WAR SAVINGS COMMITTEE

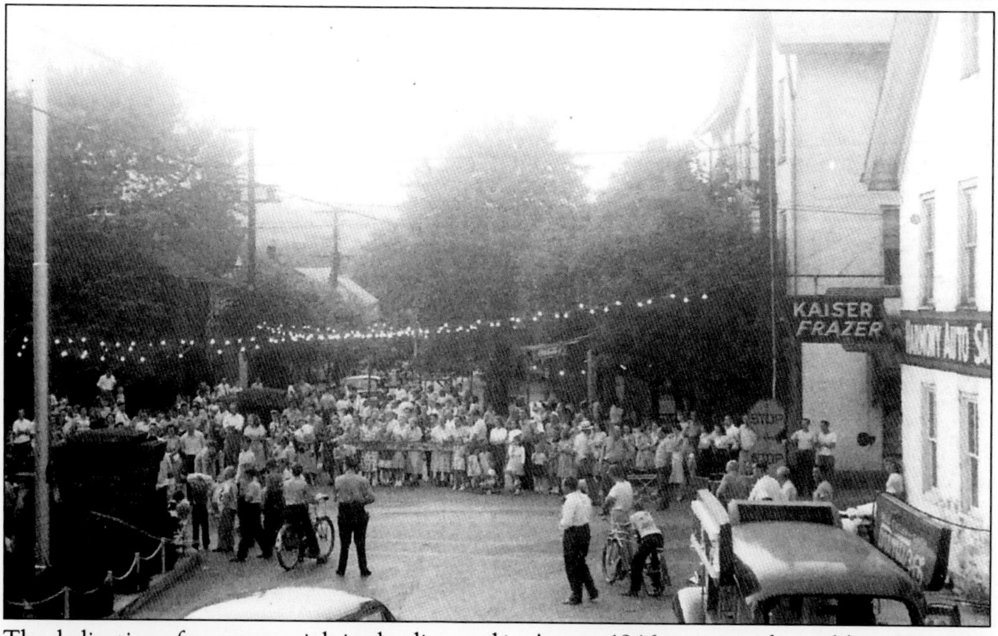

The dedication of war memorials in the diamond in August 1946 was part of a weeklong Harmony firemen's jubilee. The Harmony War Memorial Association raised funds for the markers, with the firemen donating $450. An estimated 5,000 people watched a parade that marched from West Grandview Avenue in Zelienople to Harmony. (Courtesy of Ruth Werner, photograph by Dr. Arthur Stewart.)

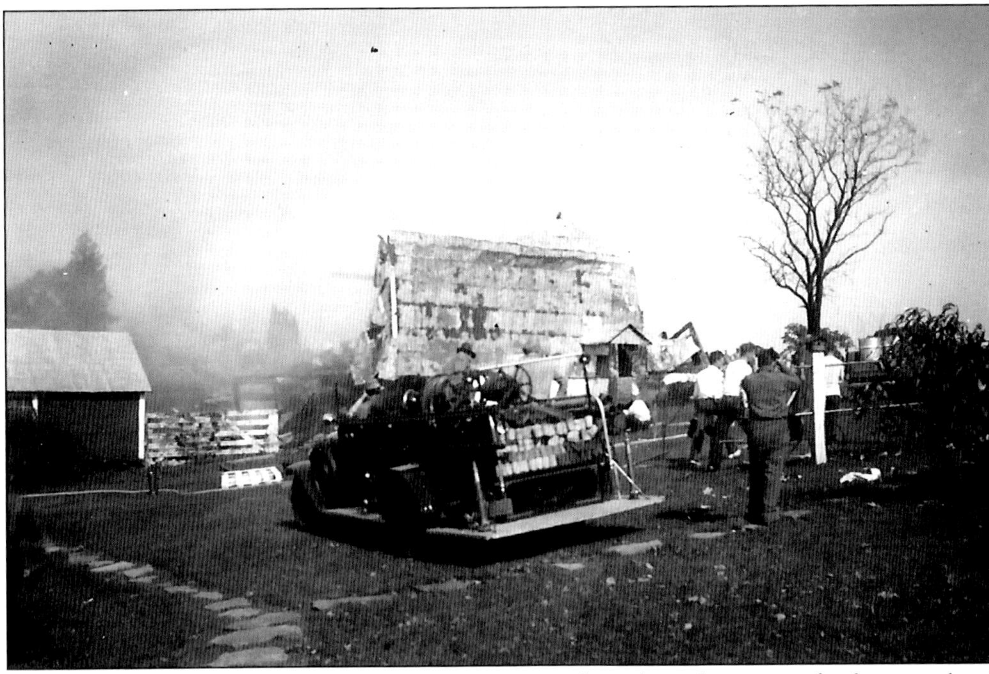

Harmony volunteer firefighters with their pumper truck work at the scene of a fire on a local farm. The action was photographed by Dr. Arthur Stewart, a member of the fire company. He noted on the photographs, "Mrs. Cowel's barn burned July 1939."

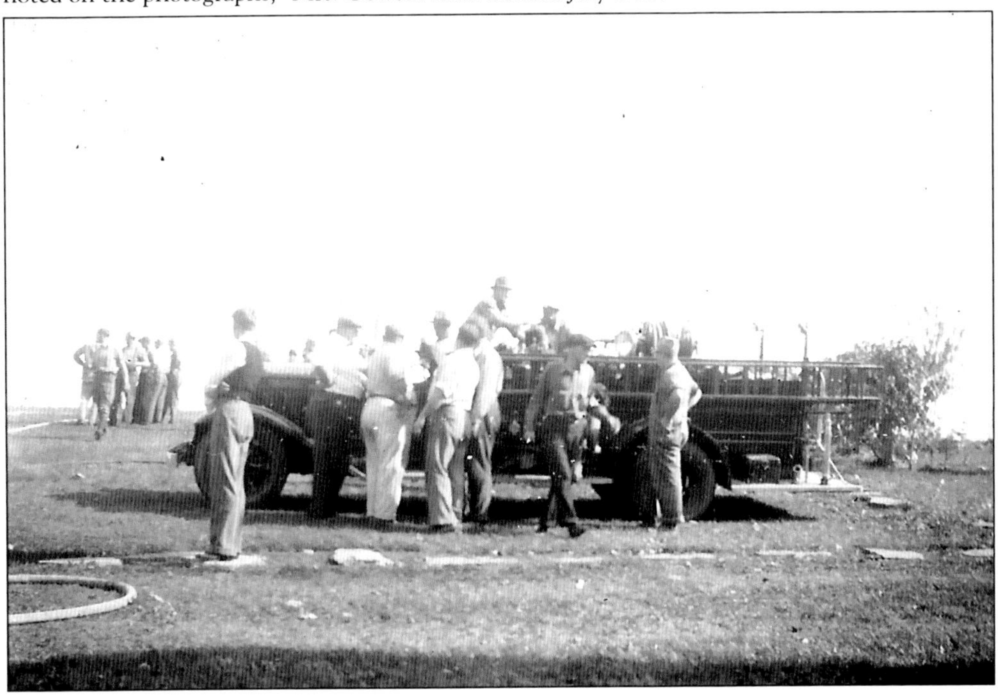

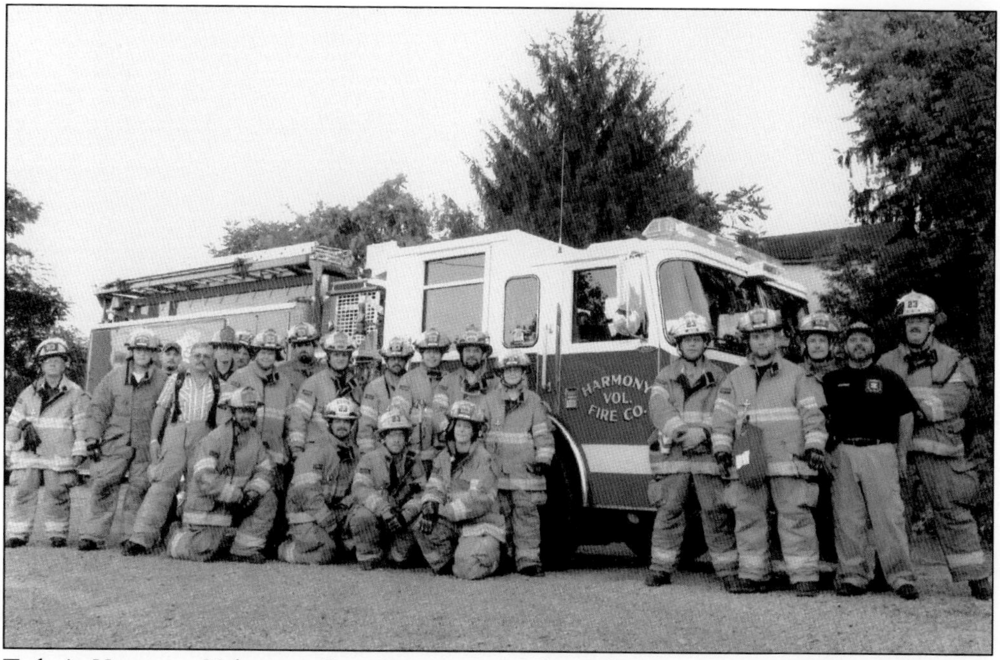

Today's Harmony Volunteer Fire Company stands ready to answer emergency calls with state-of-the-art equipment. The company numbers about 50. Tim Sapienza, standing third from left, has been fire chief since 1978. His father, Louis Sapienza, served as chief for 19 years. (Courtesy of Tim Sapienza.)

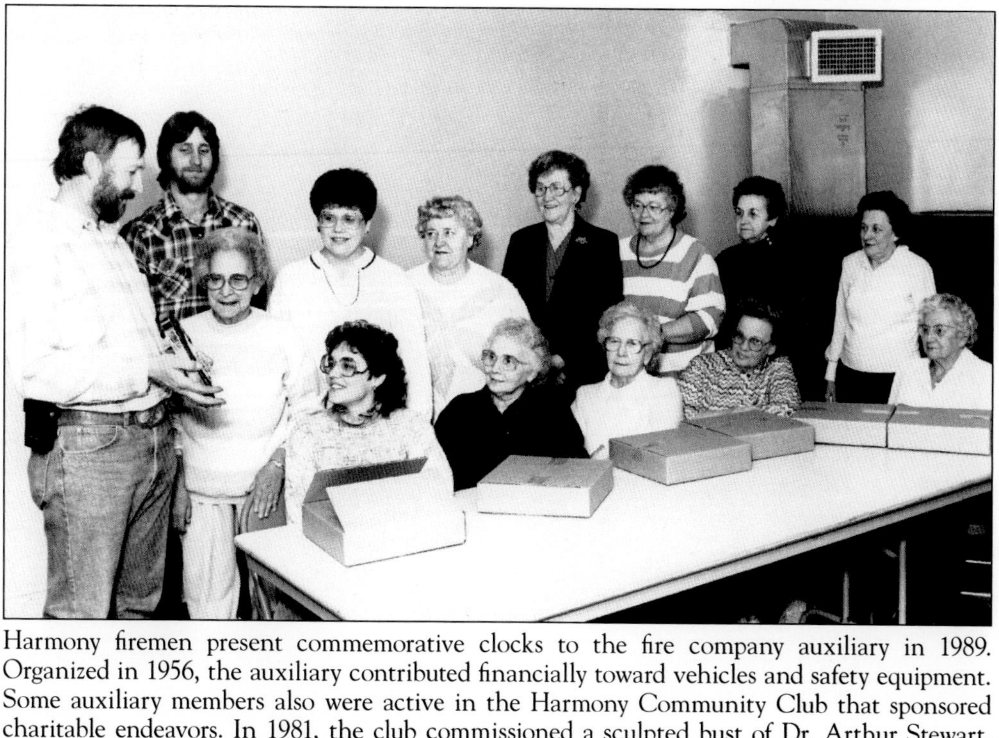

Harmony firemen present commemorative clocks to the fire company auxiliary in 1989. Organized in 1956, the auxiliary contributed financially toward vehicles and safety equipment. Some auxiliary members also were active in the Harmony Community Club that sponsored charitable endeavors. In 1981, the club commissioned a sculpted bust of Dr. Arthur Stewart. (Courtesy of the Butler Eagle, photograph by Ray Thompson.)

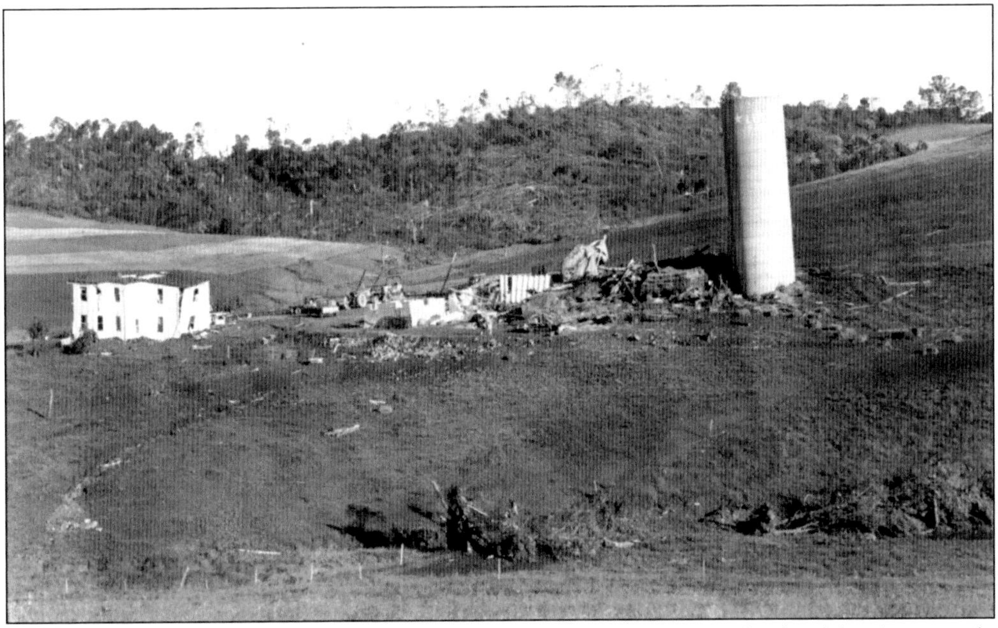

The Ronald Lutz farm on Gudekunst Road in Jackson Township was hit hard by the tornado that swept across southern Butler County in May 1985. Winds destroyed the barn while Lutz was inside with 40 dairy cows. His wife and two young children barely reached the basement before the house was blown from its foundation. The family escaped serious injury. The storm killed six people in the county, including Edward John Fink and his wife, Lorraine, of Evans City. Below, volunteer aid workers load a truck with supplies for tornado victims. (Courtesy of the Butler Eagle, photograph by Ray Thompson.)

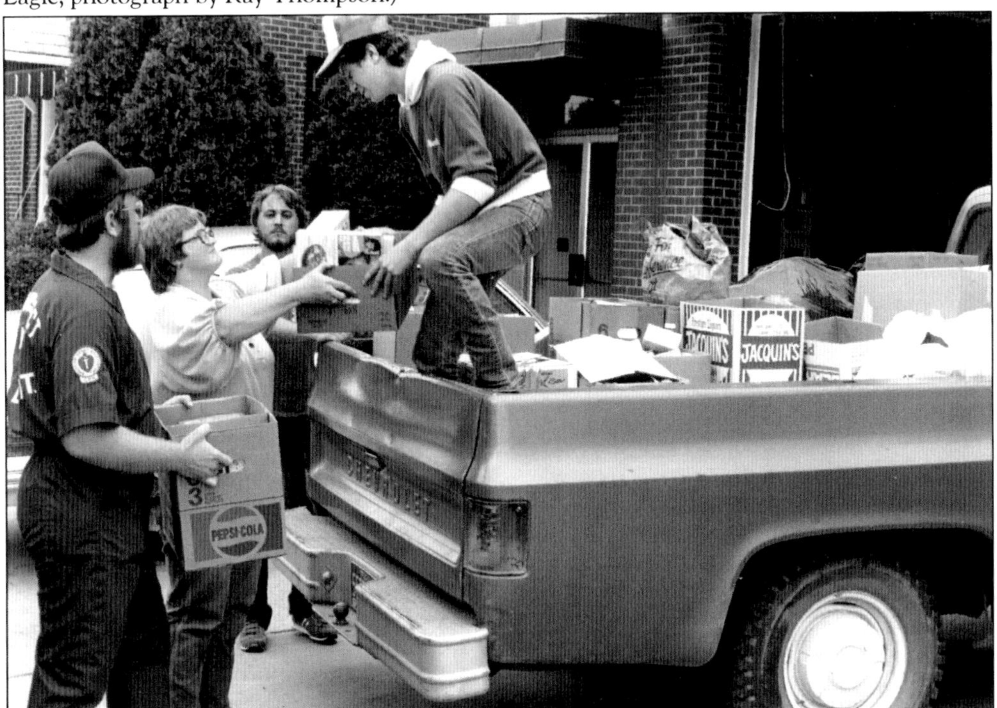

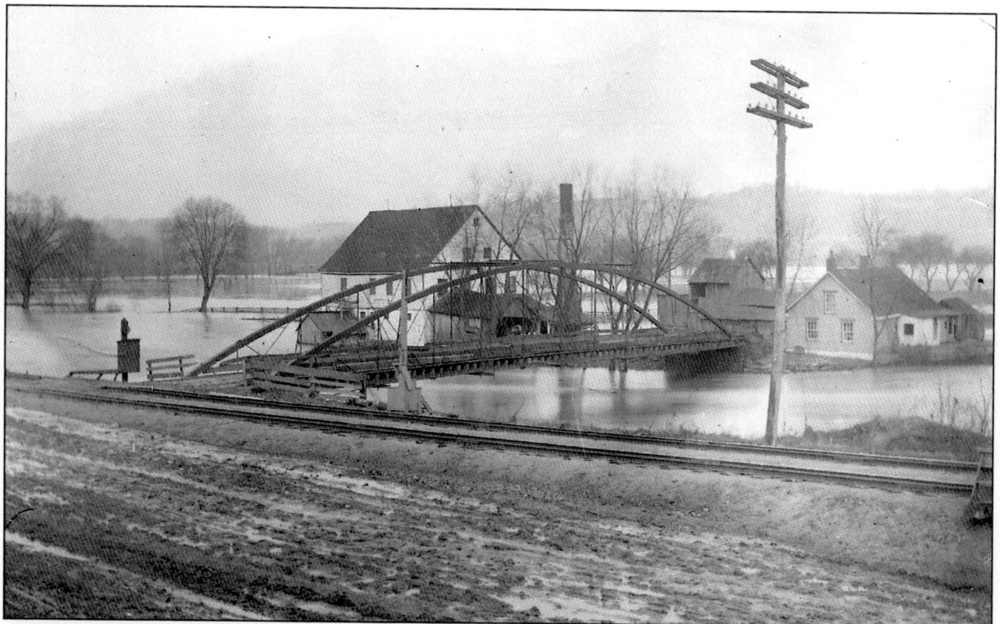

Floodwaters surround the mill and spread across the fields in Harmony Junction in this 1905 picture. In 1955, the Connoquenessing Creek overflowed again, flooding east Mercer Street. Dr. Arthur Stewart took the picture below from the corner of Mercer and Spring Streets. The opera house with the TruFlo Fan Company sign can be seen on the left behind a pole. (Courtesy of Ruth Werner.)

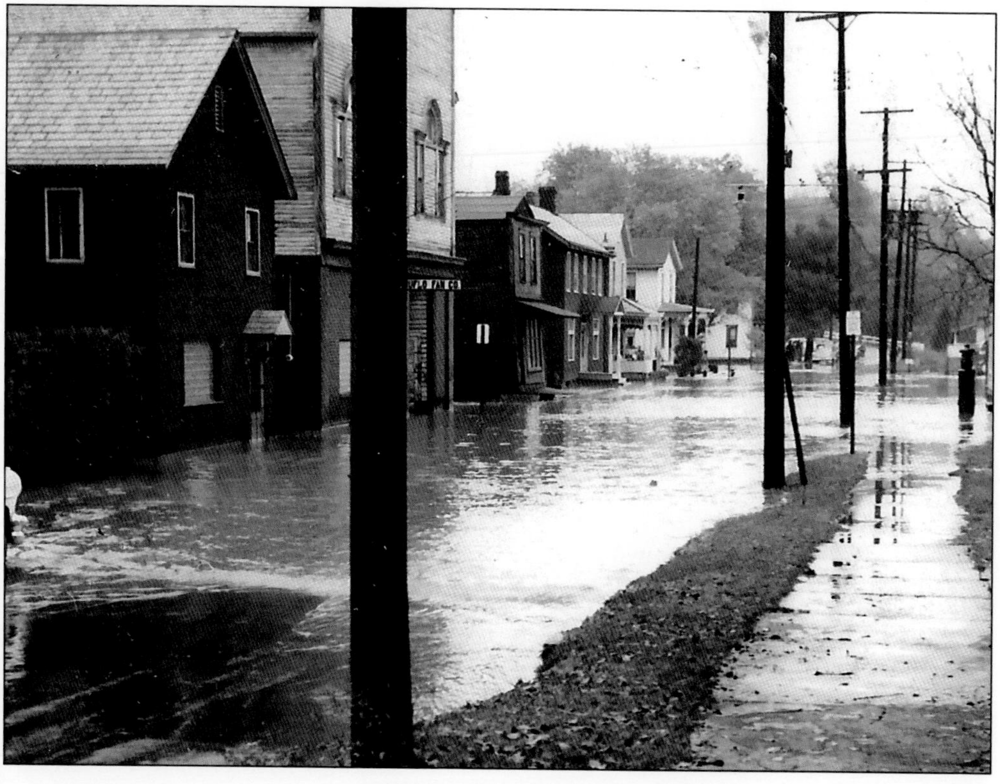

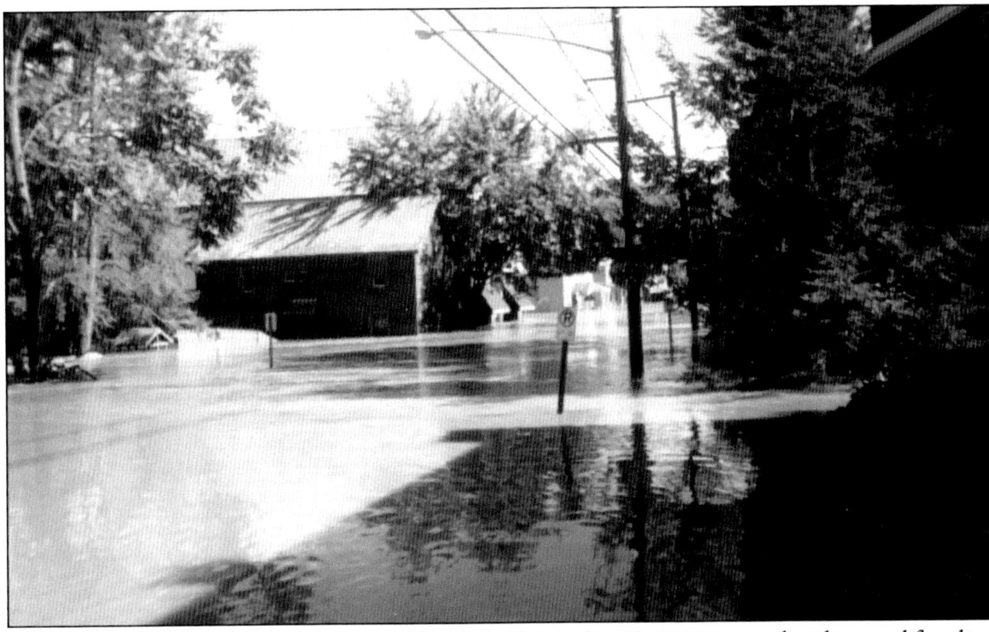

Rains from Hurricane Ivan that began falling on September 17, 2004, caused widespread flooding along the Connoquenessing Creek. This was the scene on East Mercer Street the next day, after the creek behind these buildings overflowed. The water level nearly touches the first floor awnings at Otto and Gert's in the opera house at far left. Some homes were destroyed while other residences and shops were heavily damaged.

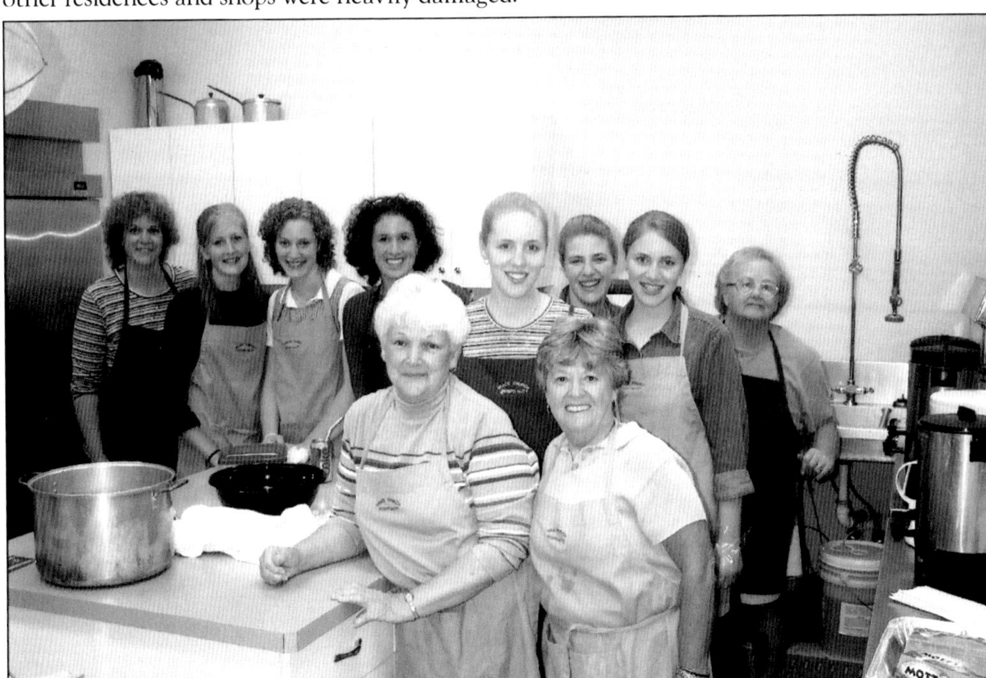

Grace Church cooks pause in the kitchen where they served food to flood victims and rescue workers for a month. The congregation also provided beds and shower facilities and collected clothing and household goods for people who lost their belongings. (Courtesy of Carol White.)

Nine

TRADITIONS AND MILESTONES

Parades, anniversary celebrations, and recognition of honored citizens have been a big part of life in Harmony. Dr. Arthur Stewart said, when he moved to town in 1906, Harmony was the largest town around and had the biggest annual parades, usually on the Fourth of July. "The units, bands, and floats would begin marching from Zelienople and end at Thompson's Dairy east of Harmony, extending more than a mile."

Helen Wiser McQuistion, who was born the year Stewart moved to Harmony, recalled, "On Decoration Day all the children paraded clear over to the cemetery. They all had flowers and they put them on the graves, and we had a service over there. On the Fourth of July there would always be a firemen's parade, a pretty big one, lots of bands in it, and at the end of the day there'd be fireworks. Nothing special for Christmas other than at church we'd have a big program—even grown-up people were in it and they'd portray the story of Christ. There was always a big party for Halloween down in what we called the hall [the opera house]."

In August 1915, Harmony celebrated the 110th anniversary of its founding and the centennial of Abraham Ziegler's purchase. A newspaper article detailed the agenda that included an old home reunion, firemen's sports meet, and a Ziegler reunion.

Before sesquicentennial week in 1955, the Harmony Veterans of Foreign Wars post directed an old timers parade that wound from Pittsburgh Street north on Main Street to the diamond and on to the firemen's carnival grounds. Lee Willets headed the committee that offered parade entry applications at Harper's and Krekler's service stations, Sapienza's Market, Stewart's Radio Shop, and McQuistion's pharmacy.

The Harmony Community Bicentennial Week in July 1976 opened with a parade followed by a songfest at Calvin Presbyterian Church. Other events were a nightly firemen's carnival, a famous women in fashion show sponsored by the Harmony Community Club, open house at the Harmony Museum, round and square dancing sponsored by the Jackson Grange, and a musical production at Grace Reformed Church.

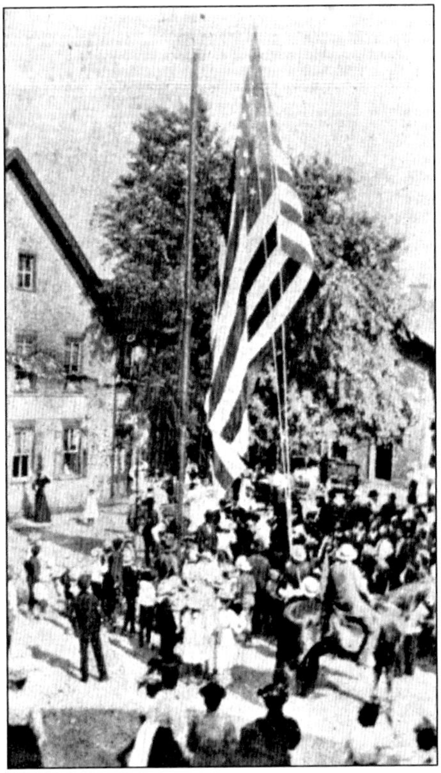

Harmony residents hoist a huge American flag onto a 100-foot pole in the diamond in 1899. The photograph was featured in a booklet printed for the 1938 centennial of borough incorporation. The celebration was a bit premature; Harmony was incorporated in 1840. Officials explained that they had checked with the state and were assured that 1838 was the correct date. Even so, Harmony put on a good show and did the town justice. Below, military personnel and residents prepare to raise the 1899 flag on Memorial Day in 1948.

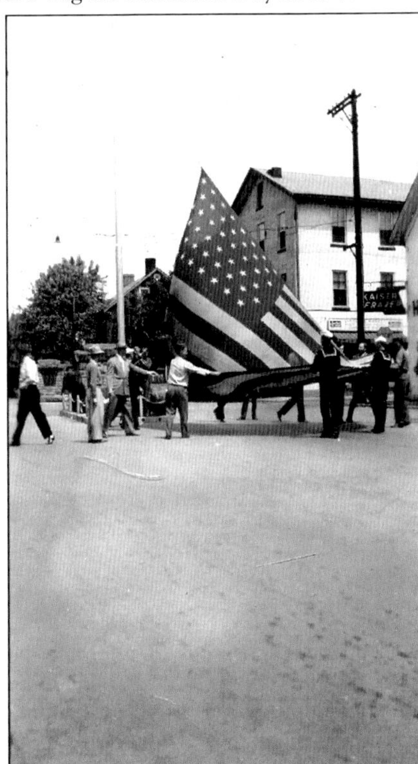

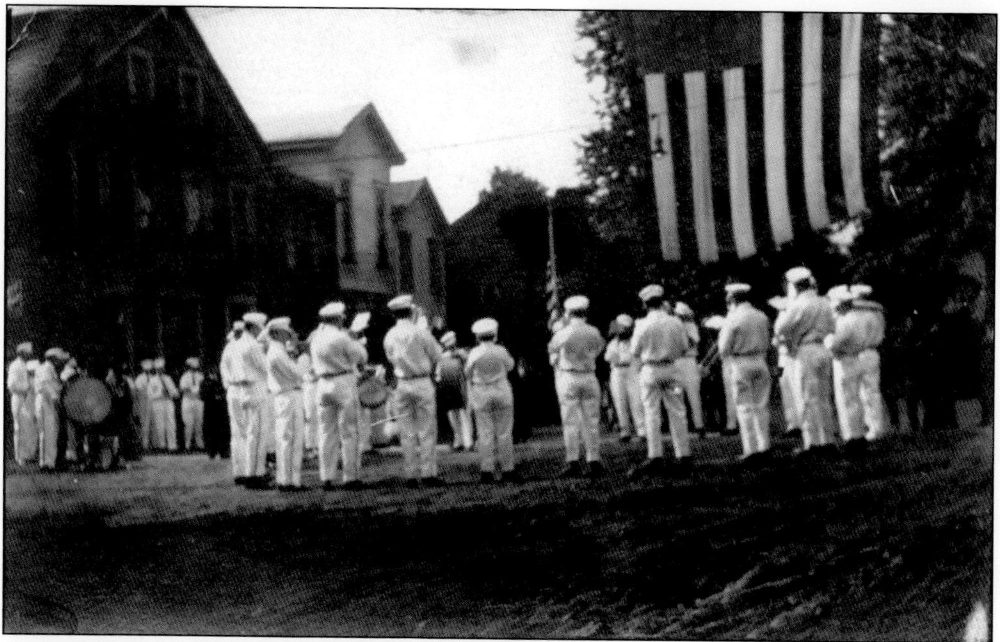

A crowd gathers as the Harmony Firemen's Band performs in the diamond. The American flag in the foreground is the same one first raised above the town in 1899 to celebrate Adm. George Dewey's victory at Manila Bay during the Spanish-American War. (Courtesy of Nancy Wiser.)

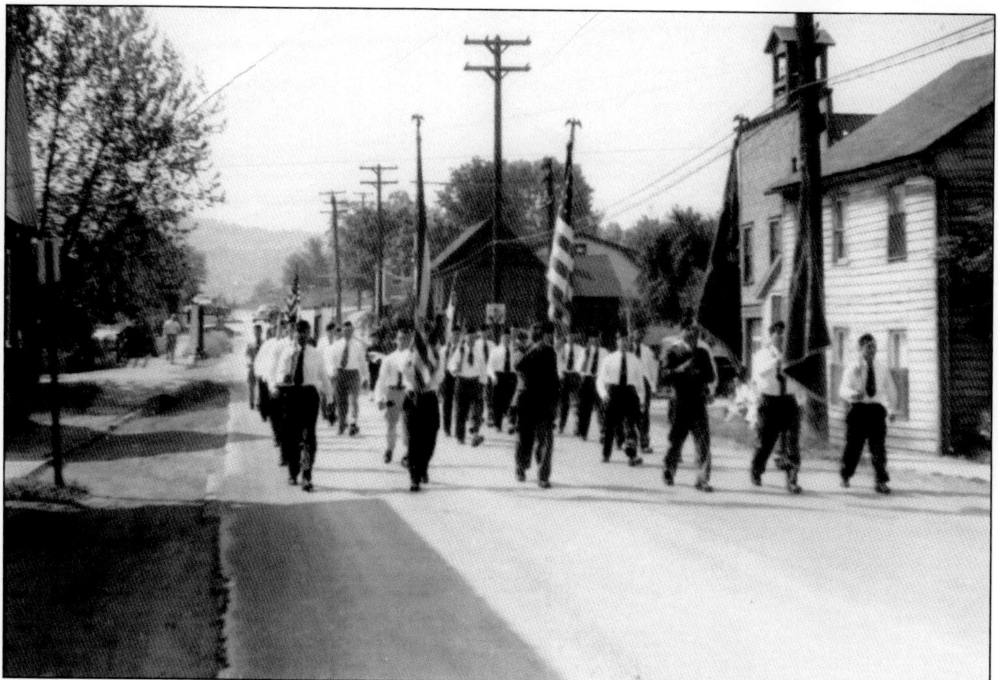

American Legion members march down Main Street to the diamond in the 1960s, probably for a Memorial Day service. At right is the old firehouse with its bell tower. (Courtesy of Tim Sapienza.)

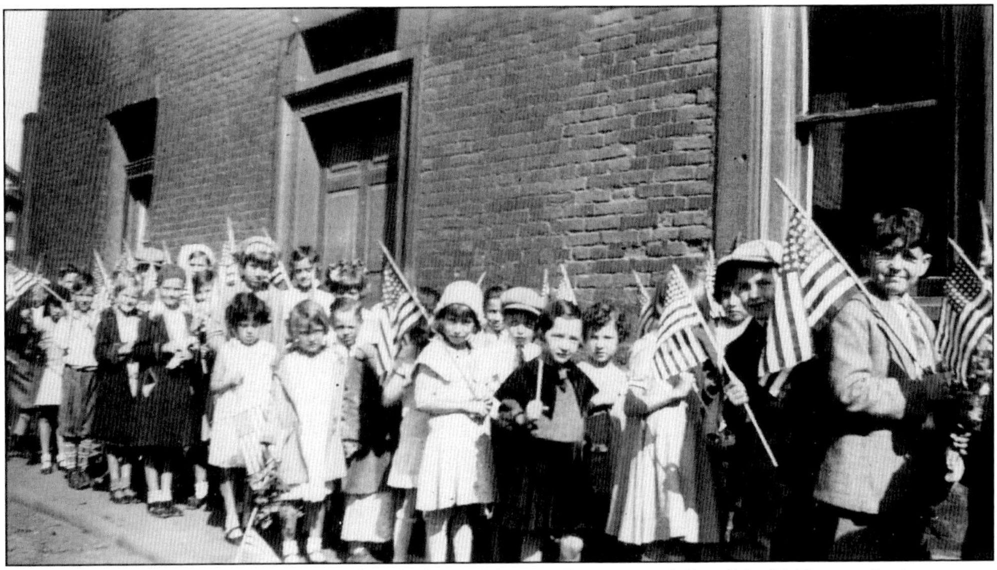

Children walk from Harmony School along Mercer Street on May 30, 1933, on their way to Memorial Day ceremonies at the Mennonite cemetery in Jackson Township. Behind them is the Harmony Society store building, with a carved stone doorway and beaded stone window trim. (Courtesy of Ruth Werner, photograph by Dr. Arthur Stewart.)

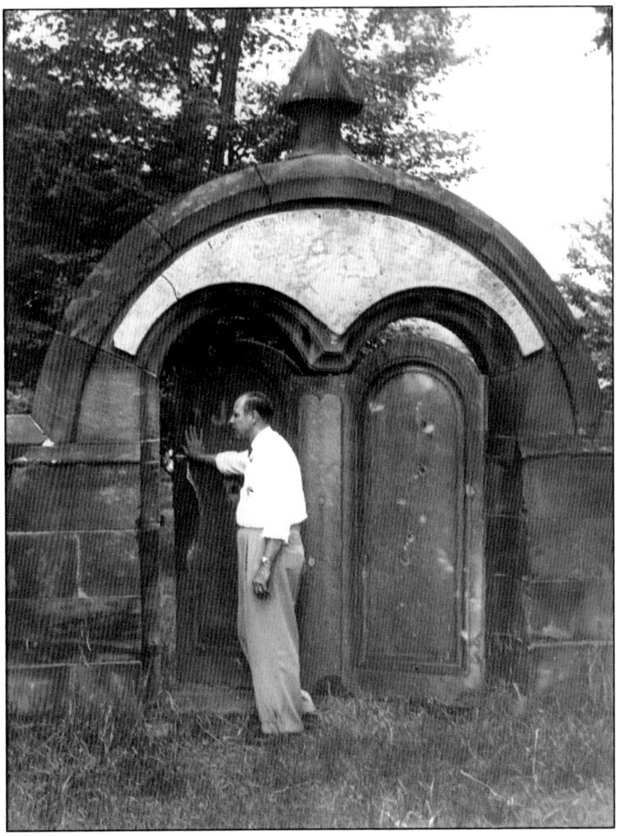

Rev. Loran Veith opens the gate of the Harmony Society cemetery for a visitor in 1955. Veith, pastor of Grace Reformed Church, was a founding member of the Harmonist Historic and Memorial Association. He and Dr. Arthur Stewart authored a history booklet for Harmony's sesquicentennial celebration. Commonly called "the green book," it has been a source of local lore for generations. (Courtesy of the Butler Eagle.)

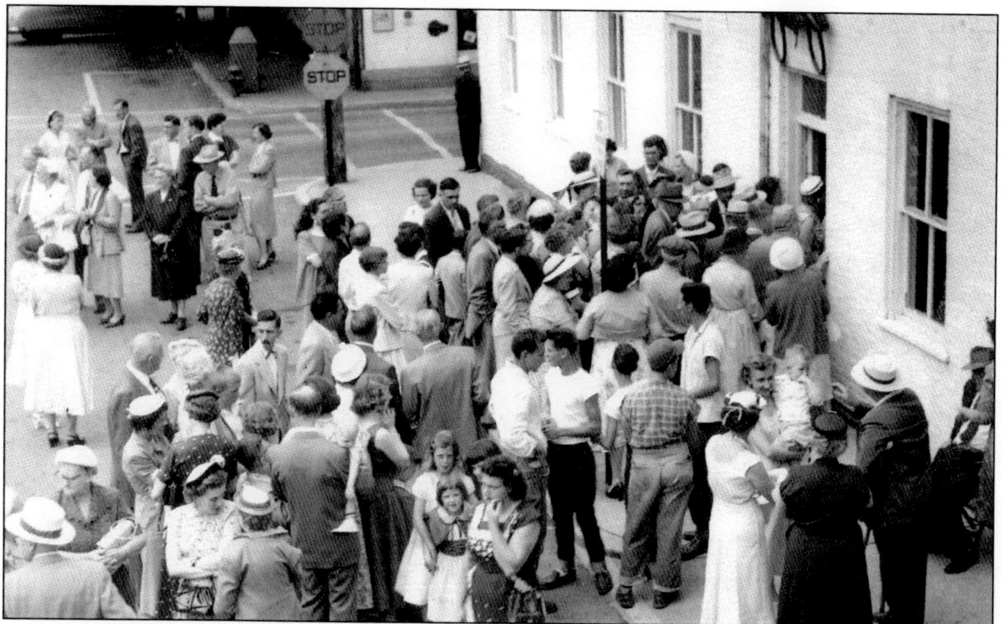

A crowd gathered in the town diamond on June 25, 1955, when the Harmony Volunteer Fire Company opened the Harmony Museum in the society's warehouse. Constructed in 1809, it had been converted for various uses including a multifamily dwelling, grocery, candy store, and car dealership. An addition served for several years as the fire station. (Courtesy of the Butler Eagle.)

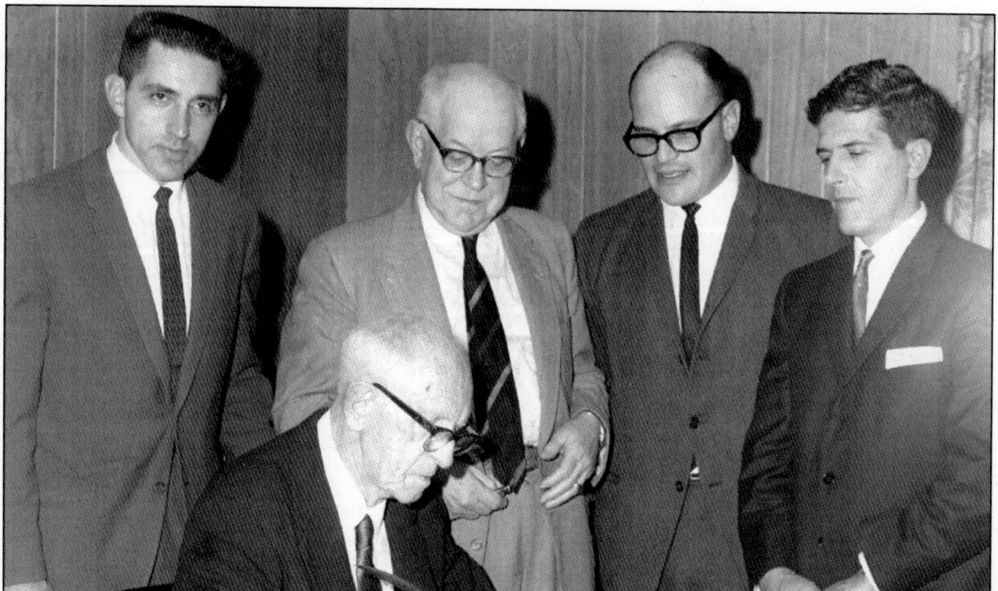

Harmonist Historic and Memorial Association board member Stewart signs an agreement with the Harmony Volunteer Fire Company in 1967 to operate the Harmony Museum. Standing from left to right are Harmonist Historic and Memorial Association president Robert Garvin, Butler County Historical Society president C. Everette Spang, Old Economy Village curator Daniel Reibel, and fire company secretary Joseph Sapienza III. (Courtesy of the Butler Eagle).

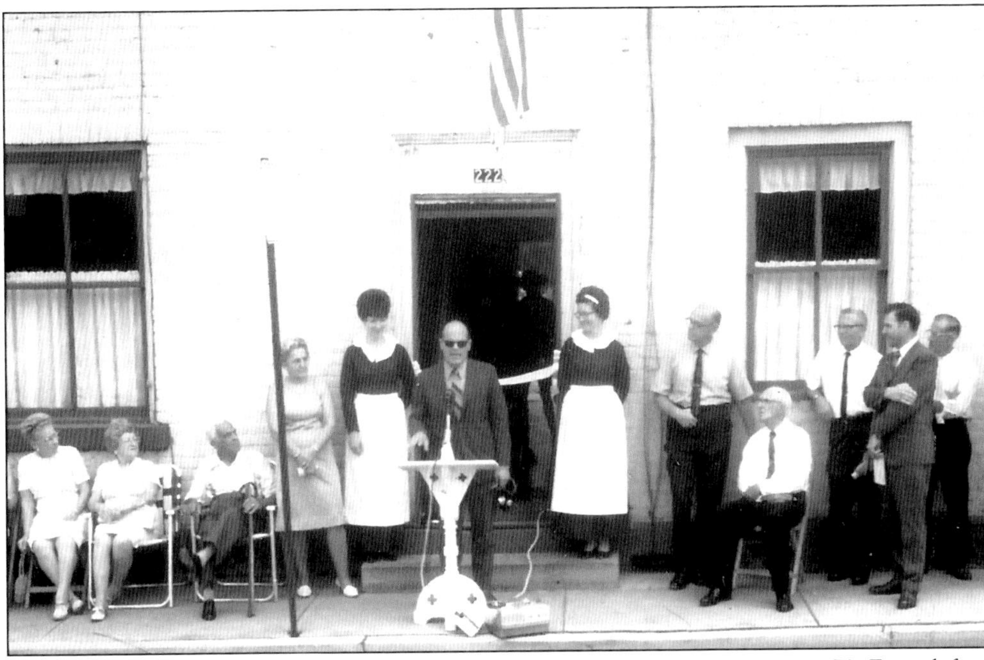

Above, Historic Harmony opens the Wagner House as a museum annex in 1970. From left to right are Louise Fiedler, Esther Fiedler Stamm, George H. Fiedler, Historic Harmony president Ruth Werner, Mildred McCormick, Old Economy Village director Daniel Reibel, Janice Barker, Rev. Philip Seiberling, Dr. Arthur Stewart, Harmony mayor Richard Voegtly, John H. Wise, and Delmont Garvin. Stewart officiated at the ribbon cutting with a pair of surgical scissors. Below, the banner across the town diamond announced another celebration, Doc Stewart Day, which followed. (Courtesy of Ruth Werner.)

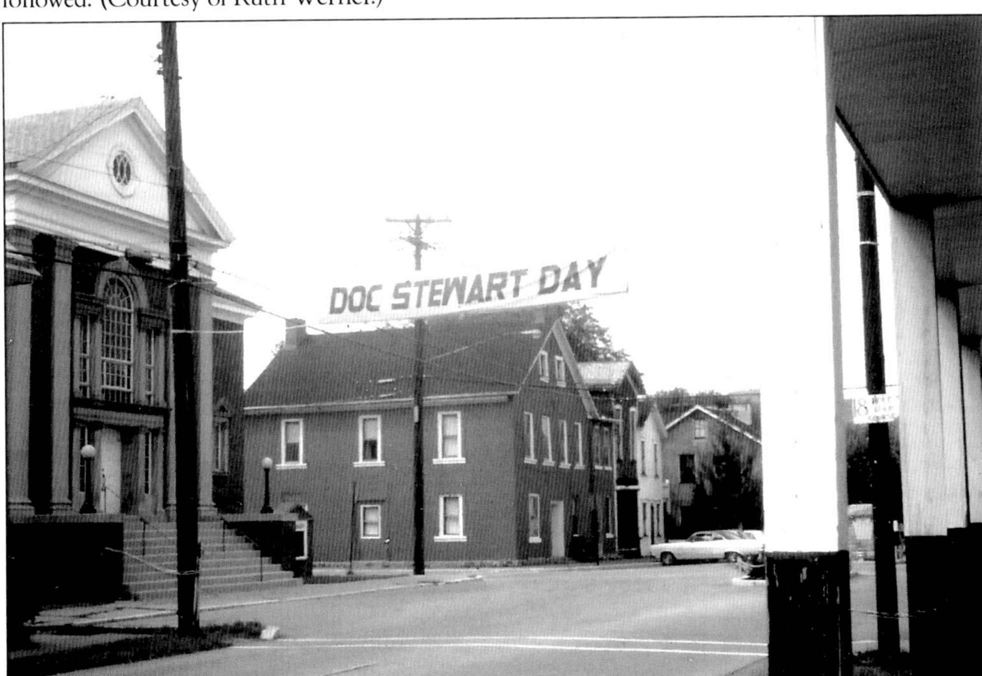

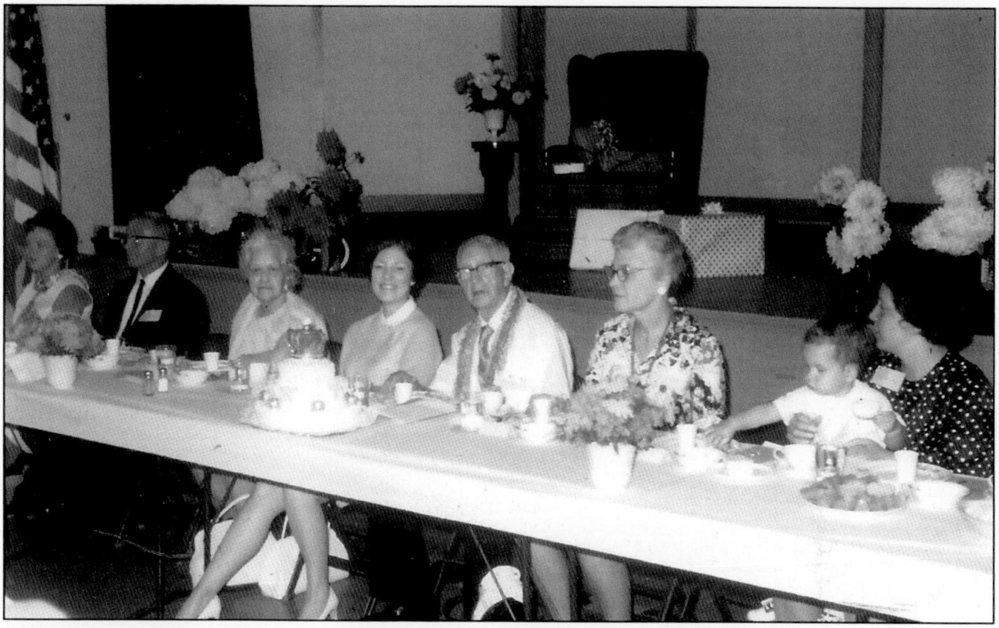

The town turned out to honor Stewart on his 90th birthday. A roast beef dinner, his favorite meal, was served by the Joy Bells Class at Grace Reformed Church. Stewart is flanked by his daughters Rebekah Johnson (left) and Jane Jennings. His granddaughter, Susan Stewart Jennings, holds her nephew, Taylor Stewart Jennings. The birthday cake was baked by Lillian Lawrence of Jackson Township and Nola Jones of Harmony Junction. (Courtesy of Ruth Werner.)

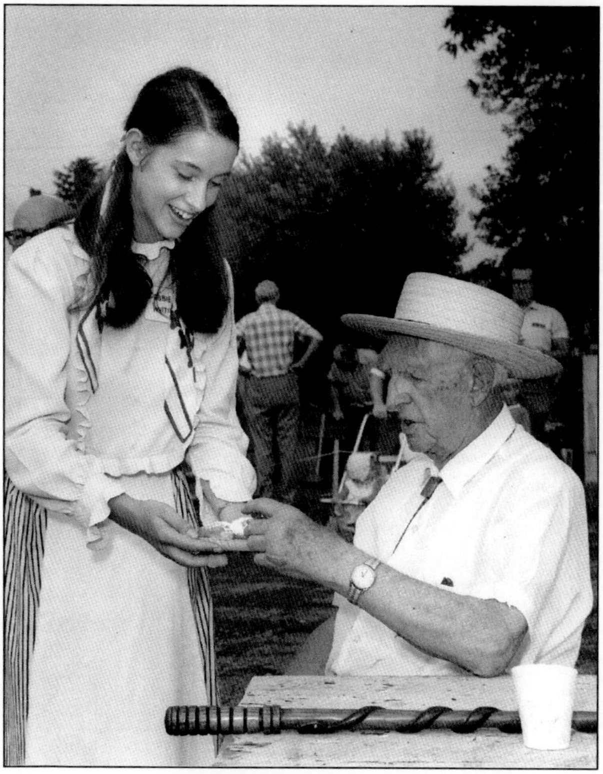

Stewart gets to sample a funnel cake at the Harmony Museum Dankfest in 1972. Museum volunteers dedicated that year's festival to him. (Courtesy of the Butler Eagle, photograph by Ray Thompson.)

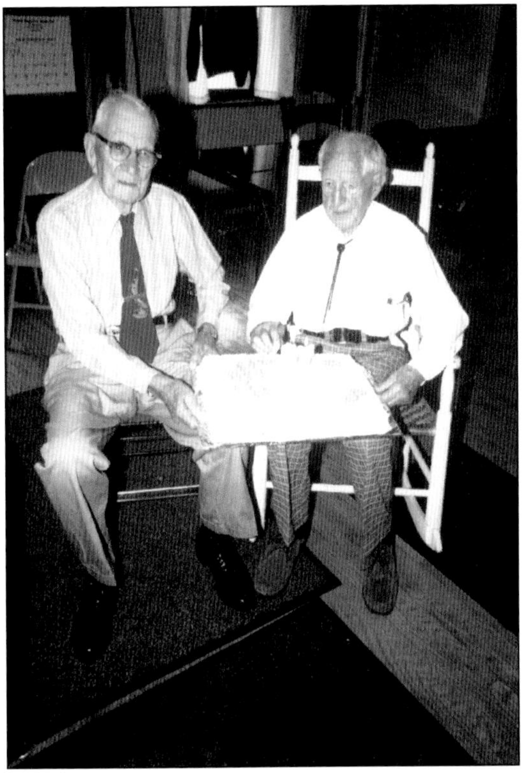

Dr. Arthur Stewart gets ready to blow out the candles on his 97th birthday cake. At left is a Harmony friend Titus Peffer, aged 100. Stewart lived to be 99, and Peffer reached the age of 104.

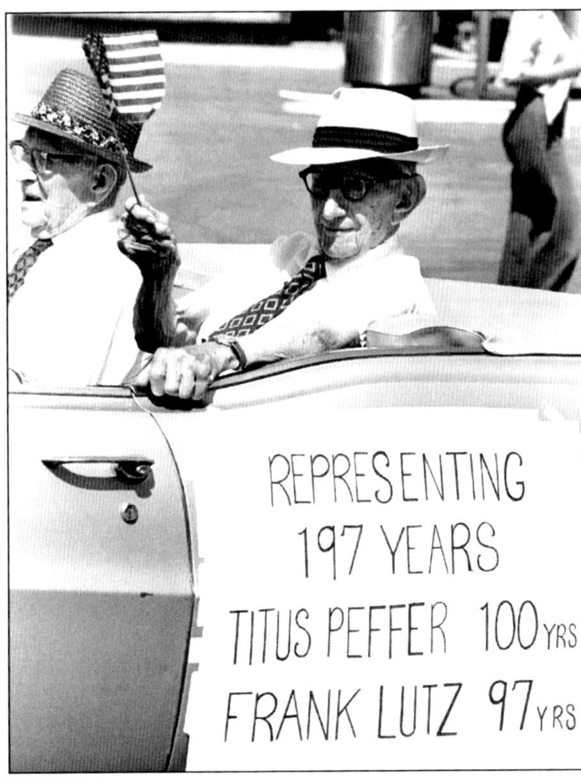

Peffer of Harmony (left) and Frank Lutz of Zelienople were honored participants in the Zelienople-Harmony Bicentennial Parade in July 1976. They were celebrating their own birthdays along with the country's 200th year. Peffer was born on July 21, 1876, and Lutz was born on July 4, 1879. Peffer lived until March 1981, and Lutz died in February 1978. (Courtesy of May Zeigler Lutz, photograph by Ray Thompson.)

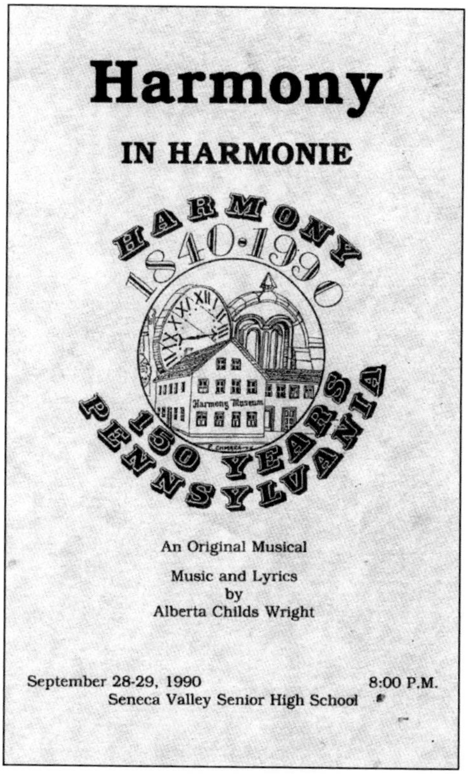

Harmony in Harmonie, an original musical, was performed September 28 and 29, 1990, during the celebration of Harmony's 150th anniversary of incorporation as a borough. The play program features the sesquicentennial seal designed by artist Paul Chmara. Images incorporated in the seal are the Harmonist warehouse, one-handed clock, and cemetery gate. Below, Alberta Childs Wright composed the music and lyrics that took the audience on a trip through Harmony's past. (Courtesy of the Butler Eagle, photograph by Ray Thompson.)

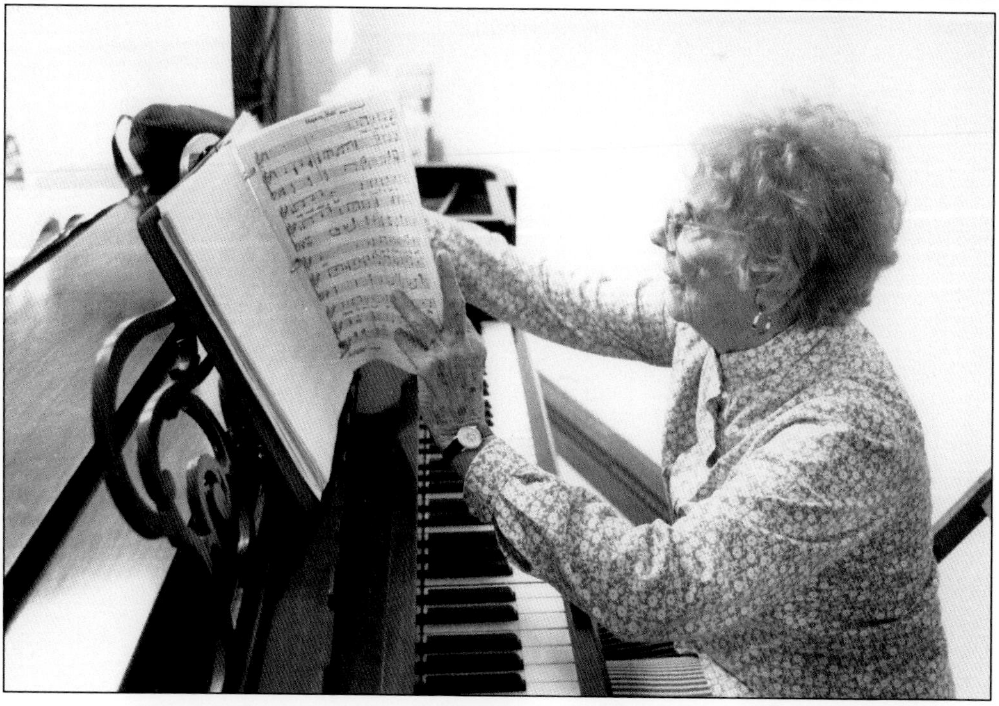

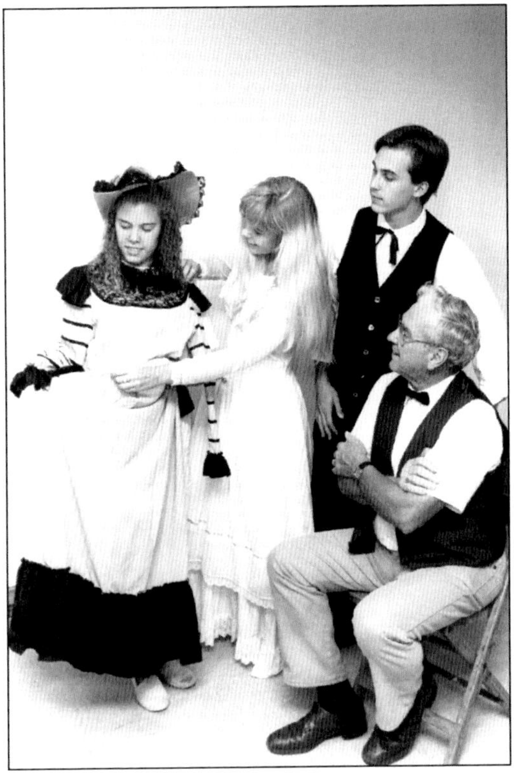

Cast members of *Harmony in Harmonie* rehearse in September 1990. From left to right are Jennifer Meeder, Heather Reeb, Shawn Miller, and John H. Wise. The musical included scenes set in Thompson's Restaurant, the Beam Hotel, Harmony opera house, Dr. Arthur Stewart's office, and the Harmony diamond. (Courtesy of the Butler Eagle, photograph by Ray Thompson.)

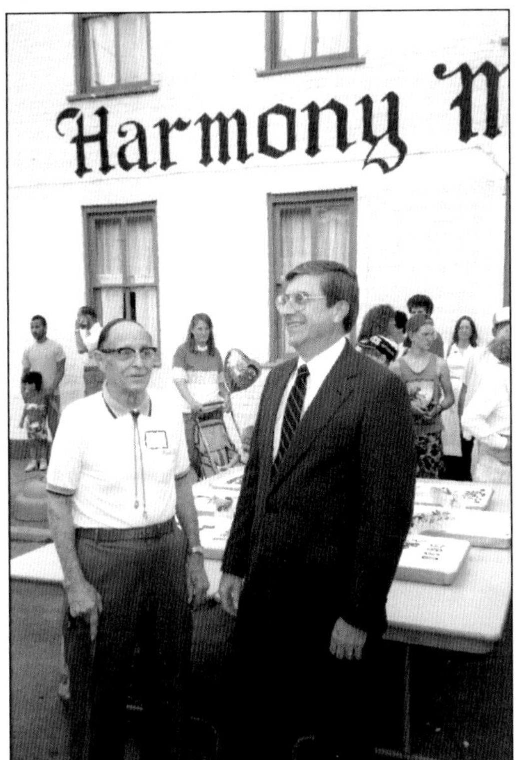

Rev. Loran Veith (left) retired Grace Church pastor, and the current pastor, Rev. David Goetschius, chat during the sesquicentennial party in the diamond. Decorated cakes representing historical eras are about to be served. Entertainment included a show of vintage fashions modeled on a runway in front of the church.

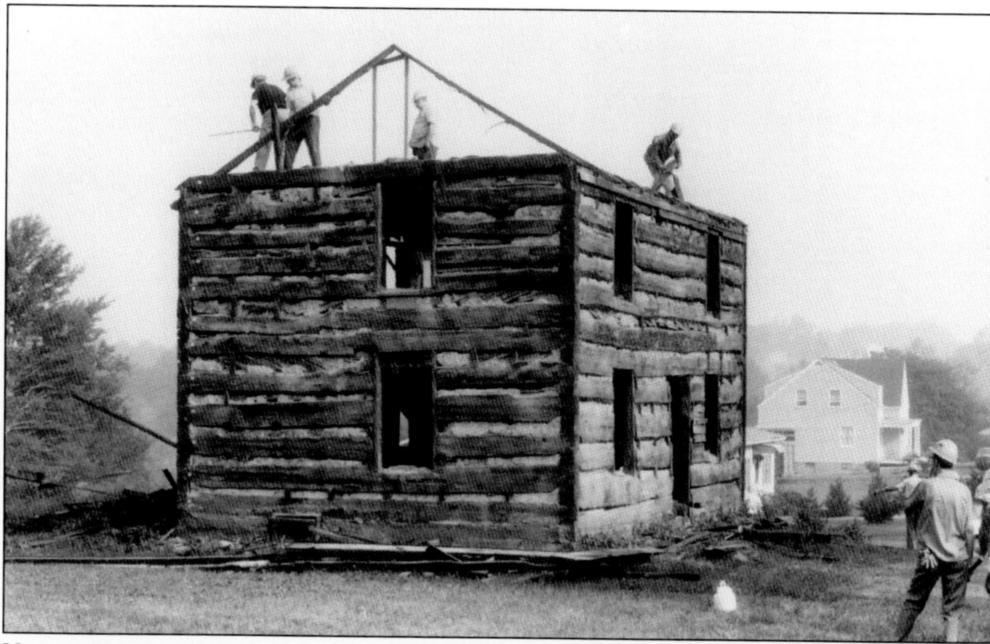

Historic Harmony volunteers work at dismantling a log house in Middle Lancaster in the 1970s. The home of Mennonite Andrew Ziegler was donated by Mr. and Mrs. Clyde Wimer of Ellwood City and moved to Harmony. Historic Harmony volunteers erected the house on Main Street as a United States bicentennial project. Reconstructed as a one-story structure with a large fireplace, it is used as an educational site. Below, students enter the log house during a museum tour. Historic Harmony members conduct a summer day camp at the log house each year, teaching local history and crafts such as spinning, weaving, and rope making.

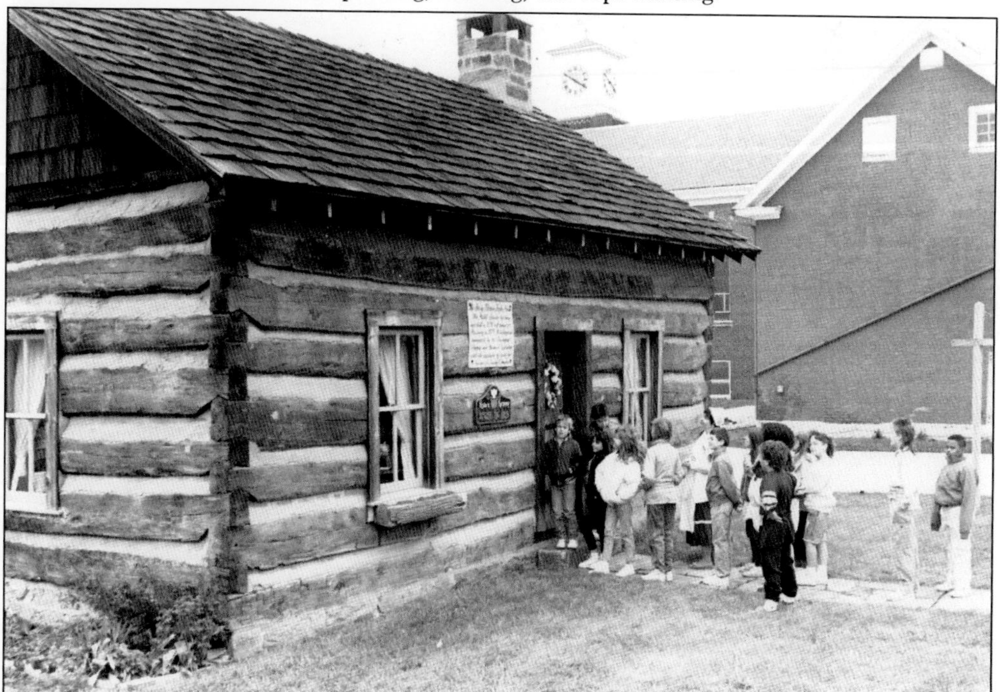

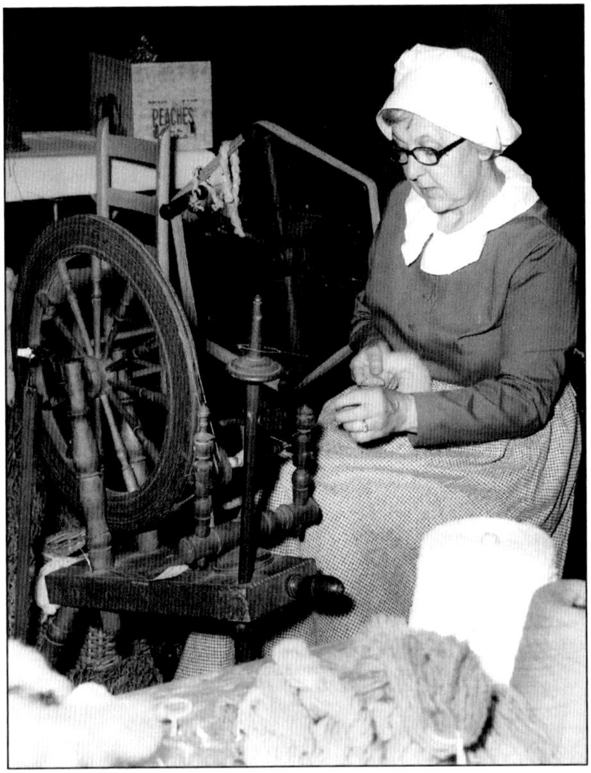

Historic Harmony volunteer Ruth Werner works at the Saxony wheel during the 1973 Dankfest. She was among the Historic Harmony members who learned pioneer ways to demonstrate at the annual harvest festival. (Courtesy of the Butler Eagle, photograph by Ray Thompson.)

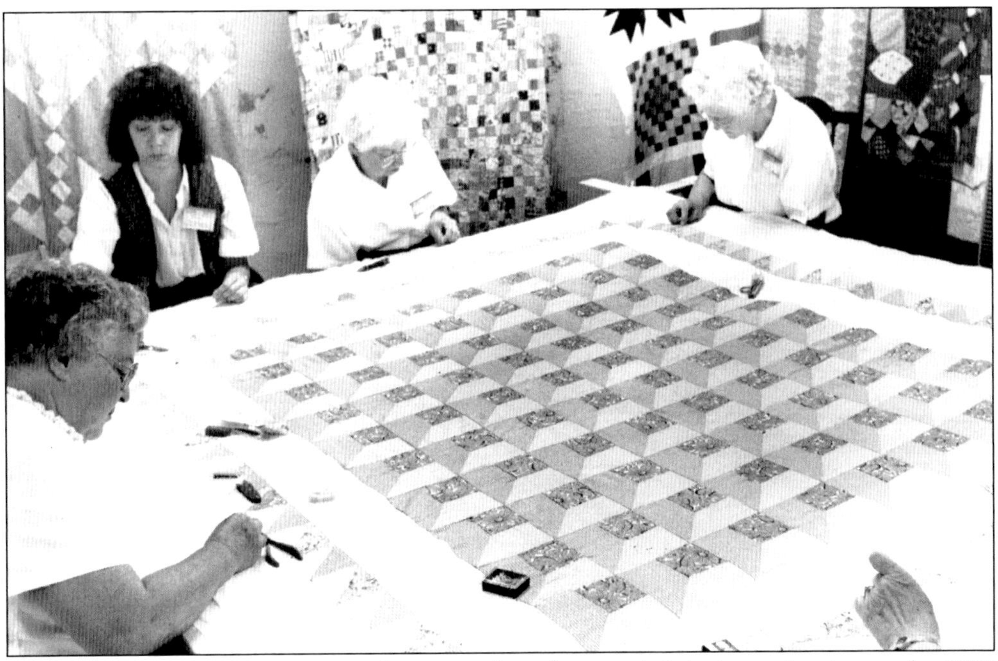

Harmony Museum seamstresses work on a quilt to be awarded during a drawing at the 1989 Candlelight Christmas. Quilting is a longtime tradition for museum volunteers who produce a hand-sewn cover each year. From left to right are Velma Cleland, Donna Hauschulz, Helen Rape, and Ruth Fox. (Courtesy of the Butler Eagle, photograph by Ray Thompson.)

The 25th Dankfest was dedicated to Historic Harmony artisan Albert Eckstein of Lancaster Township who made farm implements in the manner of 18th century craftsmen. He was one of many volunteers who learned and demonstrated pioneer methods at the annual festival for 34 years. (Courtesy of the Butler Eagle, photograph by Ray Thompson.)

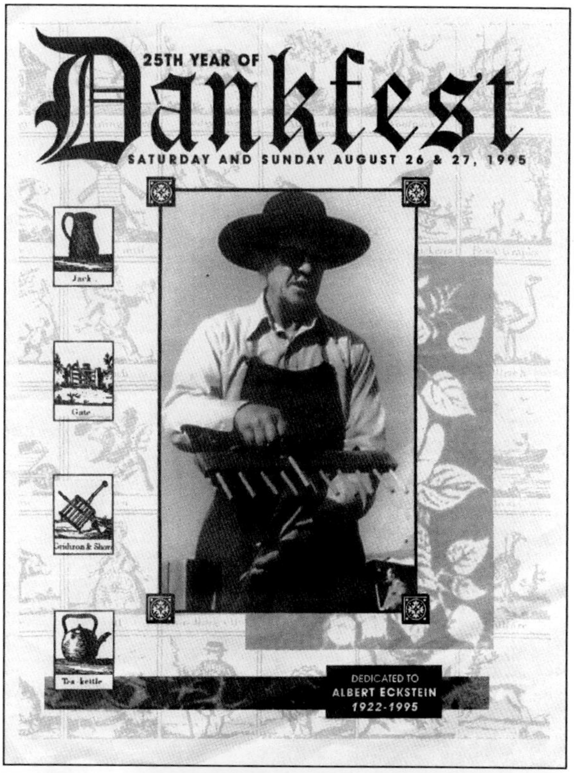

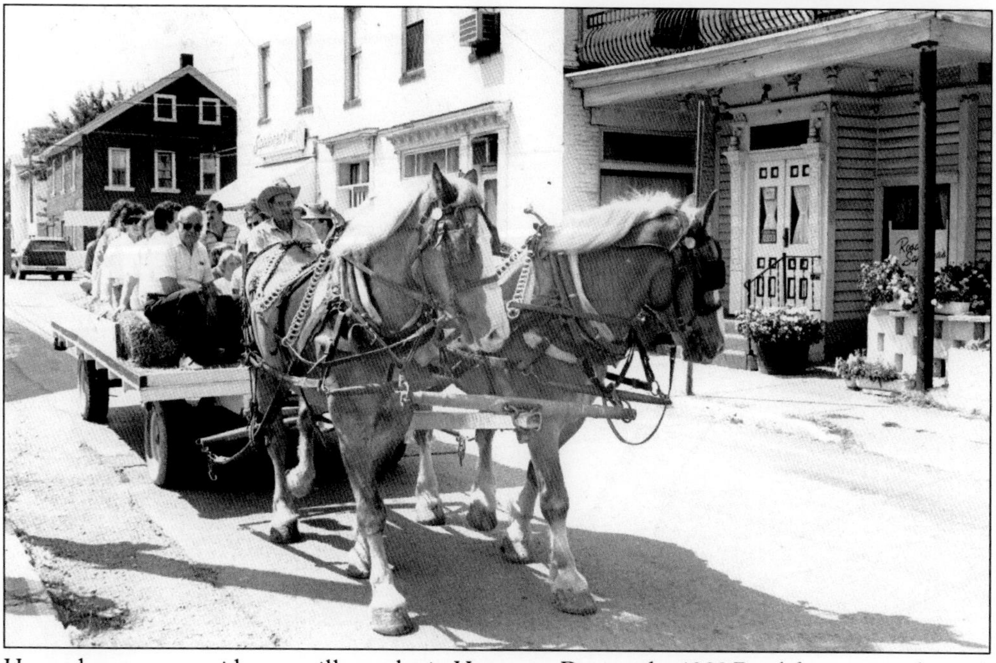

Horse-drawn wagon rides are still popular in Harmony. During the 1989 Dankfest pioneer festival, Victor Ketterer's team carries visitors along Mercer Street past Sapienza's Market and Rosalie Sapienza's beauty shop in the former Beam Hotel. (Courtesy of the Butler Eagle, photograph by Ray Thompson.)

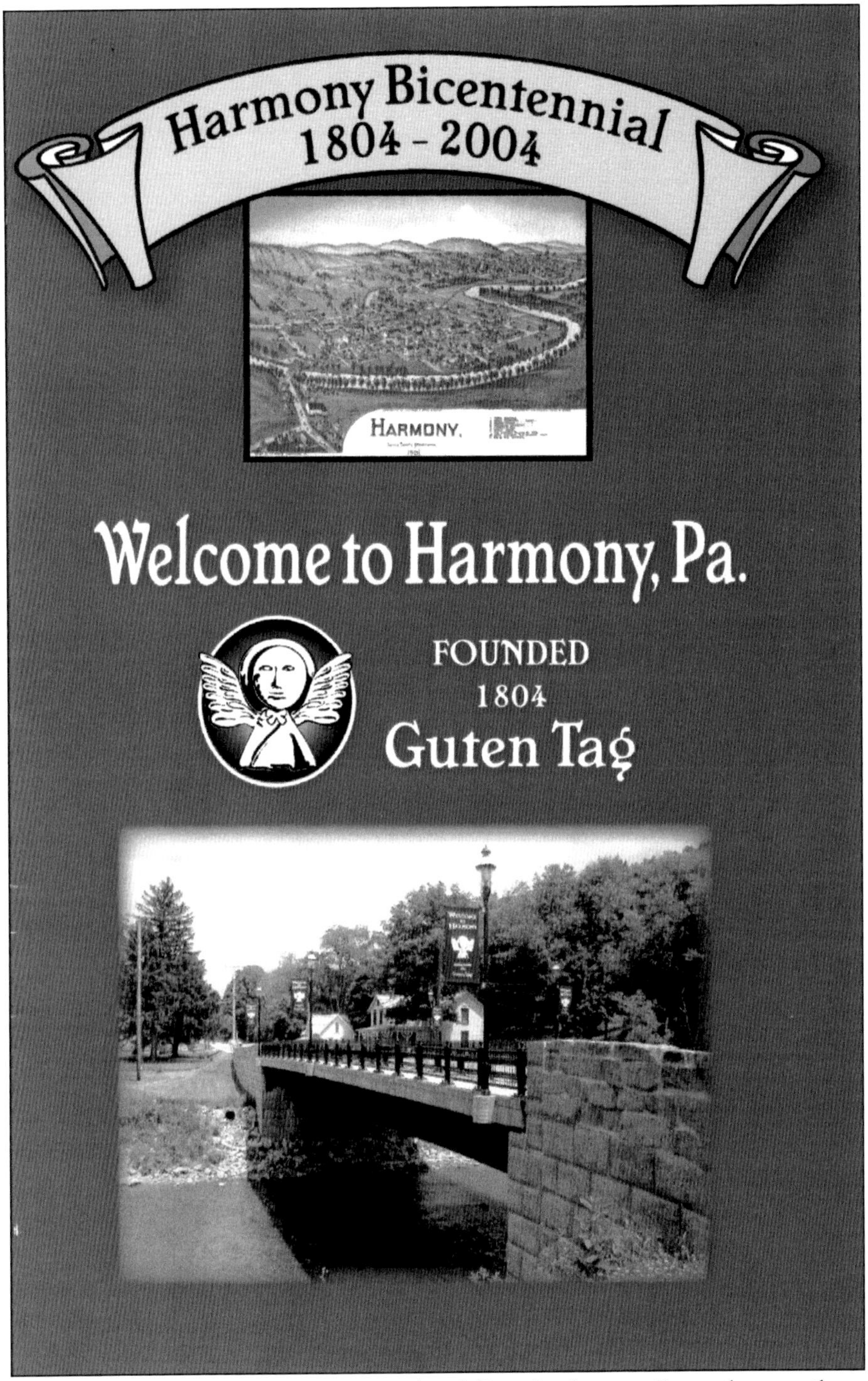

Harmony celebrated its 200th anniversary with a full week of events. Borough council president Jeffrey Smith authored this commemorative booklet that was funded by Citizens National Bank of Evans City, now NexTier Bank. Nods to the town's heritage included the cover design, a slide show about George Rapp's native Iptingen, Germany, and a German dinner at the Harmony Museum. (Courtesy of Harmony Borough.)

Former Harmony Mayor Joe Sapienza and his wife Betty were grand marshals of the Harmony Bicentennial Parade. They were the second generation that kept Sapienza's Market on the diamond open for 76 years. They answered emergency calls for years in their store and living quarters on the second floor. Sapienza served with the Harmony Volunteer Fire Company for 30 years and, with his brother, Louis, founded the Harmony Emergency Medical Service. (Courtesy of the Butler Eagle, photograph by Ray Thompson.)

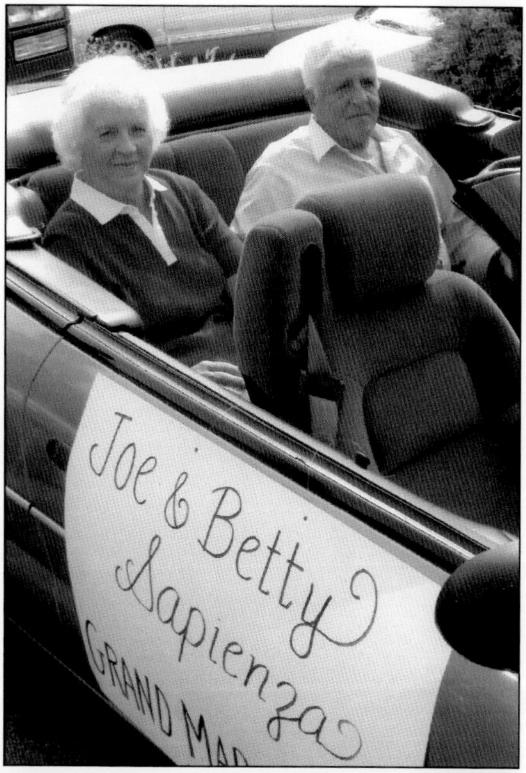

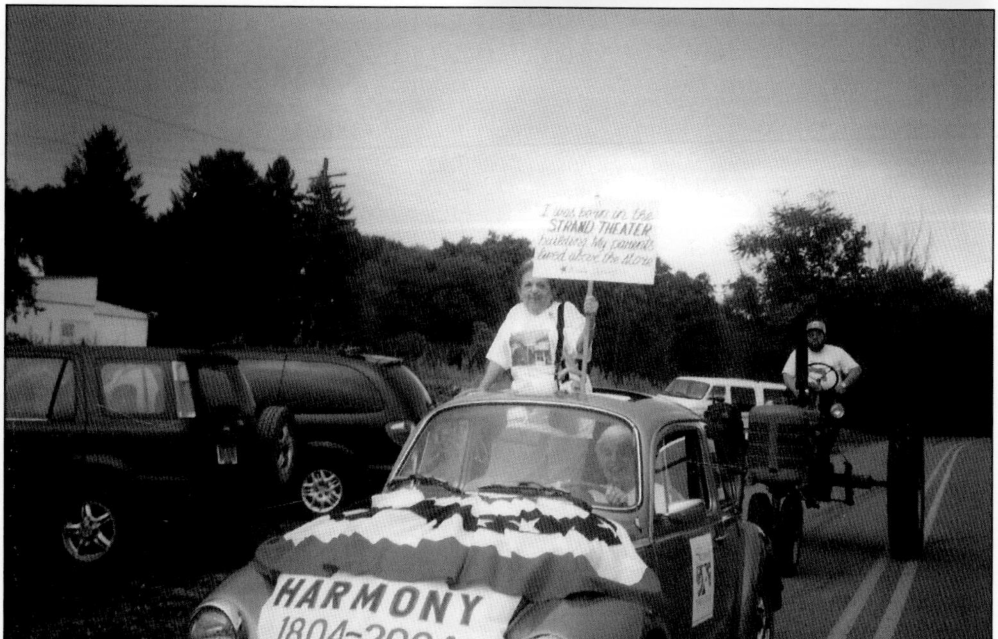

Rosalie Sapienza rides in the Strand Theater entry, driven by Joan Teichart of Zelienople, in the Harmony Bicentennial Parade. The longtime Harmony resident was born in the Sapienza's Market building on Main Street in Zelienople that later became the Strand Theater and is now being renovated. (Courtesy of Joan Teichart.)

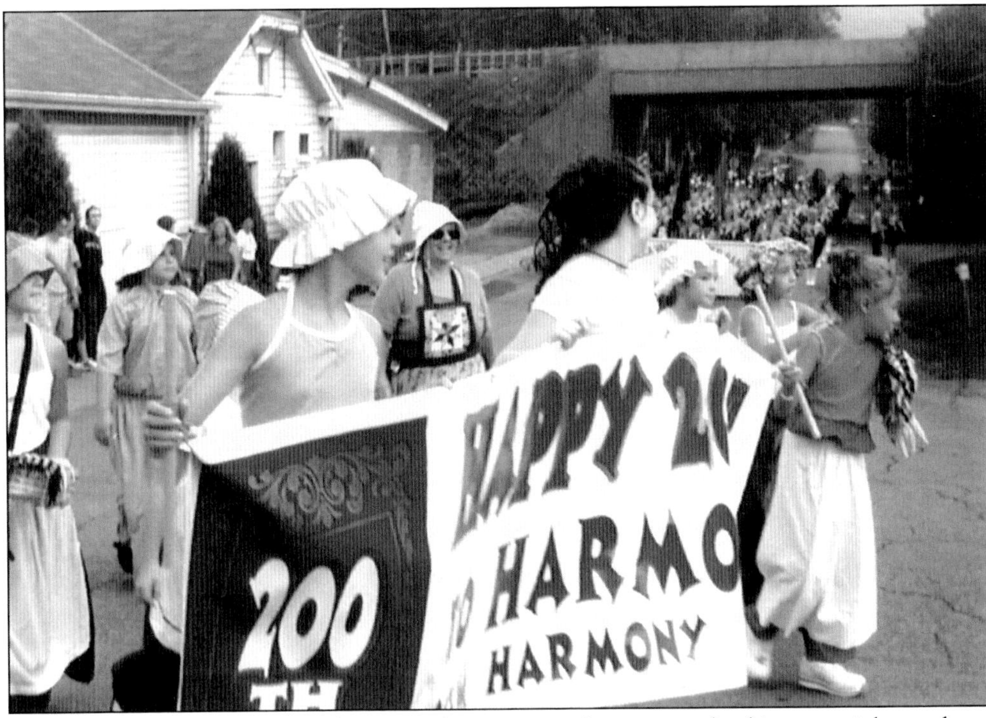

Harmony Museum junior auxiliary members carry a banner in the bicentennial parade on Saturday, August 28, 2004. Seneca Valley High School musicians can be seen marching up Spring Street. Minutes later, the marchers were drenched by a sudden cloudburst. Below, a Harmony fire truck travels down the wet pavement on Mercer Street. Despite the weather, the celebrations continued.

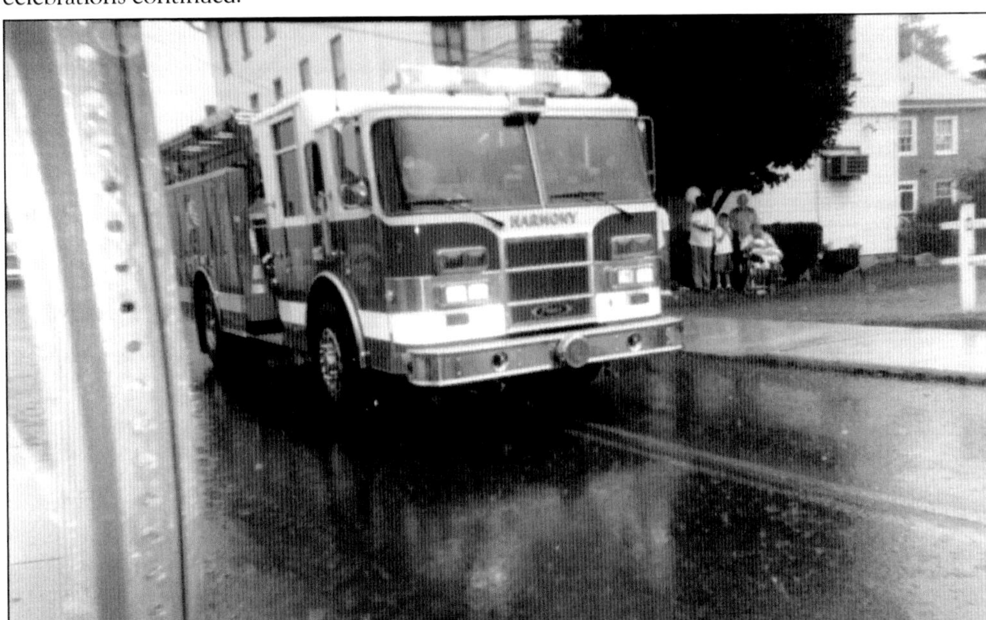

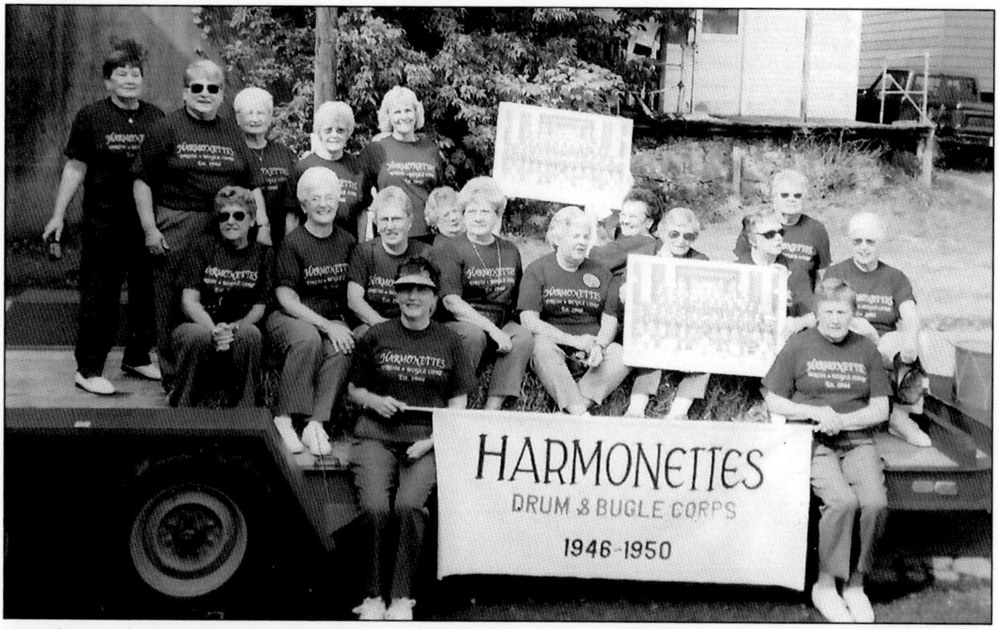

Members of the Harmonettes Drum and Bugle Corps reunited to march in the Harmony Bicentennial Parade. Their matching shirts are maroon, the color of their original uniform jackets. Other reunions held during bicentennial week were the Doc Stewart Baby Reunion, for people delivered by Harmony's longtime physician, and the Emma Farm Camp Reunion. (Courtesy of Janet Shaffer Miesel.)

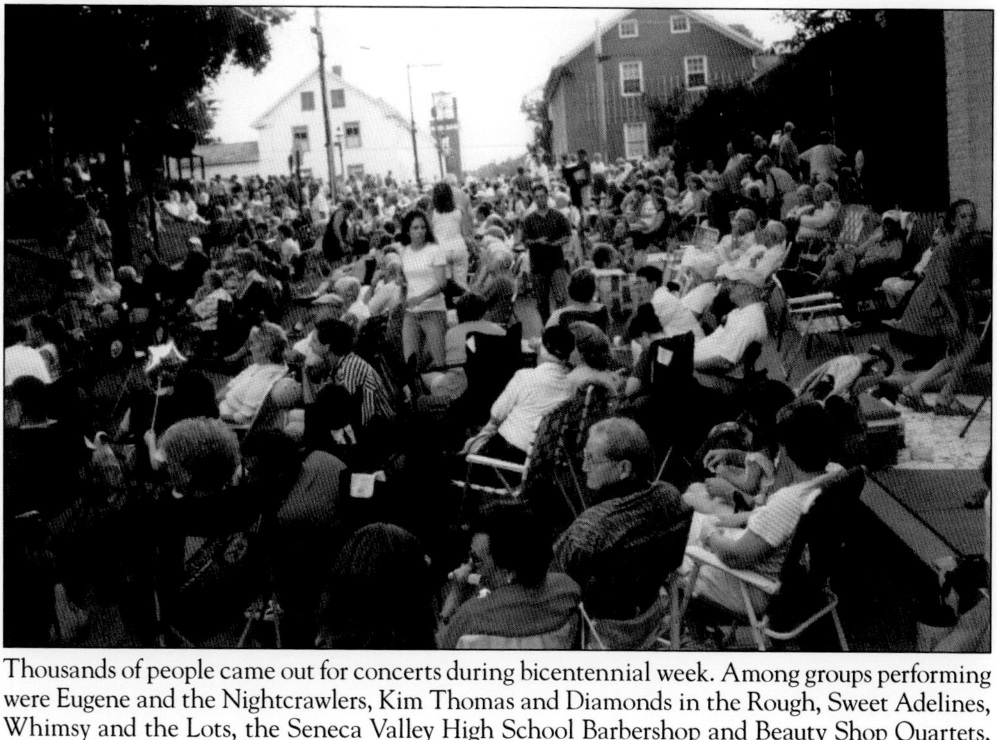

Thousands of people came out for concerts during bicentennial week. Among groups performing were Eugene and the Nightcrawlers, Kim Thomas and Diamonds in the Rough, Sweet Adelines, Whimsy and the Lots, the Seneca Valley High School Barbershop and Beauty Shop Quartets, and the John Burgh Band.

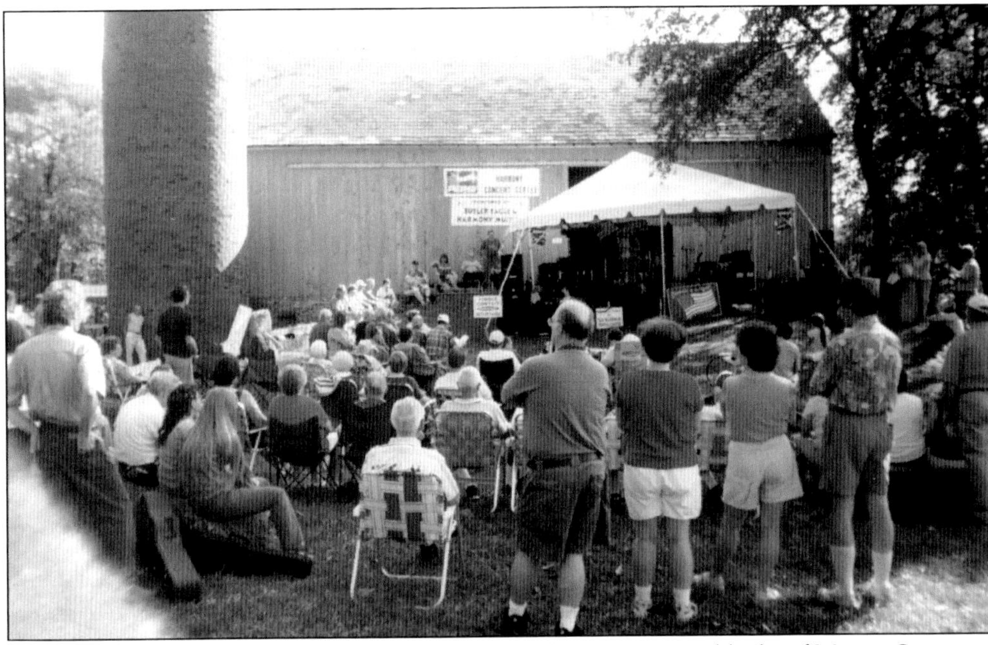

Free outdoor concerts bring crowds to Harmony each summer. Two blocks of Mercer Street are closed to traffic, allowing people to sit in the street. Occasional performances are held at the 1805 Harmony Society barn. The Bicentennial Grand Finale featuring the Old Economy Orchestra took place at the barn and was followed by a Zambelli fireworks display. Zambelli fireworks, provided by Armstrong Utilities, also cap Harmony's annual New Year's Eve celebration. Sign Innovation of Harmony created a lighted ball that is dropped in the diamond at 6:00 p.m., midnight in Germany. Below, the Allegheny Brass Band plays at the Harmony Inn, the former Hotel Ziegler. Harmony Business Association initiated the concerts with financial support of local businesses, reviving a tradition that started more than a century ago when the hotel hosted concerts on the porch.

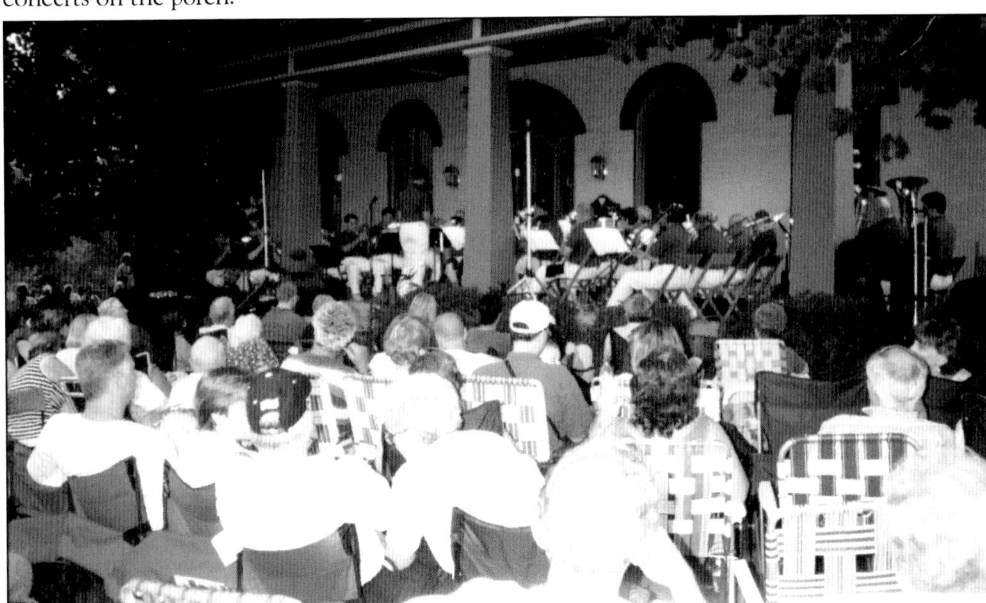

About Historic Harmony

Historic Harmony is a nonprofit, volunteer historical society and preservation advocate founded in 1943 that preserves and promotes public knowledge of the Harmony area's history and heritage through its Harmony Museum collections and outreach activities, fosters tourism in southwestern Butler County in cooperation with other organizations and agencies, and encourages preservation of historical resources in support of educational, quality of life, economic development, and associated community objectives.

Dr. Arthur Stewart and Rev. Loran Veith and his wife, Ruth, were among Historic Harmony's founders. After the Harmony Fire Company opened the museum in 1955, volunteers offered tours on request. Following a reorganization in 1965, Historic Harmony leased the building. President Robert Garvin and a small group of workers refurbished five museum rooms, built display cabinets, and organized exhibits. The next year, Dr. S. K. Stevens, executive director of the Pennsylvania Historical and Museum Commission, visited the museum and commented, "I cannot recall having ever seen an historical society and museum administered by nonprofessionals which is as well run as this one is."

Historic Harmony members learned crafts such as spinning, weaving, and woodworking, and in 1971 demonstrated their skills at the first Dankfest, a German-themed pioneer festival. They also began providing historical craft programs for local schools, an effort that continues, along with museum tours for elementary classes. Volunteers moved and reconstructed a Mennonite log house and acquired the Harmonist Wagner house as a museum annex in the 1970s. They bought the museum in 1986 and converted the attached fire company garage into a large exhibit and events facility. Honoring three Historic Harmony founders, the space is called Doc Stewart Hall, and the museum's book repository is named Veith Library for Rev. Loran and Ruth Veith. A decade ago, Historic Harmony purchased and restored an 1805 Harmonist barn. It now owns nine properties, presents a full schedule of activities each year, and offers tours year-round. Among annual events are Harmoniefest Dinner, Quilt in a Day program, Herb and Garden Fair, WeihnachtsMarkt German-style Christmas market, and periodic German dinners including a buffet during the borough's Silvester on New Year's Eve, Harmony's version of the German Silvesterabend.

The Pennsylvania Federation of Museums and Historical Organizations has honored Historic Harmony for advancement of state history, presentation of Harmony Society history and crafts, and sustained interest in public education. Learn more at www.harmonymuseum.org; Historic Harmony, P.O. Box 524, Harmony, Pennsylvania, 16037; by phone at 724-452-7341; or by e-mail at hmuseum@zoominternet.net.